ECONOMIC HIS

INDUSTRIAL SOUTH WALES
1750–1914

THE UK

INDUSTRIAL SOUTH WALES
1750–1914

Essays in Welsh economic history

Edited by

W.E. MINCHINTON

Routledge
Taylor & Francis Group

LONDON AND NEW YORK

First published in 1969

Published in 2006 by
Routledge
2 Park Square, Milton Park, Abingdon, Oxfordshire OX14 4RN
711 Third Avenue, New York, NY 10017

First issued in paperback 2014

Routledge is an imprint of the Taylor and Francis Group, an informa business

British Library Cataloguing in Publication Data
A CIP catalogue record for this book
is available from the British Library

Industrial South Wales 1750–1914
ISBN 0-415-38251-3 (volume)
ISBN 0-415-37841-9 (subset)
ISBN 0-415-28619-0 (set)

ISBN 13: 978-1-138-88076-4 (pbk)
ISBN 13: 978-0-415-38251-9 (hbk)

Routledge Library Editions: Economic History

INDUSTRIAL SOUTH WALES

1750–1914

INDUSTRIAL SOUTH WALES

1750–1914

Essays in Welsh Economic History

EDITED BY

W. E. MINCHINTON

FRANK CASS & CO. LTD.
1969

First published in 1969 by
FRANK CASS AND COMPANY LIMITED
67 Great Russell Street, London W.C.1

Copyright © 1969 W. E. Minchinton

SBN 7146 1344 4

CONTENTS

PART THREE: BANKING

PART FOUR: LABOUR

PART FIVE: HOUSING

Preface

IN July 1961 a vacation course in Welsh history was held at University College, Swansea. One of the study groups, led by Professor David Williams of University College, Aberystwyth, was on 'The industrial revolution in Wales'. In the course of the discussions on the subject of the industrialization of south Wales, it became apparent that a number of the important contributions were to be found not in books but in articles scattered in many periodicals not always easily accessible to those concerned to study or teach. It therefore seemed appropriate to collect together the more important within the compass of a single volume. Here then are gathered twelve of the more significant articles which have already been published.

The articles have not been selected at random but have been chosen to present an ordered sequence. They deal first with the problems of population and migration, then with the basic industries of iron, coal, tinplate and copper. Essays on banking, building and trade unionism follow. The whole is prefaced by an introduction which aims to put the story of the industrialization of Wales in perspective and to indicate how the individual contributions fit into the general story. No attempt has been made to provide this essay with full bibliographical references since a detailed guide is available: *A bibliography of the history of Wales* (Cardiff, 2nd ed. 1962) together with Supplement I (*Bulletin of the Board of Celtic Studies*, XX (1963), 126–64) and Supplement II (*Bulletin of the Board of Celtic Studies*, XXII (1966), 49–70).

As editor I am indebted to the authors for permission to reproduce their articles in this volume. In particular I would like to thank Lady Namier for permission to reproduce her late husband's study of Anthony Bacon and Mr. D. B. H. Jones for similar permission to reprint his father's essay on 'The Scotch cattle'. I am also grateful to the editors of the various journals concerned for permission to use material which previously appeared under their auspices. All the contributions are reprinted as they were originally published with three exceptions. Professor A. H. Dodd who most kindly has allowed me to reprint the relevant portion from his essay on 'The character of Welsh emigration', wrote bridge passages to enable the shortened version here reproduced to read smoothly. Then, in the case of the articles by T. Mansel Hodges and R. O. Roberts, the detailed references to manuscript sources have been omitted. Anyone wishing to consult such material on which the articles are based is accordingly referred to the journals in which these contributions originally appeared.

W. E. MINCHINTON

Industrial South Wales, 1750-1914

by W. E. Minchinton

IN the popular mind south Wales was regarded until recently as an area of industrial blight, of massive coal-tips, of smoking chimneys, of dark satanic mills, of crowded working-class housing in narrow valleys which were green once but are green no longer. Just as this picture is ceasing to be true of south Wales today so it was not true of south Wales 200 years ago. Then south Wales was predominantly agricultural. On the upland pastures sheep were reared, providing the raw material for the widely scattered local textile industry; while in the lowland regions of the vale of Glamorgan and the peninsula of Gower, arable cultivation was carried on to meet local needs and for sale in the nearest major market, Bristol, which served as a metropolis for south Wales. Population was still fairly evenly distributed and the towns were small. Either they were local market towns such as Carmarthen, Bridgend, Cowbridge, or Abergavenny or they were small ports, mainly engaged in coastal trade such as Newport, Cardiff or Swansea. None had more than two thousand inhabitants.

The fingers of industry had as yet touched lightly on the landscape of south Wales. In the sixteenth century the Mineral and Battery Company had operated a brass foundry and a wireworks, whose product was used for woolcards at Tintern, while the Mines Royal, which owned copper mines in Cornwall, smelted copper at Neath in a furnace there under the management of a German, Ulrich Frosse. Coal was also worked on a small scale, particularly where the coal measures came down to the coast at Swansea and Tenby and some was exported to places within the Bristol Channel and to Ireland. More widespread were the iron furnaces. Attracted like the Mines Royal by the availability of timber, Sussex ironmasters came to south Wales and set up furnaces, mostly using local iron ore, at Brecon, Monmouth and elsewhere in south Wales. After various abortive attempts, tinplate manufacture had also been established at Pontypool about 1720. But all these industrial activities were small-scale and widely scattered. They left little mark on the face

B   ix

of south Wales. The importance of these enterprises was in what they promised rather than in what they achieved. By their preliminary probings, they revealed something of the mineral wealth of south Wales which was to be exploited more systematically once industrialization got under way in Great Britain.

The development of industry in south Wales was to be based on its raw materials. Most important was coal. The south Wales coalfield is itself oval in shape. From the eastern boundary between Blaenavon and Pontypool, the coal measures extend westward across Glamorgan and south Carmarthenshire, run under Carmarthen Bay and then reappear as a narrow band across Pembrokeshire, stretching from the neighbourhood of Saundersfoot to St. Bride's Bay. The coal seams vary in thickness and are much fractured, while the quality of the coal changes from east to west. In the east bituminous coals are to be found, dry steam coals occupy a central position in the coalfield and semi-anthracite and anthracite coals are to be found in the west. The coal measures come nearest to the surface along the rim of the oval. Along the northern outcrop the strata dip gently but along the southern outcrop they dip more sharply towards the centre of the basin. All these factors have affected the pattern of exploitation of the coalfield.

While coal, which served both as a source of power and as a necessary ingredient of metallurgical and chemical processes, was the major raw material responsible for the industrial development of south Wales, other raw materials were also present. Associated with the carboniferous system of south Wales were the clay ironstones which occurred most abundantly in the lower coal series, particularly along the northern outcrop. Iron oxide ores occur in the carboniferous limestone which also provides dolomitic limestone and silica used in the iron and steel industry. The streams and rivers of south Wales, fed by a rainfall which reaches as much as 100 in. annually in some parts, provided a source of water-power to drive water-wheels for industrial processes while the grits of the overlying pennant series provided a strong and durable stone for building purposes. Such were the resources to hand when English industrialists began to look further afield for sites to carry on their projects in the early eighteenth century.

Earliest of the industries to develop was copper-smelting about which Mr. Roberts writes in more detail below. Coal had long been used to smelt non-ferrous metals and at a time when 18 tons of coal were required to smelt 4 tons of ore it was found soon to be cheaper to bring copper ore to the coalfield rather than carry coal to the copper mines. After Frosse's attempt in the late sixteenth century, copper smelting was revived at Melincryddan, near Neath, a century later by Sir Humphrey Mackworth. He also brought lead from mines near Aberystwyth to be smelted there and, by 1708, the town could boast of twelve lead furnaces and two copper furnaces. Shortly afterwards Dr. John Lane of Bristol, who already had interests in Cornish copper mines, established a copper works at Landore in 1717 and thus laid the foundation of the non-ferrous industries in the Tawe valley. Since Swansea was a better port for handling incoming cargoes of copper ore, more copper works were set up there and Swansea quickly outstripped Neath as a metallurgical centre. A little further east, a copper works was also established at Taibach, near Port Talbot, in 1727. By 1750 about half the copper produced in Britain was smelted in the Swansea area. Such activity provided a stimulus to the expansion of coal mining, mainly by drifts and levels in the Swansea area. But while copper came first, the future lay not with that metal but with iron and coal.

The subsequent industrialization of south Wales falls into three main phases. First, in the second half of the eighteenth century, an iron industry was established by immigrant ironmasters, largely with English capital on the northern rim of the coalfield. They made south Wales the most important section of the British iron industry until about 1850. In the second phase of Welsh industrialism, between 1850 and 1914, the Welsh coalfield was opened up to supply markets all over the world with steam coal and anthracite. But this time much of the capital was local and most of the coalowners were Welsh. The third phase, which is beyond the scope of this volume, is the most recent and diverse phase of industrialism in south Wales. This time the major developments have occurred along the coast, notably with the construction of large integrated steelworks and an oil refinery. Again, outside capital and entrepreneurial ability have been of importance.

THE IRON AGE, 1750–1850

Before the middle of the eighteenth century, the iron industry developed slowly because of the remoteness of Wales. By 1720 there were altogether sixteen furnaces scattered through south Wales at places like Abercarn, Brecon, Melingriffith (near Cardiff), Machen, Melin-y-cwrt (near Neath) and Tredegar, all eking out a tenuous existence based on local supplies of timber. There was little sign that south Wales would become a major centre of the British iron industry. Yet three factors, demand, technical change and transport, transformed the situation.

The turning point was the Seven Years' War. An increased demand for iron for munitions coincided with the interruption of supplies from abroad and the possibilities of iron manufacture in south Wales was looked at with new eyes. In 1757 John Maybery of Powicke Forge, Worcestershire, took a lease of a site at Hirwaun and built the first blast furnace there. In the same year Thomas Lewis of Llanishen leased a mineral site near Merthyr and in 1759, in partnership with eight others, including the Bersham ironmaster, Isaac Wilkinson, built the Merthyr Furnace at Dowlais, to which John Guest came from Broseley as manager in 1767. Other mineral leases followed in the Merthyr area, for the Cyfarthfa, Penydarren and Plymouth Works with the Cyfarthfa Works, begun in 1765 by Anthony Bacon and his associates, becoming the most important. The industry received a further stimulus from the outbreak of war with America in the 1770s. This enabled Anthony Bacon, as Sir Lewis Namier describes below, to extend his manufacture of cannon at Cyfarthfa and to lease the Plymouth works, near Merthyr, in 1777 and the Hirwaun furnace in 1780. As a result of this boom in the demand for iron there were, by 1788, 13 blast furnaces, making 10,000 tons of pig iron a year for the scattered forges in south Wales. This expansion had been made possible by the skill of Midland iron masters and the finance of London merchants, like Anthony Bacon and Benjamin Hammett, and Bristol merchants, like the Harfords and Reynolds, Getley & Company.

During the 1780s the continued growth of the Welsh industry was assisted by two technological developments. Watt's improvement of the steam engine provided a new motive power and increased the demand for iron, but of greater immediate significance was the invention of puddling. The iron industry had expanded in south Wales in the later eighteenth century because of the existence there of iron ore, limestone and water-power. It continued there because of the availability of coal also. The smelting of iron with coal became widespread in the later eighteenth century and the puddling process made it possible to reduce pig iron to malleable or wrought iron. Though credit is usually given to Henry Cort for the invention of puddling in 1784, this process was independently discovered by Peter Onions, a foreman at Cyfarthfa, and was so widely adopted in south Wales that it became known as 'the Welsh method'.

But a limitation on the growth of the Welsh industry was its poor communications. Merthyr was difficult of access and though Anthony Bacon had persuaded the local farmers to co-operate in improving road communications to Cardiff this did not really solve the problem. Neither packhorses nor the improved turnpike roads had the necessary capacity and the forward-looking men of the time therefore turned to canals. An Act was secured in 1790 for a canal from Merthyr to Cardiff and other schemes then followed. Between 1794 and 1799 four great canals were opened for traffic down the Welsh valleys, the Glamorganshire canal to Cardiff, the Neath canal from Giant's Grave almost to Hirwaun, the Monmouthshire canal which eventually reached from Newport to Brecon, and the Swansea canal which ran the length of the Tawe valley. These 77 miles of canal, with a total of 180 locks and rising at one point to over 500 ft. above sea level, were built at a cost of approximately £420,000. To these canals the ironworks were linked by tramroads along which waggons were drawn by horses. And scarcely had the canal age begun before its successor was foreshadowed. In 1804 Richard Trevithick successfully ran his steam engine drawing a load of 10 tons and 70 passengers along a tram road at Quaker's Yard.

The canals gave the Welsh ironworks direct access to the sea and enabled them to expand to meet the growing wartime demand for iron. By 1815 when there was a line of eight large ironworks and a number of smaller ones, stretching from Hirwaun to Blaenavon across the heads of valleys, on the northern rim of the coalfield, south Wales was producing about a third of the total British production of iron. Meantime tinplate-making had spread from its origins at Pontypool and by 1805 most of the 14 tinplate works operating in Britain were in the river valleys of south Wales and Monmouthshire.

The position of the copper industry was also radically changed in the third quarter of the eighteenth century. After a number of unsuccessful attempts, a rich vein of ore was struck in 1768 on the Parys mountain in Anglesey. Near the surface, this, and other veins subsequently discovered, could be worked with great ease and were enormously productive for a brief period. The ore was brought to Swansea to be smelted and production expanded in the Swansea area especially to meet the new uses for copper such as its employment for the sheathing of ships. Copper smelting spread to Penclawdd in the Loughor estuary in the 1790s and to Llanelly in 1805, where R. J. Nevill opened a works. Already the Nevills were established in Swansea and they were followed by the Vivians, a Cornish family who set up the Hafod works in the Tawe valley in 1810. Though production expanded as Mr. Roberts describes below, unlike iron manufacture, the copper industry always remained a fairly small industry, highly localized in the Swansea area where it first developed.

With the growth of industry came an influx of population to provide the labour force and the growth of towns. Most of the migration was short-distance movement. Men were drawn from agricultural pursuits in rural Wales to work in iron or tinplate, copper or coal. But there was a certain limited migration of skilled workers from further afield while some unskilled labour came from the nearby English counties. The population of Wales grew from about 480,000 in 1750 to 587,000 in 1801 and 673,000 in 1811 while that of Monmouthshire rose from 31,220 in 1750 to 45,582 in 1801 and 62,105 in 1811. Of the towns, Merthyr showed the most spectacular rate of growth. Still a small hamlet in 1750, it had become a town of 7705 in 1801 surpassing Swansea which at that date had a population of 6831. Cardiff with a population of 1870 was still, like Newport with 1087, a small town.

Between 1815 and the mid-century, the output of the Welsh iron industry expanded rapidly, once the post-war depression was over, the Welsh ironworks turnd to the production of iron for the rapidly multiplying peacetime uses. Most important was the railway. Welsh rails went first to equip railways in Britain and there was scarcely an English railway which did not obtain at least part of its railway iron from south Wales. Later they were used in the construction of railways abroad, in America, Austria–Hungary and Russia. But iron was used for other purposes too. Ballast iron for shipping, plating for high pressure boilers and cables were some of its uses. The metal used in building London Bridge came from Crawshay's Cyfarthfa works. To meet these varying needs, the ironworks were expanded. In 1823 Dowlais and Cyfarthfa each had eight blast furnaces but by 1830 Dowlais had twelve and Cyfarthfa nine, much larger and more efficient than the original ones. Dowlais quadrupled its production between 1817 and 1850 while Cyfarthfa expanded its output $2\frac{1}{2}$ times and both Plymouth and Penydarren more than doubled theirs. New works were set up in Monmouthshire at Tredegar, Ebbw Vale and Nantyglo, and the iron industry also spread to the west of the coalfield. An adaptation of the hotblast process by George Crane and David Thomas at the Ynyscedwyn Works at the top of the Swansea valley about 1838 enabled anthracite to be used in blast furnaces. In consequence further ironworks were established at this end of the coalfield and the industrialization of west Wales and particularly of the Amman and Gwendraeth valleys ensued.

By all these means production was increased. In 1823 with an annual output of 182,300 tons, south Wales made about 40 per cent of the total British production of pig iron and though capacity increased faster in some other districts, with an annual output of 720,000 tons in 1847, the region still accounted for 35 per cent of the national total. The demand for tinplate at home and abroad still increased. Production rose from 18,000 tons in 1837 to 37,000 tons (of which 25,000 tons were exported) in 1850. And more works were set up in south Wales to meet the demand. After a lean period in the 1820s copper smelting also expanded although still based on British ore, but from 1830 growing quantities of ore were brought to Swansea from Cuba and South America. In the 1840s it was estimated that between 130,000 and 150,000 tons of copper ore were smelted annually in south Wales. The production of yellow metal—an alloy of zinc and copper—which largely replaced copper in the manufacture of ships' sheathing, bolts and fastenings, was also developed in the 1840s by some of the Swansea copper firms. Nevill of Llanelly also had important sheathing contracts, particularly with Muntz.

The expansion of iron, tinplate and copper in turn provided a stimulus to coal production. It all did much to determine the location of coal-mining activity in south Wales. Wherever there were ironworks, there were collieries, mostly under the same ownership. Extensive mines were also sunk in the Swansea area for the copper industry. But alongside there grew up in the early nineteenth century a 'sale coal' trade in the hands of local businessmen. The first Welsh steam coals to attain prominence were Llangennech coals from west Wales, which were widely adopted for early steamships and also used domestically by industrialists. Amongst the major customers were the breweries, notably Meux. The mining of sale coal at the eastern end of the coalfield followed soon after and developed more swiftly. In 1829, 2472 tons of coal were exported from Cardiff, mainly to London. Within a few years, because it made less smoke, Welsh coal had supplanted coal from Newcastle in many London grates, and a number of speculators, including Thomas Powell, Thomas Wayne and John Nixon, sank pits in the Aberdare area in the late 1830s and 1840s. Powell linked his name with the two pits he sank in 1844 and made Powell Duffryn a name familiar in many parts of the world. From London, John Nixon turned overseas for markets and developed the trade with France which became an important market for Welsh coal. Coal exports sharply increased in the 1840s, of which the figures for Cardiff provide an illustration. In 1839, 21,000 tons was sent through the port while eleven years later 731,329 tons were sent out, nearly half for the foreign market.

Most of the iron, coal and copper was carried by water and in the first half of the nineteenth century the canals of south Wales which were extended to meet the growing demand, carried an expanding volume of traffic. Whereas in 1819 the Glamorganshire and Monmouthshire Canals had carried 80,333 tons of iron, in 1839 the iron trade amounted to 382,176 tons and in 1849 probably exceeded half a million tons. As a result the canals became more and more congested, and this provided a motive for the opening of the first competing railway, the Taff Vale from Cardiff to Merthyr in 1841. The inflexibility of the canals encouraged the establishment of this rival transport service. The growth of the export trade in iron and coal also led to port improvement. Burry Port at the western end of the coalfield was opened in 1831 and the West Bute Dock, the first major development at Cardiff, financed by the Marquis of Bute, in 1839, while the Town Dock was constructed at Newport in 1842.

The growth of industry and commerce and the improvement of communications was accompanied by the continued influx of workers into industrial south Wales. Most of the migrants came, as Mr. Hodges and Professor Thomas describe below, from the immediately neighbouring Welsh counties, but some came from Stafford shire, Shropshire and south-west England. Particularly in the 1840s, as a result of the potato famine, a number of Irishmen came to south Wales to find unskilled jobs there. As a result of this movement of people into the county, the population of Glamorgan rose from 71,525 in 1801 to 231,849 in 1851 and the population of Monmouthshire increased from 45,582 to 157,418 in the same period. Merthyr, which had a population of 7705 in 1801, had become easily the largest town in Wales in 1851 with 35,093 persons resident within its boundaries at that date. In the same period, Cardiff had grown from a town of 1870 inhabitants to one in which 20,258 people lived.

Though the main flood of migration was into Wales and, within Wales, from the rural to the industrializing areas, there was a trickle of migrants outwards. For most of the eighteenth century, emigration was confined to isolated individuals but the almost unbroken succession of bad harvests in the last decade or so resulted in a more concerted movement from the land, a movement which was resumed in greater volume after 1815. The vast majority of those who fled from the land in Wales went to the industrial areas of England but, as Professor A. H. Dodd describes below, a number emigrated to America, with Pennsylvania as the most-favoured destination. It is notoriously difficult to know how many actually went, but for a brief period between 1 Jan. 1841 and 7 June of the same year some figures are available. These show that 41 men and 30 women emigrated from Glamorgan in these five months, while 133 men and 80 women went from Monmouthshire across the Atlantic. A further element in the pattern of movement within Wales which deserves a brief mention, since it was largely a product of the process of industrialization, was the seasonal migration of Cardiganshire harvest-gangs to the vale of Glamorgan in the early nineteenth century, attracted by the higher wages offered there.

The inward migration was important not only for the supply of wage labour but also for the influx of entrepreneurial ability. In the expansion of iron and copper the key figures were immigrants. Bacon, Guest, Crawshay, Homfray, Kendall, all the 'iron kings', came from England bringing technical or commercial skills. Knowledge of methods and markets provided the keys to successful operation. In the copper industry, too, immigrants like the Nevills, Vivians and Grenfells dominated the scene. Though some Welshmen played their part in this first phase of industrialism, most of the entrepreneurial initiative came from outside south Wales.

Similarly the initial source of finance was largely external. South Wales can be looked on in this period as a nearby colonial area in which English businessmen invested. The original pump-priming investment in iron and copper came largely from outside south Wales. Similarly those who invested their capital in the sea-coal industry were drawn largely from the ranks of merchants in Bristol, Gloucester, Birmingham and Cornwall. But the further expansion of industry in south Wales was largely self-financed by 'the providence of steady manufacturers'. This is a classical case of industrial capital being, in Professor T. S. Ashton's phrase, 'its own chief progenitor'. In the first half of the nineteenth century, for example, both Sir John Guest and William Crawshay became the sole proprietors of their works and met the cost of modernization and re-equipment out of profits. From iron and copper capital spilled over into the more slowly developing coal and tinplate industries. The banks made comparatively little contribution to industrial finance.

The activities of three different types of bank are discussed in this volume. Mr. Hodges describes the brief life of the Cardiff Bank (1806–22) whose customers were mainly small traders from Cardiff and district or farmers and gentry; and Mr. Roberts analyses the operations of the branch of the Bank of England which was set up in Swansea in 1826. As joint-stock banking penetrated south Wales in the 1830s its discount business declined and operations ceased in 1859. Finally, catering for quite a different clientele, were the savings banks. By 1830 there were savings banks in Bridgend, Cardiff, Pembroke and Haverfordwest, and in that year another which moved to Newport in 1837 was founded, as Mr. Hodges describes, at Caerleon. This bank continued in operation until 1888.

But, as Professor John has written, the south Wales coalfield was not in general an area conducive to powerful local banking. The narrow range of its industrial activities, the relatively few concerns operating in the coalfield, and the character of its industrial communities, were factors which prevented such a development. By the middle of the nineteenth century some capital stringency was already apparent in south Wales, the consequence of the absence of appropriate institutions to mobilize it for industrial purposes rather than of an absolute shortage of funds. Though there were signs of the development of more sophisticated financial arrangements, most of the capital still came, largely through personal contacts, from private sources.

In the preceding century, south Wales had developed an impressive position as a highly specialized centre of manufacture. In iron and copper it played a major role on the British economic scene. Its contribution to exports was particularly marked. As early as 1827 south Wales provided one-half of Britain's iron exports. Such dependence on foreign markets exposed the region like Lancashire to fluctuations in trade overseas and industrial unemployment became of some significance in times of depression. It led to rather flamboyant attempts like the Scotch Cattle, whose activities are described by the late Mr. E. J. Jones below, to establish trade unionism in south Wales.

The mid-nineteenth century there marked the end of an era. By 1850 the iron industry was being seriously challenged by the faster growing Cleveland industry. The dominance of iron was fast coming to an end. Already with the expansion of coal-mining there were signs of a new age which was to produce an even more radical transformation of the economy of south Wales.

THE COAL ERA, 1850–1914

As late as 1850 industrial activity in south Wales was still highly localized. There were two main industrial areas, the eighteen-mile strip at the heads of the valleys where the iron industry was centred and the Swansea–Neath area where the copper industry and some tinplate works were situated. Cardiff and Newport had grown as ports because of their links by canal with the iron works, but elsewhere in south Wales industry was still widely scattered, disintegrated and small scale. Only slowly had the probes of industry begun to penetrate the valleys of Glamorgan and until the 1850s the upper Rhonddas, which for long have seemed almost synonymous with industrial south Wales, were secluded pastoral areas where, to quote one observer, 'a Sabbath stillness reigned'. The vital industrial experience of the Welsh mining valleys was to be encompassed within the brief historical space of less than 75 years.

The key to the exploitation of the coalfield of south Wales was the railway. Brunel built the South Wales Railway from Chepstow to Swansea in 1850 and, two years later, by the construction of Chepstow bridge, linked it with the Great Western Railway and thus provided direct rail communication between south Wales, the Midlands and London. With the construction of the Severn Tunnel, a second faster and more direct route became available in 1886. But more important were the lines which linked the valleys with the ports of south Wales, following, like the canals before them, the relief of the region. The Vale of Neath was opened from its junction with the South Wales Railway as far as Aberdare in 1851 and reached Merthyr in 1853. The first train of coal from the Rhondda to Cardiff was sent down at the end of 1855 and the line was completed through the valley in 1856. The Rhymney Railway was opened in 1858 while three lines in the western part of the region were opened in the early 1860s. In the following years the railway network was thickened as links were built between existing lines and branch lines were added, crossing from valley to valley and at high cost, breaking through the watersheds of the coalfield. Such developments allowed Swansea merchants, for example, to purchase and export coals from the Rhondda. Most of the construction was to meet obvious needs for improved transport facilities, but some was built speculatively in the hope it would generate its own traffic. But while a much more complex pattern of freight movement began to emerge, most of the traffic continued to be on a north–south axis from the valleys to the ports. Coal was overwhelmingly the most important commodity carried and the Taff Vale Railway, the largest coal carrier, was the most profitable concern. As early as 1868 the Taff Vale carried 3·54 million tons, the G.W.R. 2·25 million tons and the Rhymney Railway 659,754 tons in a year.

Apart from the railways a small amount of traffic continued to be carried on the canals up to the first world war but their contribution was a declining one. When decay started in the canal-tramroad system, it spread quickly. In 1860 the Welsh canals flourished: by 1900 they were virtually disused, the exception being the Swansea canal which as late as 1888 was passing 385,307 tons of traffic, though much of it was short-haul. By 1914 the day of the canal was past. More significant was the coming of the internal combustion engine; but road transport was of little importance for the carriage of goods in this period. Until 1914 the railways had a virtual monopoly of the rapidly expanding volume of inland traffic.

The railways tapped the valleys of the coalfield just at the time when uses for coal both domestically and overseas were expanding. Railways were being constructed at home and abroad, steamships were growing in number and coal was also in demand for industrial processes and domestic heating. Like Welsh tinplate, barbed wire and the railway, Welsh coal played a part in the outward movement of the frontier of settlement in many parts of the world. Within easy reach of the sea, the coalfield was ideally based to develop an export trade. While the whole of the coalfield came to participate, after 1860 it was the steam coals of the Rhondda which were sent in growing quantities all over the world. In the early 1870s, two million tons of coal were mined there alone and the total for south Wales amounted to 16 million tons. This provided an outgoing cargo for vessels which returned to south Wales with iron ore. Developments in the anthracite coalfield in the west occurred more slowly and output did not expand significantly until the 1880s. Then it helped to swell the rising Welsh output which reached 30 million tons in 1891 and 56 million tons in 1913. Exports provided the main engine of growth. In 1860 they amounted to 1·7 million tons, in 1880 to 9·2 million tons. By 1913, when shipments overseas totalled 38·7 million tons, they represented 92·5 per cent of all exports by volume and 82·5 per cent of the total traffic of the south Wales ports. And with expansion the structure of the industry was radically transformed. By the first world war, the Welsh coal industry was dominated by a series of large combines.

To handle the growing trade in coal the port facilities of south Wales were extended by the construction of docks. These were necessary because of the high tidal range of the Bristol Channel, of the order of 30–40 ft. At Cardiff the Bute East Dock was opened in 1859, the Roath Dock in 1887 and the Queen Alexandra Dock in 1907. Nearby, Ely Harbour was opened to coal exports in 1859 while Penarth Docks were built in 1865. Both these developments were accompanied by the construction of links to the coalfields by the Taff Vale Railway. Port development and railway construction went hand-in-hand. At Newport improvement took place more slowly. A small extension to the Town Dock had been made in 1858 but proved totally inadequate for the needs of the port. Trade growing ahead of facilities was a constant problem in south Wales in the later nineteenth century. In 1875 the Alexandra Dock was opened but pressure of shipping caused the river bank to be used for the coal trade in 1880. Soon after the construction of the South Dock was begun, to be completed in 1892 and extended in 1907. Further extensions were completed in 1914. At Swansea the first dock, the North Dock, was completed in 1852 and the South Dock in 1859, but the expansion of trade soon made further construction necessary. A portion of Fabian's Bay was enclosed to make the Prince of

Wales Dock which was opened in 1881 and extended in 1896–8. Seaward of this the King's Dock was built between 1904 and 1909. Improvements also took place at Briton Ferry where a dock was constructed in 1860, at Llanelly where the North Dock was opened in 1903, and at Port Talbot where the New Dock came into commission in 1898.

But the major event at the end of the century was the construction of Barry Docks. Periodically there were complaints about the inadequacies of port facilities, especially at Cardiff. Independent traders complained not only of congestion and delay but of extortionate charges imposed by the Marquis of Bute. A scheme was therefore promoted, with David Davies and John Cory among the spokesmen, to build a dock at Barry and to link it by rail to the Rhondda. Completed in 1889 at a cost of £2 million and subsequently extended in 1898 and 1914, the venture proved entirely justified. The shipments of coal from Cardiff had risen from 998,000 tons in 1859 to 1·9 million tons in 1867 and to 7·7 million tons in 1889, when Barry Docks in the first year of its existence dealt with 1·1 million tons. Cardiff had become the largest coal-exporting port in the world but by 1913 Barry deprived Cardiff of that title. In that year 11·05 million tons were shipped from Barry compared with 10·6 million tons from Cardiff.

The trade of the south Wales ports up to the first world war was dominated by exports which in 1913 accounted for 89 per cent of the total trade. Imports, of which iron ore was the major item, amounted to 5·1 million tons (1·7 million tons of iron ore) in that year compared with total exports of 42·1 million tons, of which coal accounted for 37·0 million tons. The lines of coal hoists along the docks bore witness to the importance of the trade in this commodity. And as the trade had grown, the size of vessels carrying the coal had increased and the freight rates dropped. The average tonnage of vessels at Cardiff in 1850 was 1000 tons, in 1880 was 3000 tons. The average coal freight from Cardiff to the Mediterranean ports in 1872 was 14s. 1d. a ton, by 1901 it had declined to 6s. 4d. It cost less to send coal from Cardiff to Port Said than it did to convey it from the Rhondda to London.

Though coalmining became the major activity in south Wales between 1850 and 1914, the other basic industries remained of importance. In the 1850s the iron industry there was still the most important single section of the British iron industry. Its core was the small group of large works centred on Merthyr. By this time, Dowlais, the 'greatest ironworks in the world', employing nearly 7000 workers, had 18 blast furnaces, Cyfarthfa had eleven, and Blaenavon, Rhymney and Tredegar had nine furnaces each. The apex of its achievement was reached in 1857 when 970,727 tons of iron were produced by the 164 furnaces then in blast. Thereafter output declined. For this change of fortune a number of factors were responsible. First, many of the leases of mineral property granted in the mid-eighteenth century fell in about the middle of the nineteenth. Whereas the old leases were at nominal rents, the new were put at more realistic figures. The Cyfarthfa lease, for example, was renewed in 1862 for a total of £7000, with royalties payable as well, instead of the annual rent of £63 negotiated in 1763. At the same time the exhaustion of the local iron ore supplies handicapped the Welsh ironmasters. Welsh iron ore production fell sharply from 1·6 million tons in 1855 to 369,000 tons in 1866. Although, with rising raw material prices in the early 1870s, a temporary expansion of production took place and 1·2 million tons were produced at high cost in 1872, this was a dying gesture. Thereafter ore production in south Wales fell back sharply and permanently, dropping to 222,000 tons in 1882. Of recent years output has been around 120,000 tons and this has all come from a different source, the haematite mine at Llanharry in the Vale of Glamorgan.

Thirdly, although the south Wales firms improved their blast furnace practice and rolling mill machinery and were among the earliest to adopt the Bessemer process on a large scale, the historic works of the northern outcrop faced increasingly severe competition in the 1870s. Imported ore was expensive to bring up the valleys and costs in the Merthyr area were higher and profits lower than in Cleveland. Moreover iron rails were everywhere giving place to steel. In consequence Welsh iron rail production fell from 534,000 tons in 1869 to less than 100,000 tons in 1879. Only the early adoption of the Bessemer process and the growth of the Welsh tinplate and sheet industries, which continued to use wrought iron till the late 1870s, helped to keep most of the older works going, though Plymouth and Penydarren had already closed. But the decline of the rail trade foreshadowed the demise of the Welsh wrought-iron industry.

Meantime the shift from iron to steel had been taking place. Discovered in 1856 the Bessemer process was adopted soon after at Dowlais and at Ebbw Vale, where Bessemer steel was used for rails, and a few years later at Rhymney and Blaenavon. By 1882, Tredegar also had convertors and Cyfarthfa as well two years later. While Bessemer steel had been making headway on the northern outcrop, Siemens had discovered successfully an alternative method of steel manufacture, the open-hearth process, and had established a works at Landore (near Swansea) in 1868. Because its future was tied closely with that of the tinplate industry, as will be described below, the production of Siemens steel grew faster in south Wales than that of Bessemer steel. In 1885, 433,000 tons of Bessemer steel were made in Wales and 138,000 tons of Siemens steel; but by 1912 the production of Bessemer steel had dropped to 328,000 tons whilst that of Siemens steel had risen to 1·36 million tons.

Along with the change in technique went a change in the source of iron ore. This led to a shift in the location of steel manufacture within south Wales. Since local ores contained phosphorous, which neither the Bessemer nor the Siemens process could eliminate, it was necessary to import non-phosphoric ore, which came mostly from Spain. Together with other iron interests, the Dowlais Iron Co. formed the Arconera Company to operate in Bilbao in 1872. Within seven years four times as much ore was being imported as was available from local sources. And the development of the Gilchrist–Thomas process—the lining of the convertor with a basic material like limestone which enabled phosphoric ores to be used—did not halt this trend. By the end of the nineteenth century, 800,000 tons of ore were imported annually through Cardiff, 340,000 tons through Newport and 170,000 tons through Swansea. The richer foreign ores increased the furnace yields in south Wales. Of the industry there in the early 1900s, J. S. Jeans wrote: 'The old Wales consisted of very small blast furnaces, producing 4000 to 5000 tons annually, and built so strongly that they seemed destined to resist even the crack of doom; of a multitude of small forges . . . of a labour community that understood no English, and was as much isolated from the rest of the British Isles in ideas, habits, and traditions, as if they had lived in Fiji. . . . The new Wales consists of blast furnace plants that produce as much pig iron per unit in a month as the old furnaces did in twelve; of ores entirely imported from abroad; of a collapsed and practically moribund finished iron industry; of a steel output exceeding a million tons of ingots annually from about 35 different works.'

The growing dependence on imported ore lessened the grip of the northern outcrop on the steel industry. Though some of the old works had turned from iron to steel manufacture, they found it increasingly difficult to operate profitably. Industrial inertia alone was responsible for the continuance of manufacture in the old areas. But changes were afoot. In 1890, the Rhymney plant was dismantled and the company concentrated on coal production. More significant was the decision of the Dowlais Co. to move to the coast and build a works at East Moors, Cardiff in 1891. And besides the shift in location there was reorganization. In the early 1900s, Guest & Company, and the Dowlais Co., amalgamated with two Black Country firms, the Patent Nut & Bolt Company and Nettlefolds, to form Guest Keen & Nettlefolds, and a few years later Baldwins, Ltd. virtually absorbed the Port Talbot Co. and so strengthened it to compete with Guest Keen's. Two years later in 1902, the Cwmfelin Steel and Tinplate Company, which was to become part of Richard Thomas & Co., acquired a stake on the east Lincolnshire orefield by the purchase of the Redbourne Hill Iron Works, Scunthorpe. Further, in 1912, John Lysaght brought the Normanby Park Works on the same Frodingham orefield into production to supply semis to the Orb Works at Newport. Such links were to be of importance later.

But the process of reorganization did not go far enough and events in the 1900s made the weakness of the Welsh hill plants increasingly plain. In the recession of 1908, when foreign tinplate bars were imported into south Wales and prices fell, the Cyfarthfa and Blaenavon works closed, operations were partially suspended at Landore and output was restricted at Dowlais and Cardiff. Renewed foreign bar imports in 1911 led to the closure of the steelworks and part of the blast furnace plant at Blaenavon and the Ebbw Vale Works (which had resisted absorption by Guest Keen & Nettlefold's in 1906) was shut down in the second half of the year. When war came, the Welsh steel industry was still in a process of transition.

Alongside the established uses of tinplate for domestic and dairy utensils and in sheets for roofing, there grew up in the second half of the nineteenth century new uses for tinplate such as food cans and petrol containers. To meet these new needs tinplate production in south Wales expanded from 37,000 tons in 1850 to 150,000 tons in 1870 and to 586,000 tons in 1890. Thus the annual output of the industry approximately doubled in each decade in this period, a rapid rate of sustained expansion. Most of the tinplate was exported. Exports rose from 25,000 tons in 1850, to 118,000 tons in 1872 and to a peak of 448,379 tons in 1891. Of this, the greater part went to the U.S.A., exports to that country totalling 325,000 tons in 1891. Since, without technical change, there were no economies of scale and tinplate works required a relatively modest amount of capital, the expansion of production was achieved mainly by the construction of new small tinplate works, operating on their own and unlinked to barmaking.

Until about 1850 tinplate manufacture had been more important in east south Wales but the second half of the century saw a shift in the centre of gravity of the industry to west south Wales. In this area there grew up a number of tinplate towns which were largely dependent on the industry for employment. Llanelly found compensation in the expansion of tinplate manufacture for the decline of the local copper and coal industries in the third quarter of the nineteenth century. Its first tinplate works, the Dafen Works, was built in 1846, and by 1880 when there were seven tinplate works in production in the town, it had earned the title of 'tinopolis'. If Llanelly was the largest, Pontardulais, Morriston and Briton Ferry with five works each, Port Talbot with four and Neath, Pontardawe and Gorseinon with three works, all relied for their prosperity on tinplate manufacture. They were essentially one-industry towns, shopkeepers and service industries being dependent for their well-being on the state of the tinplate trade.

For this concentration of manufacture west of Port Talbot there were a number of reasons. West Wales was particularly adapted for tinplate making: local supplies of the particular coals required, of limestone and of sulphuric acid were available; water from the rivers Afon, Neath, Tawe and Amman was plentiful; and the coastline possessed ports, notably Swansea, which were well placed for the import of iron ore and tin and for the export of the finished product. But these factors do not completely account for the dominance which west Wales obtained. The operative reasons lie elsewhere. First, there was the growing concentration of the ironworks in east Wales on rails. Then there were few competing outlets for the kind of labour the tinplate industry required. Tinplate makers were able to recruit workers from the copper industry and from the old charcoal iron industry, both of which began to decline just at the time when tinplate-making was expanding most rapidly. Finally, the development in west Wales of the Siemens open-hearth process of steelmaking after 1875 provided the tinplate industry with a convenient local source of bars.

Tinplate makers had found the early Bessemer steel too unreliable for their purposes but had quickly adopted the use of Siemens steel after the success of its first commercial production at the Landore Works (near Swansea). By 1890 there were 12 Siemens steelworks in west Wales which had been erected to meet the needs of the tinplate industry. The two developments interacted. Steelworks were built to supply the local tinplate industry and then, because a supply of bars was available, further tinplate works were built in west Wales.

The expansion of the tinplate industry in south Wales was checked in the 1890s by the loss of its main export market, the U.S.A., because of the increased tariff placed on imported tinplates by the

McKinley Tariff of 1890. Production fell from 586,000 tons in 1891 to 450,000 tons in 1896 and exports from 448,000 tons to 267,000 tons in the same period. A few tinplate works closed permanently while others changed hands, in particular, Richard Thomas & Co., seized their opportunity and by purchase became the largest firm in the industry. Yet a few other works were converted to the production of blackplate or galvanized sheet. From the 1890s galvanizing grew in south Wales and by 1902 there were eighty mills there making galvanized sheets and blackplates. As there seemed to be advantages in ensuring a secure supply of tinplate bars, most tinplate firms invested in steel manufacture once trade improved with the upturn of the trade cycle in 1896. The Lewises of Gorseinon built the Bryngwyn Works to serve their group of tinplate works, the Grovesend Company built a steelworks in 1900, and Gilbertson's added to their steel capacity by building a works at Port Talbot in 1906. The Llanelly Steel Co., founded by two Llanelly tinplate firms, in 1898, was reorganized to include eight other independent tinplate producers in 1907, and another group of independents built the Bynea Steel Works (Loughor) in 1912. The expansion of production of tinplate which reached a pre-war peak in 1912 of 848,000 tons led to the construction of new mills and works. To begin with mills were added to existing works but from 1909 new works were built at Swansea, Gorseinon, Pontardulais and Llanelly. 'In the Swansea district,' reported *The Economist* in 1913, 'more capital has been expended in the last seven years than in any corresponding period in the history of the trade.' All these works were built near the coast, within easy reach of the steelworks which supplied them with their major raw material and within close reach of Swansea docks through which they obtained their tin and exported their product.

While the tinplate industry expanded, the copper industry prospered and then declined. At the mid-century Swansea was the copper capital of the world. Of the eighteen copper works in Britain in 1860, seventeen were in the Swansea area and the Swansea Metal Exchange was the centre for the world trade in copper. The production of British copper ores reached a maximum about 1860 and then fell from 210,000 tons in 1863 to 42,000 tons in 1880. Meanwhile imports of foreign ores and regulus rose rapidly from small beginnings in the early nineteenth century to reach a peak in the period 1885–90. Some cargoes came from Cuba, Australia and South Africa but soon Chile became the major source of supply. The Cape Horners who brought the wooden sailing ships laden with ore to Swansea have become a legend. But Swansea's dominance was threatened by two important developments. Great new sources of supply were found in the U.S.A. south of Lake Superior and American firms entered the market, breaking the hold the Swansea smelters had long held, and copper-smelting was begun in Chile and Australia so that it was no longer necessary to bring the ore to Swansea for refining. One by one the Welsh copper works closed and the chemical industry which was linked with copper smelting also declined. The fabrication of copper had never become established in the Swansea area but had been carried out in London and Birmingham so that with the collapse of copper-smelting, Swansea's stake in the copper industry was lost, apart from two or three works in which sheet and wire production took place. Important though the discovery of new sources of ore and the development of smelting overseas was, a major factor in the decline of smelting in south Wales was the monopolistic practices followed by the industrialists there. By combining to keep up the prices of manufactured copper and to drive down the prices of imported ore, they encouraged ore producers to set up their own smelting works.

Though copper waned, Swansea retained an interest in non-ferrous metal production. In the 1860s two erstwhile copper works, the Old Forest (Morriston) and the Upper Bank (Landore), were converted into spelter works and spelter manufacture flourished at the Landore works before it was taken over by Siemen in 1868. New spelter works were built at Port Tennant, Llansamlet and Landore, all in the immediate neighbourhood of Swansea, between 1870 and 1913 at which latter date there were seven zinc-smelting works in active production. In the mid-nineteenth century most of the zinc ores came from Sardinia but from 1885 the Swansea industry largely relied on ores from the Broken Hill mine in New South Wales, Australia. The need for water, for skilled labour and for access to a port combined to make zinc-smelting a highly localized industry. Certain other non-ferrous industries were carried on in the Swansea area in the later nineteenth century. Arsenic refining was carried on at three works and tin smelting at two, but the most important development was the establishment of the Mond Nickel Works at Clydach in the Swansea Valley in 1902. The local skilled labour, the accessibility of anthracite fuel, the availability of water and of sulphuric acid (from the local chemical works) made the Swansea Valley a most suitable location for the refining of the nickel matte brought from Canada. Within a short period, the Clydach works became the largest of its kind in the world.

One ingredient which made the growth of industrial output possible in south Wales in the later nineteenth century was the considerable increase in the size of the labour force. Though output per head rose in the steel and tinplate industries there were no major labour-saving developments. And productivity actually fell in the coal industry. As late as 1913 it was still in the pick-and-shovel stage, while the seams being worked were much leaner than those previously exploited. More coal was therefore produced only by employing more miners. These developments in coal, steel and tinplate, and the expansion of ancillary industries, affected the structure of industrial employment in south Wales, as Mr. Mansel Hodges describes below.

Some of the growing numbers of workers were a consequence of natural increase, but migration also played a part. Almost alone of European countries Wales gained population in the later nineteenth century and at the beginning of this century was absorbing immigrants at a rate not much less than the United States. As more capital was invested in sinking new pits, workers were drawn from a wider area. In 1871 the English counties provided, as Mr. Hodges indicates, 9.6 per cent of the population of south Wales but this proportion had increased to 13 per cent by 1881 and to 16.5 per cent by 1891. Few Scots, however, came to south Wales and the influx of Irish, of whom nearly 16,000 lived in south Wales in 1861, declined as the century wore on. The figures of migration into south Wales in this period have been analysed by Professor Brinley Thomas and Mr. Hodges in articles printed below. Not all the movement, however, was into south Wales. The growth of employment there was predominantly for men. Women in search of work were forced to leave south Wales and go into occupations, such as domestic service, in England. And when trade was bad there was some migration of male workers overseas, especially to the United States.

Migration fluctuated from decade to decade, as Professor Brinley Thomas has pointed out, in harmony with the British export sector. Within the coalfield the most remarkable example of headlong expansion was provided by the Rhondda which in 1831 had only 1636 inhabitants. Population there grew from 4000 in 1861 to reach 127,980 in 1891 and a peak of 163,000 in 1921. In the same period the population of Cardiff, the main coal-exporting port, rose from 41,422 to 220,827. Such was the extent of migration that only half the 182,259 people living in Cardiff in 1911 had been born there. Nevertheless, the picture throughout the region was not one of continuous growth. The population of the old iron region on the northern outcrop reached a peak in the 1860s and then declined. With wages higher in coal than iron, workers migrated. Between 1871 and 1911, Merthyr lost 18,000 for this reason. Towards the end of the century with the expansion of demand for anthracite the western end of the coalfield (which had similarly lost population in the 1870s and 1880s) began to attract people again. Thus between 1891 and 1921 the population of Ystradgynlais rose from 4346 to 11,061. The pattern is not one of simple growth but is complicated by local increases and decreases as the fortunes of different parts of the region fluctuated.

The consequence of population growth became quickly visible on the face of south Wales. Though overcrowding persisted, the mining valleys were filled with long rows of houses, usually built of stone quarried from the pennant grit and blackened by grime, which extended in untidy lines along the valley sides. The whole of the industrial valleys became straggling urban settlements. Older industrial centres, like Morriston or Brynmawr, which had been originally planned as a unit, were surrounded by a less orderly accretion of houses. The ports like Cardiff and Swansea broke free from their ancient limits and expanded into the surrounding parishes. An Act of 1875 brought both Roath and Canton within the borough of Cardiff while by Acts of 1867 and 1888 Swansea absorbed Morriston. Using material in the hands of local authorities, Mr. Hamish Richards and Professor John Parry Lewis have shown, in the article printed below, how housebuilding fluctuated from year to year in south Wales between 1850 and 1913. Particularly after 1880 they argue the experience of south Wales differed from that of Great Britain. In the country as a whole construction of houses took place when building in the U.S.A. declined. The converse was true of south Wales, that is, the south Wales building cycle was export-determined.

On the fringe of industrial south Wales resorts developed at Tenby, Llandrindod Wells and Porthcawl. Once the railways had been constructed works' outings came to be organized. On a number of occasions, for example, nearly 2000 workers from Crawshay's at Merthyr were brought to Swansea for the day. Meantime, while the mining valleys throbbed with life and the ports buzzed with activity, the vale of Glamorgan slumbered on. The population of Cowbridge was 1134 in 1871 and no more than 1202 in 1901.

Entrepreneurially the outstanding characteristic of this period was the dynamic response of local industrialists to the opportunities of expansion which became available in both manufacturing industry and transport. Apart from Powell and Nixon already mentioned, outstanding in this age of rugged industrialism were Samuel Thomas, a grocer of Merthyr, whose collieries later formed the Cambrian Combine and whose son became Lord Rhondda; David Davies of

Llandinam, the son of a small Montgomeryshire farmer, who founded the Ocean Coal Company, built railways and launched the construction of Barry Docks; and John Cory who established a network of bunkering depots throughout the world. Unlike the iron kings in the previous period, the leaders in the age of coal were predominantly Welsh in origin. The contrast has never been fully explored but the difference between the metallurgical industries, in all of which outside entrepreneurs were of importance, and the coal industry may lie in the technical needs and capital requirements of the respective activities.[1] Certainly in the tinplate industry when the industrialists, most of whom were of local origin, were faced with the problem of technical change, they proved for reasons set out in my article below, reluctant to innovate.

Though there was some maturing of financial arrangements, south Wales remained a backward region in this respect. Until the outbreak of the first world war, some capital continued to be mobilized on a personal basis rather than through the more impersonal machinery which was adopted in more advanced sections of the British economy.

While Welsh industrialists continued to be paternal despots, intermediate forms of labour organization such as the butty system —a form of subcontracting for labour—continued to be common and truck, despite successive Acts, still prevalent until the early years of the twentieth century. With expanding trade, the fifties and early sixties were relatively free from industrial strife and trade unionism made little progress. In 1867 the Trade Commissioners reported that trade unionism had no hold among the miners of south Wales. The new burst of unionism there was to come as the result of a stimulus from outside. In 1869 a visit of Thomas Halliday, the Lancashire miners' leader, led to a period of militancy which resulted, as John Morris and L. John Williams relate below, in the establishment of a sliding-scale agreement to regulate wages. From the subsequent regulations, William Abraham (Mabon) emerged as the dominant figure amongst the miners. Under his leadership slow advances were made by the coal-miners who became the best organized: but trade unions also grew up in the iron and tinplate industries and amongst the crafts. As with industrial leadership, in all except coal, outsiders provided the knowledge and organizing ability. In iron and tinplate, for example, Ben Tillett and John Hodge played a major part both in organizing unions and also in establishing conciliation machinery. They had much greater success than the coal miners who on the eve of the first world war became more militant. With the coal owners organized in great combines, the coalfield was seething with unrest and a stormy period of industrial relations seemed in prospect. It was this sequence of events which gave rise to the belief that Welsh labour was unruly, a belief which was later to be of importance when attempts were made to encourage new employers to come to the region. Visions of the 'Red Rhondda' did not provide the most inviting prospect.

In the later nineteenth century, south Wales had developed extremely fast, it was a boom economy, organized by unrestricted private enterprise, based on the export trade and facilitated by massive immigration. South Wales was at once a major centre of iron production and the greatest coal-exporting region in the world. But its prosperity was based on extreme specialization. Before 1913 the benefits of this position were apparent not least in rapid growth: after 1913, for a quarter of a century, when conditions changed, the concomitant weaknesses were to be ruthlessly exposed.

NOTE

1. Recent work suggests this contrast has been exaggerated and that in the coal industry immigrant entrepreneurs were also important.

PART ONE:
POPULATION

CHAPTER ONE

The Peopling of the Hinterland and the Port of Cardiff (1801-1914)

by T. M. Hodges

I. 1801-31

ONE of the outstanding features of the Industrial Revolution in Great Britain was the rapid increase in the population during the nineteenth century which doubled from 9 millions in 1801 to 18 millions in 1850, and again doubled itself by the end of the century. Another outstanding feature was the attractive power of industry, which drew the population from the countryside and concentrated it on the coalfields. This process changed the whole face of the countryside, and new densely populated regions came into being in Lancashire, Yorkshire, the Scottish Lowlands, the Midlands, and parts of south Wales which before had been distinctly rural in character.

At the opening of the nineteenth century the hinterland of the port of Cardiff was already beginning to feel this attractive power of industry, but its influence was as yet relatively small and restricted to a few localities only. The two sharply divided regions of the hinterland, the one agricultural, of long standing and more or less static in character, and the other industrial, new and vigorously expanding, showed the trend of the future distribution of its population.

The extent of the hinterland at that date amounted to about 504·4 square miles and consisted of the eastern part of Glamorganshire, bounded on the east by the Rhymney river from the hamlet of Rudry to the sea; on the north by the Glamorgan–Brecknock boundary; and on the west by a line running from the Avon in a north-north-east direction to the head of the Neath valley. The westerly and easterly margins were vague, however, since the area in the west from Bridgend to Neath overlapped with that of the natural hinterland of the ports of Neath and Swansea, while that in the east overlapped with the natural hinterland of Newport. So scanty

3

was the population, however, that for census purposes there were only six administrative districts, each composed of one or more civil parishes which sprawled over several valleys bearing no likeness to future urban districts.

Of the total area of 504·4 square miles, the Merthyr and Aberdare districts accounted for 177 square miles, or just under 40 per cent, and this represented the extent of the industrial hinterland, except for isolated pockets of industry as at Llantrisant, Whitchurch and Caerphilly. At the turn of the eighteenth century, there were no more than 40,000 people dwelling in the whole of the hinterland and its port, of whom a little more than one-quarter lived in the industrial districts of Merthyr and Aberdare.[1] The only places which could boast of more than a thousand inhabitants were Merthyr Tydfil, Cardiff, Aberdare, Llantrisant, and Coyty (near Bridgend).[2] The bulk of the population outside of these small townships lived in hamlets and villages dotted over the vale of Glamorgan and in scattered hill farms. Though the iron industry was well established in Merthyr and to a smaller extent in Aberdare, the demand for iron had not yet reached the dimensions of future years when machine tools made the manufacture of iron goods easier, and steam-engines, iron bridges, and railway lines caused a wave of intense industrial activity in iron-making districts.

As yet, too, the mining of coal was confined to the needs of smelting, and mines were really small levels burrowed into the hillside where the depth of the valleys exposed the upper coal seams. The great demand for labour which characterized later years had yet to come, and the growing of wheat, oats, barley, and the making of dairy produce still absorbed nearly three-quarters of the total population of the hinterland. The vale of Glamorgan, which for centuries had been more advanced economically than the area occupied by the coalfield, contained many villages and hamlets with ancient histories; but broadly speaking the population was scanty and fairly evenly distributed, as one would expect where agriculture was the sole occupation.

During the first thirty years of the century the tempo of the iron-making industry quickened, and most of the increased population can be attributed to its development in Merthyr and Aberdare, but more particularly the former. By the year 1831 the population in the port and hinterland amounted to 71,998, an increase of approximately 80 per cent in 30 years. By this time the Merthyr and Aberdare iron-works were producing four times as much iron as they did at the end of the previous century.[3] Coal-mining for sale purposes had also started in the vicinity of both these towns during the late twenties. The effect of this increased industrial activity was to cause a rise in the population of Merthyr Tydfil from 7705 to 22,083 and in that of Aberdare from 1486 to 3961.

The port of Cardiff, too, benefited from increased port activity as a result of the rise in its export trade. This was reflected in a rapid rise in its population from 1870 to 6187. These increases were confined to the immediate vicinity of the places named. The remainder of the Merthyr and Aberdare districts, for example, which extended over 92·6 square miles and 83·7 square miles respectively, embracing the Upper Taff, the Cynon, and the Rhondda valleys, together contained only 4365 people, or about 25 to the square mile. The only other places in the hinterland to show relatively rapid increases were those which contained coal-mines or iron-works. These accounted for the relatively greater concentrations of population around Treforest, Llantrisant and Whitchurch.

Despite the promise held out by these widely scattered iron and coal workings, however, exploitation was relatively small, supporting only a population of a little over 30,000 people in 1831, of which over 22,000 were concentrated in the town of Merthyr Tydfil, by far the largest town in the whole of Wales.

Of the total increase of 32,619 people in the whole of the hinterland from 1801 to 1831, the Merthyr, Aberdare and Cardiff districts contributed over 23,000 while the remaining 9000-odd represented the normal natural increases of the rural districts.

Where did this increased industrial population come from? Apart from natural increases, migration from outside supplied the answer. In the absence of exact statistics of births and deaths for the period and of reliable information on migrations of population, how much was due to the one cause and how much to the other must rest largely on conjecture. Lack of good roads and the absence of rail communication were undoubtedly factors limiting influxes from long distances. Consequently, migration from outside was largely confined to the nearby rural counties of south Wales and south-west England, such as Somerset and Gloucester, and to such iron-working districts as Shropshire and Staffordshire. An exception to this, however, was the number of Irishmen who came over in returning coal boats to Cardiff. Most of these went to Merthyr Tydfil where they found unskilled work in the iron-works.

Migration from the nearby rural districts of the Vale must have been relatively small and slow as yet, since there was no marked depopulation. On the contrary, small percentage increases were registered in all areas without exception.

5

II. 1831–61

Between 1831, when the population of the port and its hinterland was 71,998, and 1861 population increased to 208,145, a rise of 189 per cent. Three outstanding factors contributed towards this development: the rise in coal production for sale purposes; the construction of rail transport; and the opening of the Bute Docks. Of these three factors, though the first was a *sine qua non*, the second and third became so closely related with each other and with the first that the resultant economic advance was due to their mutual reactions.

As one would expect, the increases in population were most marked in the coalfield and in the port itself. Whereas in 1831 the combined population of these two amounted to 59,215, representing 82 per cent of the total population of the port and hinterland, by the year 1861 their populations had increased to 196,954, a rise of nearly 233 per cent, representing 94 per cent of the total population. Of this population the port of Cardiff represented 7486 in 1831 and 46,954 in 1861, an increase of 528 per cent.

The outstanding increase in the coalfield was that in the Aberdare valley, where by 1861 population had risen from 6393 in 1831 to 37,487 an increase of 490 per cent, while the population of the town of Aberdare itself had increased by 715 per cent. This phenomenally rapid growth was due to the development of the steam-coal seams during the forties and fifties, when the greatest activity in sinking took place. This period also saw the establishment of the export trade in steam-coal with France, based upon coal from this valley.

The Merthyr district, however, made its greatest increase in population during the thirties due to the expansion of iron-making there during those years. Population in this valley increased from 24,016 in 1831 to 69,618 in 1861, a rise of nearly 190 per cent, over 81 per cent of which took place up to 1841. Development was almost entirely in the near vicinity of the town of Merthyr itself where all the iron-works were situated. Coal-mining for sale purposes had not really become general in this valley despite the fact that it was here that the first steam-coal for sale had been produced.

In 1845, John Nixon sank 'to the deep' at Merthyr Vale, about 5½ miles south of the town of Merthyr. But owing to the fact that the steam-coal seams lay deep beneath a thick pennant overlay, coal-owners were deterred from further exploitation as yet. Consequently, the population of the valley outside of the town of Merthyr itself was meagre and more or less static in growth. Even in Merthyr the rate of development was much slower after the forties when the iron industry had reached the zenith of expansion. Whereas population increased by 81 per cent from 1831 to 1841, the rate of increase declined to 33 and 19 per cent respectively in the next two decades.

Though a start had been made in the fifties to open up the upper part of the Rhondda valley, the real development of this valley did not take place until the seventies. In 1831, the valley was almost completely rural in character. Only 1636 people inhabited the whole valley, of whom 542 lived in the parish of Ystradfodwg, the location of the greatest concentration of coal-mining activity in the country some years later. The remainder dwelt in the parish of Llanwonno which included the lower Rhondda valley, in the vicinity of the village which was to grow into the flourishing town of Pontypridd. This meagre population represented only 14 people to the square mile in the upper valley, and barely 53 to the square mile in the lower valley.

During this period up to 1861, coal-mining began to develop rapidly in the neighbourhood of Pontypridd by the sinking of a number of shallow pits for the production of upper seams, but the pits were relatively small. Even so, population increased to 11,735 by 1861, a rise of 617 per cent in 30 years, of which nearly 180 per cent was made in the decade 1851–61. Other less spectacular increases in population were made in minor parts of the coalfield, all associated with coal. Mining in the vicinity of such places as Caerphilly, Llantrisant, Bridgend and Maesteg caused increases in their populations, but development in these areas was as yet relatively small.

Expansion in coal-mining meant an increasing demand for labour far beyond the means of existing populations to provide by natural increases. The nearby rural counties of Wales naturally provided the most accessible source of supply, but population statistics show that most of the rural counties of England contributed a share in the supply from outside. Of the latter, Somerset and Gloucester easily ranked first. Of the total 74,735 migrants into south Wales by 1861, over 40,000 were born in these two English counties. The prospect of relatively high wages for work requiring no previous training proved an attractive bait to these country folk, while rail transport brought the industrial valleys within easy travelling distance. Another source of supply, particularly after the potato famine of 1846, was Ireland. Large numbers of Irishmen gravitated to the ironworks at Merthyr Tydfil. By the year 1861 nearly 18,000 Irish lived in south Wales, where they set up colonies of unskilled workers either at the ports or in the iron-making districts. Of the total population of Glamorgan of 317,752 in 1861, non-natives represented 23 per cent; those born in Welsh counties other than Glamorgan

7

represented 11 per cent, while the remaining 66 per cent were native born.

SOURCES OF MIGRANT POPULATION INTO SOUTH WALES 1861

Birthplace	Total male and female
London area	3,989
Southern counties	2,967
Home counties	1,415
East Anglia	1,218
Somerset, Wilts., Devon, Cornwall	23,685
Gloucester, Shrops., Staffs., Worc., Warw.	16,478
Leic., Linc., Derby	945
Ches., Lancs., Yorks.	2,969
North-east coast	856
North-west coast	363
Scotland	1,824
Ireland	17,926

Total 74,735

Source: 1861 *Census of Population.*

Coal-mining and iron-manufacture engaged by far the greatest proportion of the population for single occupations. Exact statistics of this proportion for the hinterland are not available, but the numbers for south Wales give a rough indication. In 1861, there were 29,292 people engaged in coal-mining above and below ground, or 12 per cent of the total number employed in mining in the United Kingdom, while iron-manufacture gave occupation for 11,051, which was 11 per cent of the total number of people so engaged in the United Kingdom.

In order to attract experienced workers at a time of new development in any particular part of the coalfield, coal-owners offered a tempting bait of higher wages. Since the question of wages was entirely a matter for settlement between individual coal-owners and their employees, many different rates were in operation at any one time not only throughout the coalfield but even within the same valley. For example, rapid development took place in the Aberdare valley in the forties, and coal-owners there attracted miners and others from the Merthyr Tydfil district by offering rates of pay 15 per cent in advance of those paid by the Merthyr iron-masters to workers in their mines. Later on, when intense mining activity took place in the Rhondda valley, coal-owners there offered wages 10 per cent above those paid in the Aberdare valley, and thus 25 per cent higher than those offered in the Merthyr valley for similar work.[4]

Owing to the rural character of these valleys when they were

8

first opened up for coal-mining, there was a complete lack of housing accommodation and other amenities. Consequently, workers often had to walk many miles to and from work. In fact, it was the distance of these isolated pockets of industry from the more settled communities and the general lack of social amenities there, which were given as reasons for higher wages to work in them.[5]

This problem of providing dwellings and other necessities of an ordered social existence was not easy of solution. In some valleys, particularly in Monmouthshire, the employers found it to their own advantage to erect miners' cottages themselves and even to provide shops for the sale of the necessities of life. This practice was not common, however, in Glamorganshire. Where it did operate, the coal-owners soon became the universal providers, and the 'Company' shop more a curse than a blessing. In due time, however, as these communities became more settled, 'free' or privately owned shops made their appearance, while the problem of house building was left to private builders.

The shortage of housing accommodation remained a perpetual problem during the development of all the mining valleys and was largely unsolved in 1914. It is not surprising therefore that overcrowding and part-letting of available houses became common. The general topography, of course, did not make the task of house construction any easier. It compelled the construction of dwellings in long streets rising tier upon tier up the steep valley slopes from the valley bottom which usually housed the few shops catering for the needs of the community. Nearly every dwelling contained its 'lodgers', and such was the shortage of sleeping accommodation that beds worked double time—day and night.

There is no record in south Wales of the 'padrone' system of soliciting labour, which provided the United States employers with much of their immigrant labour. But the same result was achieved in south Wales by early immigrants encouraging relatives and friends to leave their native villages in England and elsewhere for Welsh mining villages. Much of the Irish and Spanish quota came via boats putting in at Cardiff for coal.[6]

III. 1861–91

People are drawn as if by magnetic attraction to every scene of intense industrial activity. These influxes are composed not only of migrants from the countryside with no previous knowledge of industry, but also of experienced workers from other industrial areas. Thus every spate of new sinkings in the coalfields resulted in an inrush of workers eager to participate in their exploitation. The reason for this is not hard to discover, since those who were first in the field secured the pick of the best 'places', where high wages could be earned. In this respect coalmining in the pioneer days of the last century bore close resemblance to goldmining in the days of early gold rushes. Experienced miners trekked over the intervening mountain ridges into new valleys, urged by the prospect of big money to be earned with a smaller expenditure of effort than in the older mines where the best and easiest seams had either been worked out or were already being operated by older employees. Similarly, those who were raw to mine work were impelled by the prospects of high wages in an occupation which demanded at first no other qualification than the ability to work hard. Moreover, coal-owners in their eagerness to secure adequate labour stimulated these movements to new areas by offering higher wages than elsewhere.

Those were the days when wage rates differed not only from valley to valley, but even from one district to another in the same valley. This accounted for the parochial character of mining disputes and agreements, and proclaimed the intense individualism which ruled supreme. The effect on the population was that, whereas each valley, on reaching its full industrial development, became settled and more static in character, it experienced in its early stages of development a period in which its expanding population was mobile and constantly changing in composition.

Just as Merthyr Tydfil was the mecca to which all newcomers drifted during the period up to the forties, and just as Aberdare exercised a similar influence from the forties to the sixties, so the Rhondda valley eclipsed both as a power of attraction from the seventies onwards. Both the Merthyr and Aberdare valleys had achieved maturity by that time, and therefore their populations remained more or less static from 1860 to 1890. In fact, both experienced a slight decline in their populations during the seventies owing to the attraction of workers to the Rhondda.

Year	1861	1871	1881	1891
Merthyr Valley	69,618	54,741	51,712	61,135
Aberdare Valley	37,487	38,637	38,137	43,314

Note: Without a local knowledge it is almost impossible to compute an accurate estimate of the population of these valleys from the Census figures, since the various parish populations given overlap into several valleys. Thus it is only by means of many cross-calculations coupled with local knowledge of the places mentioned that approximate valley totals can be computed.

On the other hand, the Rhondda valley, from 1861 to 1891, experienced an eleven-fold increase of population as the direct result of intense coal-mining activity, particularly from the seventies onwards. In 1861 its population was 11,737; in 1871, 41,458; in 1881, 81,895; and in 1891, 127,980. Its aspect during those years changed from one of extreme rural loneliness broken here and there by isolated small coal-workings, and a population of less than 12,000, to one of an almost continuous ribbon of dwellings from Pontypridd at the bottom of the valley to Blaenrhondda at the head of the Rhondda Fawr, and Ferndale at the head of the Rhondda Fach. New townships sprang up where several mines were concentrated in those parts in which the valley happened to be wider than elsewhere, and places like Porth, Penygraig, Tonypandy, Llwynypia, Treorchy and Ferndale were born during those years. Pontypridd too came into being out of the older place name of Newbridge and developed as a shopping and commercial centre. From a small township of 2000–3000 inhabitants in the sixties, it grew to be the fourth town in size in the hinterland by 1891 with a population of over 24,000.

The Rhymney valley, which had been brought into the hinterland of the port by means of the Rhymney railway, also witnessed a five-fold increase in its population from approximately 8000 in 1861 to over 40,000 in 1891.[7]

The western valleys comprising the Maesteg–Bridgend districts which were brought more securely within the hinterland by Great Western railway connections with Cardiff actually suffered a slight decline in population in the sixties, owing to migrations to other mining districts; but a spurt of mining activity took place there in the seventies and eighties, especially in the Cwmddu area of Maesteg and in the Ogmore valley, with the result that these valleys witnessed a two-fold increase in population and registered in 1891 as many people as either the Aberdare or Rhymney valleys.[8]

Not less spectacular were the increases in the size of the ports of Cardiff, Barry and Penarth. Cardiff had been growing rapidly throughout the century—every expansion in the hinterland had stimulated a similar increase in the size of Cardiff. From 1861 up to 1891 its population multiplied four-fold. By 1871 it became the largest town in Wales, having surpassed Merthyr Tydfil, the previous largest town for many years, and in 1891 it contained more people than the whole of the Rhondda valley, which was itself the most thickly populated valley in south Wales.[9]

Barry and Penarth were, until the opening of their docks, merely tiny villages. Barry, whose docks were opened in 1889, had only 85 people in 1881, but experienced a phenomenal growth in ten years

and by 1891 had a population of 13,278. In 1865 a dock was opened
in Penarth, and its population jumped from 273 in 1851 to over
12,000 in 1891 not only on that account but also because it became
a residential district for the growing class of well-to-do Cardiff
docksmen.

The hinterland continued to attract immigrants from all the
counties of England, and also from both Scotland and Ireland,
though there were wide differences in the numbers coming from
each. The counties of south-west England and the west Midlands
provided by far the greatest number of any area outside Wales. Of
the non-Welsh population, these two groups of counties accounted
for 60 per cent in 1871, 64 per cent in 1881 and 66 per cent in 1891.
The reason for this is not hard to find, since they consisted of agricultural areas which could not hold out prospects of wages as high as
the nearby industrial area. Other agricultural counties farther afield
had nearer industrial areas of absorption, and only relatively small
numbers came to south Wales.

The English counties as a whole provided 9·6 per cent of the population in 1871, but this proportion was increased to 13 per cent by
1881, and to 16·5 per cent by 1891, owing to a spurt of immigrants
from the counties of Gloucester, Somerset, Devon and Hereford in
that order. People of Scottish birth, though equal to several of
the more distant English sources, contributed only a fraction of 1
per cent, but Irish immigrants continued to outnumber any single
area outside the two groups mentioned above. They formed a body
of unskilled workers who readily took to mining and general labouring. Though they formed only a relatively small percentage of the
total population—about 2 per cent—yet they represented in 1871
about 20 per cent of the non-Welsh. The influx of Irish was, however, on the decline throughout the period, and in 1881 fell to 7 per
cent of the total non-Welsh and represented 9 per cent in 1891.

Despite these influxes from outside, the bulk of the population remained predominantly of Welsh extraction, though growing less and
less so with each succeeding decade. In 1871, about 87·9 per cent of
the total population were Welsh born, but by 1881 the percentage
had dropped to 81·7 per cent, and still further to 79·5 per cent by

Year	1871	1881	1891
Native born (Glamorgan)	279,955	330,639	426,534
Other Welsh counties	71,483	91,059	121,653
English counties	34,015	70,230	114,451
Scottish counties	1,216	2,019	3,289
Irish counties	9,478	11,958	4,256

1891. Of this native population, migrants from other Welsh counties formed 17·9 per cent in 1871, 17·7 per cent in 1881, and 17·5 per cent in 1891, with Carmarthenshire, Pembrokeshire, Monmouthshire and Brecknockshire easily leading the rest of Wales. Though north Wales supplied a quota it never exceeded that of any one of the above-mentioned south Wales counties probably on account of the nearness of the big city of Liverpool which has always maintained a large quota of north Walians in its population.

As one might have expected, industrial occupations absorbed most of the working population, of which coal-mining was easily the first, followed by iron and steel manufacture. In 1871, there were 32,274 persons engaged in the mines, of whom 761 were women, and a further 1018 were engaged in the coal-mining service. By 1881 the number had increased to 44,864 representing about 50 per cent of the total industrial population. By 1891 the number of mine-workers spurted to 76,948 with an additional 3640 engaged in the coal-mining service. This doubling of the numbers between 1871 and 1891, and almost trebling since 1861, was largely due to the activity in the Rhondda, Rhymney and Western valleys during these years. As for iron and steel manufacture, the numbers declined gradually throughout the period, partly due to the decline in industry and partly due to the adoption of mechanical devices in operations previously performed by manual labour. Whereas in 1871 there were 14,906 engaged in this occupation including 676 women, the number declined to 11,396 by 1881 of whom 220 were women, and to 10,133 by 1891, all of whom were registered as being males. The Merthyr Tydfil district absorbed the largest number of these iron-workers, just as the Rhondda valley contained the highest number of mine-workers.

A third group of occupied persons, second in number only to the coal-miners, was the general labouring class, but as it absorbed labourers of many kinds, working in many different trades as widely apart as agriculture and railways, it cannot strictly be put second to coal-mining as a distinctly separate occupation.

The great problem of adequate housing accommodation in the industrial valleys remained largely unsolved throughout the period, though a great deal of building of small cottages went on as witnessed by the great increase in the number of masons, carpenters, etc. from 6290 in 1861 to 15,458 in 1891, and also by the increased quantities of constructional timber imported into Cardiff. Loads of timber and deals imported into Cardiff rose from 27,761 in 1861 to 65,000 in 1871, to 85,599 in 1881 and to 129,796 in 1891.[10]

IV. 1891–1914

The intercensal increase in population for the whole of the county of Glamorgan was 25·1 per cent between 1891–1901, 31·1 per cent between 1901–11; and 5·8 per cent between 1911–14. In 1891, the number of people living in the county was 687,218, and by 1914 this had increased to 1,186,489, a rise of 72·6 per cent in 23 years. Urban population in 1891 amounted to 549,941 and in 1914 to 956,164, an increase of 73·6 per cent. Rural population increased in the same period from 137,277 to 221,352, a rise of 61·2 per cent. This relatively large increase in rural population, despite the higher degree of industrialization, was due to the large number of miners who lived in rural areas owing to the shortage of accommodation in the mining communities. Nevertheless, rather more than 80 per cent of the total population remained urban in character. A feature of this urbanization was the birth of a number of urban districts in certain well-defined parts of the county. These new districts were largely governed in size by the existence of the long, narrow transverse valleys, shut in by intervening mountain ridges, which characterized the topography of the coalfield.

Each of these valleys became a natural entity for the formation of an urban district. Thus many of the old civil parishes, which had formerly sprawled over several valleys, were broken up to make way for new urban areas representing compact communities, more suitable for the purposes of local administration.

Within the exact limits of the natural hinterland there was a population of approximately 485,000 in the year 1891. By 1914 it had increased to over 885,000, a rise of 82 per cent. This represented about 81 per cent of the population of Glamorganshire, or 64 per cent of the combined populations of Glamorgan and Monmouthshire. The bulk of the population was concentrated either in the industrial valleys or in the ports of Cardiff, Penarth and Barry. The districts showing greatest increases over the period were: Caerphilly (360 per cent); Bedwellty (281 per cent); Gelligaer (215 per cent); Maesteg (191 per cent); Barry (168 per cent); Mountain Ash (152 per cent) and Ogmore and Garw (106 per cent).[11] The large percentage increases in certain of these was not entirely due to greater coal-mining activity than elsewhere in the coalfield, for some of it was due to the absorption of surrounding communities in order to form urban districts. Nevertheless, the increases were either directly or indirectly attributable to coal-mining development.

The Rhondda valley had already experienced its most rapid development in the seventies and eighties when its chief collieries were sunk. By 1891, its tempo of development had slowed down as the margin of new production was reached, and expansion from that date onwards consisted of a fuller development of existing undertakings. Nevertheless, its population increased from 88,351[12] in 1891 to 162,592 in 1914, a rise of 84 per cent over the period.

This population was evenly spread along the valleys, and no very large single township had developed. This was due to the exigencies of natural configuration, since the long narrow valleys confined lateral expansion to a few spots where the valley widened sufficiently to allow high local concentration, e.g. as at Porth and Tonypandy.

Of the total population of the county of Glamorgan in 1901 (859,931), 562,098 were born within the county, a rise of 135,564 since 1891. In 1911, 607,801 were native born, a rise of 45,703 in 10 years. A further 134,939 of the 1901 population were born in other Welsh counties or in Monmouthshire. This was a rise of 13,286 since 1891. In 1911, well over 100,000 were born in the same counties. This high proportion accounted for the fact that about 50 per cent of the people either spoke Welsh as their sole language or were bi-lingual.[13] Of the migrant population, the counties of Somerset and Gloucester still provided the highest proportions. In 1901, Somerset supplied 21 per cent and Gloucester 15 per cent of the English-born population in the county. By 1914, the latter county, as the result of interim increases in its number of migrants, provided 19 per cent, while the former had dropped to 17 per cent of the total.[14] Together with neighbouring counties, these two counties provided about 74 per cent of the English element. There was a notable drop in the numbers of Irish immigrants after 1901. From 1891 to 1901, the number had only declined by 150, but from 1901 to 1911 there was a remarkable falling off from 11,106 to 5980. This may be attributed to the decline in the iron and steel trade at Dowlais and Merthyr which had attracted most of the Irish element in previous years. On the other hand, the number of Londoners showed an increase of 1531 from 7604 during the decade 1901–11.

An examination of the distribution of these migrants shows that the number of females exceeded the number of males going to Cardiff (presumably into domestic service), whereas the reverse was true of the mining valleys (due to the nature of available employment there). Devonshire men, however, preferred the sea-ports, particularly Cardiff; by 1911 there were nearly 6000 Devonshire-born people residing in Cardiff. Outside of Cardiff, the Rhondda took the greatest number of migrants, particularly from Monmouthshire and Somersetshire. On the other hand, the Irish quota went to Merthyr as usual, or to Cardiff where they provided the labouring element of the docks and the iron-works.

15

Mining easily absorbed the greatest proportion of the working population for any single occupation, taking more than one-third of the total occupied population. The number engaged in mining above and below ground was over 154,000 within the hinterland in 1914.[15] This was an increase of over 64,000 since 1895.

Other occupations which absorbed large numbers of the working population were transport (48,739 in 1911) and the iron and steel industry (50,618 in 1911). Railway workers formed the bulk of the former, while tinplate workers represented a quarter of the latter, most of whom were engaged in the Swansea area. Building also ranked high as a single occupation, absorbing 26,452 in 1911. These were spread evenly over the county, forming fairly constant relative proportions over each district population. Agriculture, however, took declining numbers, as one might expect from the tendency towards increasing urbanization, and in 1911 absorbed only 11,028 people, most of whom were to be found in the rural areas of the vale of Glamorgan.

There was still an extreme shortage of dwelling-houses, particularly in the coalfield, and overcrowding and part-letting of houses was still common. The position, instead of improving, got gradually worse in the mining areas. In 1901 there were 103,980 inhabited houses in the urban districts of the hinterland. This worked out at 5·6 persons per house. In 1911 there were 135,416 inhabited houses or one inhabited house for every six persons. Such was the shortage of miners' dwellings that David Davies (Ocean Coal Co.) in 1913 paid for a survey of south Wales in respect of housing; a task carried out on his behalf by the Garden Cities and Town Planning Association,[16] but the shortage was as acute as ever at the outbreak of the Great War 1914–18.

Throughout the period 1891–1914 house building failed to keep pace with increases in population in every part of the hinterland. In all cases, the number of separate occupiers was much in excess of the number of inhabited houses. In 1901 there were throughout the urban areas of the hinterland 11,722 part-let houses, or 11·2 per cent of the total inhabited dwellings, and 16,724, or 12·3 per cent of the total, in 1911. The report of the Garden Cities and Town Planning Association put the number as high as 20,000–25,000 in 1913.

When it is considered that most dwellings in these areas were of the cottage type, usually with two bedrooms and rarely more than three, the cramped living accommodation can be readily imagined. Furthermore, such modern amenities as flush cisterns in lavatories and bathrooms were almost non-existent in the mining valleys.

In fact, in many of the older houses one outside closet (without a cistern) between five or six houses was common.

Whereas house building increased only by 3·2 per cent between 1901–11, the population increased by 44·9 per cent during that period. Taking the average number occupying one dwelling-house as six persons, this meant that for every new dwelling-house erected during the period there were nearly 7·5 persons waiting to occupy it. The cause of the shortage of houses may be largely attributed to the lack of available capital for building. Most building was speculative, or sponsored by local building societies in the case of the small number of better-class houses. In the Rhymney valley, however, the building of workmen's houses had been carried out largely by the employers as part of an almost all-embracing truck system,[17] but elsewhere in Glamorganshire this was not done on the same scale, although every mining town contained its street or two of what were known locally as 'colliery houses'.

NOTES

1. Merthyr district, 8945; Aberdare district, 2758. Year 1801, *Census of Population*, 1831.

2. Population in 1801: Merthyr Tydfil, 7705; Cardiff, 1870; Llantrisant, 1715; Aberdare, 1486; Coyty, 1018, census cit.

3. Production of pig-iron (tons): 1796, 18,049; 1828, 89,839; see H. Scrivenor, *Hist. of Iron Trade* (1841).

4. A. Dalziel, *The Colliers' Strike in South Wales* (Cardiff, 1871); *Western Mail*, 1872.

5. Ibid.

6. A. Redford: *Labour Migration in England*, 1800–50 (Manchester, 1926).

7. Rhymney valley: 1861, 8000; 1871, 29,470; 1881, 32,988; 1891, 40,748.

8. Western valleys: 1861, 19,979; 1871, 19,703; 1881, 33,959; 1891, 43,997.

9. Cardiff (including Llandaff): 1861, 32,954; 1871, 56,911; 1881, 82,761; 1891, 128,915.

10. *Stat. Tables*. Bute MSS. (Cardiff Library).

11. These new groupings render comparisons of periodic population changes very difficult, since the old civil parish boundaries bore little or no relationship to the new urban district boundaries. In this text the difficulty has been largely evaded by treating the valleys as individual entities from the start. In this way, it is possible to trace the close relationship between coal development and corresponding population increases through the whole of the period 1830–1914. This has necessitated slight adjustments in calculation, which a knowledge of local configuration has made possible. For geographical reasons the ports of Swansea, Neath and Port Talbot became in due course the natural outlets of that part of Glamorganshire lying west of the vale of Neath. For this reason the population of places lying in that part of Glamorgan has not been included in the population of the natural hinterland of the port of Cardiff. Similarly, since only the Rhymney valley and parts of the Bedwellty district of Monmouthshire lie within the natural hinterland, no places lying father east have been included. For the intermediate

region, which includes the Western, Rhondda, Taff and Rhymney valleys together with the vale of Glamorgan, the port of Cardiff can legitimately be considered as the natural outlet. If we broaden the conception of the term hinterland to include those areas within easy rail communication, then the hinterland includes nearly 1½ million people within a radius of 25 miles of the port and nearly 9 million people within a radius of 90 miles.

12. This figure represented the population of the newly formed urban district. It is thus much less than the figure of 127,000 given for that year earlier in the text. The discrepancy is explained by the fact that Pontypridd and parts of the parish of Llantrisant were then included in the 127,000. The census of 1901 was the first to give figures for the Rhondda Urban District as such.

13. *Census of Population, 1911. Preliminary Report.*

14. *Census of Population.* Somerset 1901, 28,756; 1911, 20,881; Gloucester 1901, 20,827; 1911, 23,782.

15. *South Wales Coal Annual* (1915).

16. *Colliery Guardian* (1914), p. 420.

17. W. S. Jevons, *The Coal Question* (1865), p. 26.

CHAPTER TWO

The Character of Welsh Emigration to the United States to 1840

by A. H. Dodd

THE Hungry Forties produced that mighty boom in emigration which ended by peopling the open spaces of the United States from the Mississippi to the Pacific. Wales suffered her full share of the tribulations of those dismal years, and if official figures are to be trusted the effects on migration were more startling here than in the country as a whole.[1] But behind the sudden spurt which carried Welshmen to every corner of the States there lay two centuries of sporadic migration, simpler in pattern if subtler in incentive, and it is with the broad character of these earlier movements and their lasting effects that the present study is concerned. The attractions of the New World, however strongly felt in later years, left Wales almost unmoved for three-quarters of a century after the first batch of emigrants settled at Jamestown. There were a number of early settlers with Welsh names, mostly classed as 'servants' and doubtless accompanying English households to which they were already attached.[2] Of the more substantial emigrants who went out under their own steam as it were, very few before 1680 remained to found families on American soil. Various attempts have been made to explain this surprising deafness to the call of the Atlantic on the part of a people who eventually made such excellent colonists, and who had so recently put out the legend of the first discovery of America by Madoc and his followers.[3] J. A. Doyle, in his work on *The Middle Colonies*, sees the explanation in the language barrier on the one hand, and an 'underpeopled and prosperous country' on the other.[4] Doyle was a historian of standing, and he knew Wales well, having lived there most of his life; but his diagnosis hardly carries conviction. No language barrier kept the Welsh from flocking to the court of Henry VII or from taking full advantage of the Elizabethan and Jacobean plantations in Ireland; and as for the alleged under-population,

William Vaughan of Llangyndeyrn draws precisely the opposite picture when he is urging the claims of his ill-fated Cambriol colony in Newfoundland, a decade after the first successful planting of Virginia.[5]

Welsh backwardness is to be attributed, I think, to quite other factors, partly geographical, partly religious. Among the former must be ranked the Irish plantations just referred to; why tear up one's roots and cross the Atlantic to wrest a home from the primeval forest when land-hunger could be appeased across the Irish Sea without the preliminary pioneering and without the pain of permanent exile from all that was dear and familiar? Many a Welsh squire was able to maintain and even to enhance his position in local society by the acquisition of Irish estates worth three or four times as much as his lands at home—to say nothing of peerages and knighthoods to be won there.[6] It is true that the Irish plantations did not meet the problem of the impoverished small peasant for whom Cambriol was planned; but Cambriol failed just because its colonists never freed themselves from dependence on the founder's capital, and for this class there was even less chance of prospering on the more distant mainland of America, unless they went out as indentured servants or under the headright system, by which fifty acres of land were offered to anyone bearing the expense of transporting a needy but able-bodied settler. The Welsh had long been prized as servants in the gentle and noble households of England, whether as stewards and secretaries or in more menial capacities, and they were equally in demand in the New World (as, for that matter, in Victorian London).[7] We can know little of this class, but it clearly accounts for a high proportion of Welsh emigration before the nineteenth century. A very occasional Welsh name is to be found among planters and headrights in early Virginia and Maryland, and a sprinkling of Puritans from south Wales joined the exodus to New England from 1639 onwards; but most of the latter returned to Wales after 1650, when their religious views were in the ascendant at home.[8]

The first extensive and lasting emigration came in 1682, when a body of Quakers, mostly from central Wales, established themselves in what was long known as the Welsh Tract of Pennsylvania, with a Welsh population which had reached about 2000 by the end of the century.[9] From about 1700 they were joined by other religious migrants (mainly Baptists), and these in turn filtered into Delaware, Maryland and North Carolina (where another extensive Welsh Tract had appeared on the map by 1747), and eventually South Carolina too.[10] The success of the first settlers attracted kinsmen and neighbours to join them, and Pennsylvania as the instinctive goal of Welsh emigration long outlived the original religious impulse and the disappointed initial hopes of maintaining an autonomous and self-contained Welsh community.[11]

Emigration from Wales slackened off in the middle years of the eighteenth century. As long as conditions remained adverse for the setting up of New Jerusalem at home, men went on seeking it overseas; but when the Great Awakening came to Wales the outward flow dried up. Not for long, however; for Whitefield's influence on the newly founded colony of Georgia on the one hand, and among the leaders of the Welsh revival on the other, formed a new bond of union. A few years before the American Revolution, a small group of students from the new Methodist college at Trevecka (Brecon) went out to Georgia to study at a similar institution just opened by Whitefield to train missionaries for the 'back settlements' and the Indian territories. One of them, Lewis Richards, became a Baptist minister successively in South Carolina, Virginia and Maryland, remaining at the same time in close touch with his old spiritual leaders in Wales, with whom he exchanged news of the progress of the Welsh revival and of the evangelization of the backwoodsmen of 'Caintucky'.[12]

By the time America had won her independence, Methodism at home was undergoing a period of stress which gave fresh currency to the old apocalyptic vision of the New World as the 'wilderness' prophesied in the Book of Revelation where a place was 'prepared by God' for His Church. Thomas Charles, like many of the Methodist fathers, had his doubts, and hoped at least that any of his flock who emigrated would go 'beyond ye confines of ye American republic' to virgin soil where they could 'erect a standard for ye Lord of hosts'; rather than 'get rich and great' in the materialistic atmosphere of the settled states, let them be content to 'eat barley bread and oaten Cakes in Wales'.[13] Wales indeed contributed little to the stream of emigrants that now sought the shores of the new republic[14] until after the revolutionary fever had spread to France, and Wales herself had begun to experience a national *risorgimento* in which democratic ideas from America and France and the social distress of the resulting wars all played their parts. These often conflicting impulses converged on America as the land of promise. The myth of the Welsh Indians was now revived and became a sort of contemporary counterpart of the Prester John *motif* of the early explorers. It was as acceptable to the missionary zeal of the Methodists as to the national pride of the Welsh radicals in London who sponsored the patriotic movement and re-founded the eisteddfod; for one of them it offered the additional prospect of a new and cheaper source of the furs in which he traded.[15]

It was with the encouragement of Thomas Charles, as well as of the London radical group and some of their correspondents in both Wales and America, that John Evans, son of a Methodist 'exhorter' from Caernarvonshire, crossed the Atlantic in 1792 on that quest of the Welsh Indians which was to end in the exploration of the upper Missouri and Evans's premature death seven years later.[16] His mission aroused for the first time a widespread interest in America in his own county, which had hitherto contributed little to the peopling of the States beyond a few indentured servants in mid-seventeenth century, a number of 'apprentices' at its close, and some individual emigrants during the War of Independence itself. A group of local bards who had been active in the re-establishment of the eisteddfod formed the plan of following Evans up, but only one of them actually crossed the ocean—Abraham Williams, who reached Philadelphia by slate boat in 1793; he soon forgot the Welsh Indians in the attractions of his new home, where (unlike Goronwy Owen, whose muse did not survive transportation) he was still writing Welsh poetry 'in the dark forest by the banks of the Susquehanna' a quarter of a century later. His glowing eulogies of this land of religious freedom and social equality attracted others from the neighbourhood to join him there; for a time they went on collecting and transmitting Welsh Indian lore, till these fancies were swallowed up in the grim economic realities of war time, and in a few years emigration from this one county shot up to more than 40 per cent of the total from Wales.[17]

A more surprising adherent of the Madoc myth was the sceptical and self-taught scholar William Jones, of Llangadfan in Montgomeryshire. This interest, however, was only incidental to his ambitious scheme for founding a sort of Voltairean version of Penn's Holy Experiment (which was still attracting emigrants a few miles from his home to within a decade or two of his birth) by the acquisition of a block of Pulteney lands in New York state. For the last five years of his life (1791–5) he devoted himself to the prosecution of this scheme by approaches to the Pulteney interest and the American government on the one hand and propaganda at eisteddfodic and other gatherings in north Wales on the other. He had more success in the second field of endeavour than in the first, for his apotheosis of America as the land where feudal and religious tyranny were unknown had a timely appeal even for those most liable to be shocked by his supposed heterodoxy, and a few from the neighbourhood of Bala, the very Mecca of north Wales

Methodism, and others from east Denbighshire, took his advice and sailed for New York in the years 1791-4.[18]

The tale was taken up from south Wales by the Baptist minister Morgan John Rhees, who had first booked his passage (abortively) for South Carolina at the end of the American war, and now returned to his early love with a crusading zeal inflamed by a visit to Paris (as Protestant missionary) during the Revolution, a resultant enthusiasm for its political ideals, and a more hesitant belief in the Welsh Indians. In 1794, when the war with France was making it increasingly dangerous to sympathize with the Revolution, he set sail for Pennsylvania to make one more bid for a Welsh settlement there. For this purpose—with the help of Benjamin Franklin's friend, Dr. Benjamin Rush—he founded the Cambria Company, under his own presidency, two years later. Shares were offered at $100 each, and two officials of the company (one of whom had just come out from Llanbrynmair and eventually settled in Ohio) were appointed to 'see the country and give information'. Rhees himself joined in the search (trying at the same time to keep track of John Evans), and eventually the newly opened Allegheny tract of Pennsylvania, still known as Cambria county, was chosen for the settlement, with its capital first at the now vanished Beula, then at Ebensburg. Not content with founding a colony, he promoted all sorts of educational, journalistic and philanthropic ventures, and the foundation of an undenominational church and an undenominational missionary society for work among the Indians show that the evangelistic motive was as strong with him as the political or the economic—if he ever found it possible to separate the strands.[19]

The struggle with revolutionary France made the emigration movement, with its republican and radical associations, more distasteful than ever to the conservative-minded leaders of Welsh society, and the heads of Methodism and the older Dissent in Wales joined hands with Anglican parsons and Tory newspaper editors to decry it;[20] but by his use of both pulpit and press Rhees gained a considerable following (especially among his own denomination) in north and south alike. Close on his heels went a party of a dozen farmers' sons from Llanbrynmair in Montgomeryshire, once a scene of the labours of Vavasour Powell and later to be a fruitful recruiting ground for Samuel Roberts's scheme of a Welsh settlement in Tennessee; indeed S. R.'s own uncle and aunt were among the emigrants.[21] These also included a number of Dissenting ministers—no longer fleeing from persecution, but in search of a wider and more promising field for evangelism. In the same year (1795) as many as seventy emigrants left Caernarvonshire for New York, and in 1796

23

a party of Rhees's South Wales disciples went out to form the nucleus of a congregation for his new pastorate, first in Philadelphia, then at Beula, the metropolis of the new Cambria settlement, where thirty houses and a public library of a thousand volumes had been provided by 1797.[22] Some of the more adventurous spirits pushed still further west into Ohio. David Jones, a Cardiganshire immigrant to the Pennsylvania Baptist community, had visited the area as a missionary to the Indians just before the Revolutionary War, but instead of settling there he returned to serve in the American army and then as chaplain to Wayne in the Indian wars,[23] leaving to Ezekiel Hughes and Edward Bebb, thirty years later, the honour of pioneering a community which long continued to attract the Welsh emigrant. Edward Bebb's son William, born in Ohio in 1804, was destined to become a governor of the state and a powerful advocate of S. R.'s schemes.[24]

The rural distress of 1797 extended 'the spirit of emigration' till it was believed to have 'infatuated a great part of the Principality'.[25] Well over a thousand left Wales for the States between 1794 and 1801, some of them to regions which had seen no Welsh and few European settlers before. A favoured goal of those from the northern counties was the Mohawk valley in the hinterland of New York state, over much of which backwoods conditions still prevailed, although development had begun (chiefly through German pioneers) soon after the winning of independence. Welsh settlers formed a substantial element in the populations of such rapidly growing urban centres as Utica (laid out in 1797 and rising during the next quarter-century to 'a very smart thriving village . . . of nearly 600 dwellings'), or the more westerly Steuben. By 1812 an area extending ten to fifteen miles round Steuben had 700 Welsh inhabitants; sixteen years later the area of settlement had nearly trebled and the Welsh settlers increased tenfold. Some came from rural Merioneth, where agricultural distress was rife; others from the Conway valley and the Creuddyn peninsula, where economic pressure was less urgent. Such districts had been powerfully affected by the religious revival, and the newcomers were often shocked by the godlessness of the backwoods, the neglect of Sunday, the disrespect for the dead, above all the prevailing drunkenness.

Soon after 1800 they began building their own chapels, served by Welsh-speaking ministers from Snowdonia or west Wales or the industrial south-east. Utica had two Welsh chapels by 1817, and Steuben two a few years later. Sometimes the same minister served both areas, and though they were a hundred miles apart, a joint annual *cyfarfod* was organized, lasting two days at each of the two centres. New York city, credited with only five Welsh inhabitants in 1793, had enough to hold an occasional Welsh service two years later, and to support a Welsh chapel early in the next century. At Remsen the first Welsh Calvinistic Methodist cause in America was established in 1826. For those who lived too far afield, services in Welsh were arranged (as earlier with the Pennsylvania Episcopalians) in private houses. Many cultivated small holdings to supply the New York market with 'Welsh butter', or set up smithies, shops or inns. Two North Wales immigrants attempted in 1794 to turn to account their skill as quarrymen by developing the unexploited slate resources of New York state and freeing it from dependence on New England supplies; and twenty years later many found work in navvying for the new Erie canal. With very few exceptions, they found economic conditions easier than at home—whatever they might think of the morals of their new fellow-citizens—and kept pestering old neighbours to come out and join them.[26]

As long as emigration was centred on Pennsylvania, and emigrants were drawn from the regions of Wales that had fed it so long, the newcomer could generally be assured of a welcome and sound advice from relatives or friends on the other side. In 1729 the Welsh Society of Philadelphia was founded by Robert Weyman, the Pembrokeshire incumbent of St. David's, Radnor—members marching in procession 'with Leaks in their hats' to hear a sermon by Weyman in the 'Ancient British Language' at Christchurch, Philadelphia.[27] About 1760 there followed the St. David's Society, catering for Welshmen throughout Pennsylvania, but it fell a casualty to the Revolutionary War. No sooner had the Cambria Company been formed than the Pennsylvania Welsh founded (in 1798) a Welsh Society 'for the Relief of such Emigrants as may arrive in this Country from Wales.' One of the founders of the older society lived to help in organizing its successor, and did not pass from the scene till 1822, at the age of 86. Another prominent member was Dr. Samuel Jones, the Baptist minister of Pennepek, who had left Glamorgan for Pennsylvania as an infant in 1737 with one of the later parties of Baptist emigrants and became (with Lewis Richards) a cautious American adviser in the search for the Welsh Indians.[28] Similar societies for the protection of newly arrived 'foreigners' were to be found in New England by 1793. Where protection of this sort was lacking, the Welsh settler too often became a prey of the sharks who infested the ports on both sides of the Atlantic, and so liable to find himself working in conditions not far removed from slavery, as a lumberman or labourer in the 'back settlements' of New York or Vermont.[29]

As the struggle with France grew more intense, the flow of emigrants was kept in check by lack of shipping, government restrictions, and the demand for manpower in the armed forces, though the Peace of Amiens caused a temporary boom.[30] Flood tide came in 1817, when the war was over and mass unemployment began. Hitherto the Pennsylvania Welsh Society had had no extensive calls on its funds, except for occasional relief of the sick (for which purpose two honorary physicians were part of its regular establishment), since most of the new arrivals were already provided for; it was even proposed in 1811 to seek legislative sanction for the diversion of its accumulated funds (now nearing $7000) to educational purposes.[31] But from 1817 to 1823 (with a few lulls) and again from 1829–32, the pressure became intense. The disillusionments of 1818–19, which severely checked the general flow of immigration for a whole decade, were not experienced by Welsh settlers in Pennsylvania; here the stream reached flood proportions in 1821 and stayed in spate another two years before it began to abate, till in 1826 there were no calls at all on the society's funds.[32] Although the steadiness and frugality of Welsh emigrants generally, and the strong bonds of kinship spanning the Atlantic itself, still kept most of them independent of organized help, and despite efforts in 1823 to make known in Wales the limited objectives and resources of the Welsh Society, over forty Welsh settlers passed through its hands in 1818, and nearly twice as many in 1832, while the amount spent in relief might rise as high as $500 in a single year.[33]

To meet these new demands it was necessary to have a clear-cut policy. Where the immigrant had a trade and could speak English (and as a rule the two went together), work could generally be found for him in or near Philadelphia or in Cambria county, the society often advancing money to set him up in business or to pay his children's apprenticeship fees;[34] but the unskilled and the monoglot were encouraged to make their way to the unsettled regions further west—either to the rapidly developing neighbourhood of Pittsburgh or on to the still newer states of Ohio and Indiana—or occasionally to upstate New York. For this purpose sums up to $40 (according to the number of children and the distance to be covered) were when necessary advanced to meet the cost of transport, and occasionally the younger children were boarded with a member of the society in Philadelphia until their new home was ready.[35] By 1812 the Welsh in Pittsburgh were strong enough to have their own Baptist chapel, and when nine years later the vice-president of the society paid a visit he found most of the Welsh settlers 'profitably engaged in the manufactories of the neighbourhood' and eager to repay their loans.[36]

This was the time when Robert Owen was trying to establish his New Harmony community in Indiana, but there is no evidence that his fellow-countrymen who settled in Indiana were attracted to it, at least not until unemployed weavers in his native county of Montgomery took up with Chartism in the early years of Victoria and (according to a local satirist) 'preach'd New Harmony was heav'n'.[37] Yet an enterprising Welsh pioneer had left his mark there as early as 1786, before it had even been organized as a territory. This was the Merioneth-born lawyer John Rice Jones, who abandoned his practice in Brecon in 1784 to sail with his family to Philadelphia, then, after fighting the Indians in Kentucky, played a great part in consolidating the new states of Indiana, Illinois and Missouri and in developing their mineral resources. His numerous descendents were long prominent in the political and military affairs of the Middle West.[38]

From 1830 onwards increasing numbers of Welsh arrivals at Philadelphia were provided for seventy miles up-river at the newly incorporated town of Pottsville, in the heart of the anthracite belt (where the first settlers had been massacred by Indians only half a century earlier). Here they were 'established under the guidance of our benevolent fellow member and true-hearted Welshman Joseph Simmons'—evidently a big employer in the area. What Hansen calls 'the Welsh era in the history of American mining' had begun, and another region became dotted with Welsh chapels.[39] Apart from getting the newcomers settled, the society performed invaluable services in advancing loans to tide them over a time of sickness such as often resulted from the rigours of the crossing, protecting them from the knaveries of agents and sea captains, assisting wives to rejoin husbands who had gone ahead, or facilitating their repatriation if they were left stranded.

Endless examples could be quoted of the benevolent work of the society, but a few must suffice. A Montgomeryshire man arrives in 1822 with his wife and eight children; the four youngest are boarded with a member while the rest go on with their parents to Ebensburg, the father returning, after getting them settled, to take the youngsters with him on foot. Here, however, the society intervenes and insists on advancing $20 for transport. Seven years later a family of six from Denbighshire, bound for Ohio, is caught in a storm at sea in which all their goods are lost; the wife is prostrated with illness and the youngest child dies. The society finds lodging for the stricken family in Philadelphia, gets a situation for the girl of eleven with the son and namesake of Morgan Rhees (who followed his father's calling and was elected a member of the Welsh Society next year), and medical attention for the mother from Rhees's doctor brother Benjamin Rush Rhees (named after his father's partner in the Cambria venture), while the two youngest children are boarded with yet another member of the society, who sees to their schooling. An even more distressing case was that of the wife who went out to join her husband at Pottsville in 1831, only to find that he had returned to Wales without sending her word. The society cared for her till she heard from him and then (since he sent no remittance) paid $45 to a ship's captain for her passage home. On the other hand, a Welshman who, having lost his wife through yellow fever in Baltimore, came to Philadelphia to seek work but fell ill himself, was refused the passage money to take him back to his seven children in Baltimore in 1822; but the year was one of exceptionally heavy calls.[40]

Pennsylvania's primacy as the goal of Welsh emigration was still unchallenged; its industrial development gave increasing scope to skills in which Wales abounded (to the point of redundancy in times of depression) and broadened its appeal beyond the regions which had been the sources of the original Quaker and Baptist migrations, though the old connection was maintained long after the resumption of large-scale emigration in the last decade of the eighteenth century.[41] Richard Crawshay's scheme for settling Welsh ironworkers there in 1800, soon after the first discoveries of iron ore, was an early pointer; the rise of Pittsburgh from a backwoods *entrepôt* to a great centre of the heavy industries attracted a steady stream of Welsh artisans and labourers, enabling it at one time to support four Welsh newspapers[42]; while in the eastern part of the state the balance of Welsh population shifted northwards of the original Welsh Tract with the development of the anthracite belt and subsequently of the slate industry, the latter chiefly by Caernarvonshire immigrants in the forties.[43] But by this time the helter-skelter flight from a hungry countryside to the New World was obscuring the original pattern of Welsh migration; it is significant that this increased influx is not noticeably reflected in the activities of the Pennsylvania Welsh Society during the decade 1841–50, for other regions were receiving a larger and larger proportion of the total, till in the course of the next generation the Welsh population of New York state and of Wisconsin (which with its mines and its boundless prairies was cried up in the forties as 'ideal for Welsh settlers') was already threatening to rival that of Pennsylvania.[44]

In these new and more widespread migrations economic motives usurped the place that religion had occupied ever since serious migration from Wales began, though even now the apocalyptic *motif* peeped through once more in the great Mormon exodus from south Wales between 1840 and 1870, and was not without its influence on the schemes of two more Welsh Dissenting ministers, Samuel Roberts and Michael D. Jones, for a Welsh settlement across the Atlantic in the fifties and sixties.[45] To counteract the croakers, the Welsh had new mentors like the Rev. B. W. Chidlaw, who, with an experience of America that pioneers like William Jones or Morgan Rhees had lacked, preached emigration on his visits to Wales in 1835 and 1840, and in the latter year published at Llanrwst a Welsh handbook for emigrants; and instead of having to suffer the endless delays and frustrations involved in the search for transport, the prospective settler was now canvassed by shipmasters announcing the departure of vessels from creeks and harbours near his home —beginning with fast sailing brigs between Bangor and Boston or Caernarvon and Charleston, or similar craft leaving Cardigan or New Quay, and culminating in the steamboat direct from Portmadoc to New York announced in 1830.[46] Caernarvonshire emigration was no doubt stimulated by the ease with which a passage could be booked in one of the slate boats which began to ply to America with increasing frequency from the closing years of the eighteenth century.[47]

In these conditions Morgan Rhees's dream of a new Wales which would 'flourish under the auspices of a free and enlightened people' when 'the old Cambria is neglected and despised',[48] was as unattainable as the Quakers' vision of a self-contained Welsh Tract had proved a century earlier. Although the plan was revived for Tennessee in mid-century (and later still for Wisconsin) before it was partially realized in the Argentine, it proved incompatible alike with the growing mobility of American society and the natural reluctance of the federal government to consolidate its racial groups. And so the Welsh settlers were soon swamped by Germans and Irish, both of whom had been subjected to similar disappointments. Both had formed a substantial element in the population of Pennsylvania since the early eighteenth century, the former growing to nearly half the total in fifty years; both had their national societies in Philadelphia, with which (as well as with the St. George's and St. Andrew's Societies) the Welsh Society began to exchange courtesy visits from its early days; both took part in the westward movement across the Alleghenies, the Irish on a scale that imposed an intolerable burden on the Pennsylvania Hibernian Society during the post-war rush.[49] Without a local habitation and a name, it became increasingly difficult for Welsh settlers to fulfil the aspiration of the inhabitants of the Welsh Tract in 1690 'to preserve our Language,

29

that we might ever keep Correspondence with our friends in the land of our Nativity',[50] although in fact the language survived for several years after all hope of autonomy had faded.

When the Pennsylvania Welsh Society was founded in 1798, nearly half a century had passed since Welsh was commonly spoken in the Quaker state, and what little migration from Wales had taken place during that period had been mainly to other parts of America. Its early members were so much out of touch with the motherland that the secretary (though obviously a man of education) had difficulties with the simplest Welsh place name. 'Anglisie', 'Denbrickshire', 'Lamorganshire,' and 'Merthytyd' are a few samples of his transcriptions of the place of origin given him by emigrants receiving help; 'Balla Manora' and 'Aberyshire' are still heavier disguises—possibly for 'Bala, Merioneth' and 'Aberystwyth.[51] The founders (with a few exceptions like Samuel Jones of Pennepek) thought of Wales in terms of geography and kin rather than of culture; they took endless pains to satisfy themselves of the Welsh origin of any prospective member or client,[52] but although the society's annual dinner was from the outset held on March the First, it took over twenty years before this was referred to in the minutes as 'St. David's Day', and a quarter of a century before the dinner took the character of a celebration of the patron saint.[53] Of the language itself not a word appears in the minutes for nearly seventy years. The established Welsh settlers who founded the society were men of substance, and their foundation was small and exclusive, with membership generally hovering round thirty, and confined to such as could afford high subscription rates and lavish honoraria of plate for services rendered—yet after heavy disbursements boasting a reserve fund of nearly $10,000 at the end of the first thirty years.[54] The monoglot Welshman was too migratory and too poor to enter such a circle, and the upper strata of the Pennsylvania Welsh adopted towards him the patronizing tone of a generation untouched by the national revival now gathering strength in Wales. It was probably among these 'poor relations' that a second society, naming itself (like the pre-revolutionary Welsh organization) after the patron saint, was formed some time before 1811, when a proposal from it for co-operation in buying a Welsh burial ground in Philadelphia was somewhat brusquely rejected by the senior society. The latter proceeded separately in the matter more than twenty years later, when the flow of immigrants had temporarily subsided, moving to a fresh plot in 1862.[55]

Long before this, the Cambria settlement had brought fresh Welsh blood to Pennsylvania after the long lapse of immigration.

Morgan Rhees's church at Beula was bilingual from the start; the neighbouring congregation at Ebensburg, also founded in 1796 (by his companion Rees Lloyd), was the first in America to hold all its services in Welsh, and went on doing so for more than half a century. It was here that Lloyd's successor (and S. R.'s uncle) George Roberts published in 1834 an English translation of Theophilus Evans's *Drych y Prif Oesoedd*,[56] a century-old work on Welsh antiquities, written by one of the earliest sponsors of Morgan Jones's 'Welsh Indian' romance. Each of these settlements became a new Welsh nucleus, constantly recruited from classes and areas with a newly resurgent Welsh life of their own, and between them they evoked a new spirit among the Welsh settlers, manifesting itself in such novel ways as the issue in 1875 of a St. David's Day message in Welsh by the governor of Pennsylvania, at the prompting of a senator who was a lifelong member of the Pennsylvania Welsh Society.[57]

For the new immigrants were of very different stamp from those who responded in an earlier generation to the call of William Penn. Seeking jobs rather than lands, and needing for the achievement of their aim not a substantial outlay of capital (their own or a patron's), but only the savings a labouring family might put by in a year or less, they could be conveyed almost direct from work, with neighbours and fellow-worshippers, to where they would find old neighbours, a rude replica of the familiar Bethel, and (if they were lucky) their old job. The monoglot would be kept in countenance by other groups even less at home in English, and there were frequent opportunities for keeping up communication with friends at home in the mother tongue.[58] Emigration was thus far less of an uprooting than in earlier days—but by the same token the new local roots were shallower and more easily pulled up again, leaving the Welsh life of the neighbourhood to wither as fast as it had sprung up, once the next generation had moved on. For example at Paddy's Run (Ohio) the first Welsh sermon was preached in 1803, the last in 1886; thirty years later only one inhabitant was left who could read Welsh, and a dozen more who could speak it. Similarly at Ebensburg Welsh services were abandoned in the eighties, although the Welsh community had been strong enough in 1859 to hold an eisteddfod.[59] At Utica they have continued to fight a losing battle against increasing pressure from English during the present century. Many Welsh churches have been closed in recent years owing to shifts in population and a monoglot English younger generation.[60]

Outside the more populous centres the survival of the language depended on the strength and persistence of personal or family sentiment. Even those who settled far from any existing Welsh group might be strong-minded enough to carry their own atmosphere with them—like the Welsh lady settled near the foot of the Great Smokies in North Carolina (possibly a straggler from the Welsh Tract further east), who having lost her husband in the war of 1812, trekked with her two young sons (of seven and three) two hundred miles across mountain and river to western Tennessee (not long since wrested from the Cherokee, who still roamed at large there), then migrated another two hundred north to southern Illinois—and through it all went on reading her Welsh Bible till her death in 1852.[61]

On the whole it has been by the accidents of dispersion rather than by pursuit of the will-o'-the-wisp of concentration that the Welsh have made their special contribution to the United States, and this has been largely the legacy of the original migrations. The indentured servants of whom they contributed so many tended to become a mobile class, since it generally behoved them to look far afield for good land when their term of service was over. Equally important was the gravitation of Welsh settlers to the Middle States rather than to New England or the South; for as F. J. Turner pointed out in his classic essay on 'The significance of the frontier', this middle region—an 'open door to all Europe' through its great harbours, and hence from the earliest times the receptacle of a mixture of nationalities, religions and institutions (in contrast with the original homogeneity of New England and the South)—was at the same time the most natural gateway to the west, 'with no barriers to shut out its frontiers from its settled regions'.[62] Through these two factors it came about that again and again—in the provision of a labour force in seventeenth-century Maryland, in the peopling of North Carolina and of the lands between tidewater Virginia and the mountain barrier in the early eighteenth century, in the movement forty years later from North Carolina to the upper tributaries of the Tennessee river, in the settling of the Mohawk Flats and the trans-Allegheny regions of Pennsylvania during the late eighteenth and early nineteenth centuries, and later still in the colonization of Wisconsin—Welshmen are to be found in association with Ulstermen, Germans and occasionally French Huguenots, more often than with the settled English Puritans of New England or the settled English and Scots planters of the South.[63] In each case their early provision for religion and education, their acceptance of hardship, their industry and sobriety—even their worship of respectability—left a mark on the communities they founded, and made a modest but effective contribution towards building up a civilized life in the backwoods.[64]

The predominance of the religious note in the early migrations appears not only in the character and aims of the first settlements but also in the strength of Welsh participation in evangelistic drives of every colour—whether to convert the Indian or to minister to the white man in the wilds, whether to arrest the drift of Maryland from Rome or of Virginia from its Anglican heritage, to plant the Anglican gospel in Pennsylvania or that of the Baptists and Methodists in the South. In comparison with this host of obscure pioneers, the hypothetical Welsh origins of distinguished Americans, from Jefferson downwards, pales into insignificance; and the pattern of the earliest migrations in a sense persisted even when the dream of a transatlantic New Jerusalem or New Wales faded away.

NOTES

1. The figures given in Brown and Roucek, *One America* (3rd ed., 1952), p. 663, show an increase just under threefold for total immigration, and nearly sevenfold for Wales; but reasons will be given for distrusting the figures for Wales. See also M. Hansen, *Atlantic Migration* (1941), pp. 141–4.

2. E.g., Hotten, *Original Lists of Emigrants* (1874), pp. 83–4, 121–3, 125, 133, 161–89, 201–74; *American Colonists in English Records*, 1st ser. 1932, 2nd ser. 1933.

3. David Williams in *Transactions Cymmrodorion Society* (*T.C.S.*), 1948, pp. 110–12.

4. 1907, p. 499.

5. W. Vaughan, *Golden Fleece* (1626), II. vi. 29–36.

6. A. H. Dodd, *Studies in Stuart Wales* (1952), p. iii.

7. *T.C.S.* 1948, pp. 12, 14; cf. J. E. Griffith, *Pedigrees of Anglesey and Caernarvonshire Families*, pp. 122, 277, *Cal. S. P. Dom.*, (1644–5), pp. 221, 615, A. E. Smith, *Colonists in Bondage* (Chapel Hill, 1947), p. 281.

8. *Bull. of Bd. of Celtic Studies*, xvi (1954), 30–1.

9. *Merioneth Hist. Soc.*, iii, 1959, 111–12.

10. D. Benedict, *General History of the Baptist Denominations* (Boston, 1813), i. 580–93, ii. 3–6; E. Bowen, *Complete System of Geography* (1747).

11. *Pennsylvania Archives* I. i. 108–10, xii. 279–80; *Hist. Soc. of Pennsylvania*, Penn Papers, letter of 15 March 1691.

12. Benedict, *op. cit.*, ii. 16–17; D. E. Jenkins, *Thomas Charles* (Denbigh, 1908), i. 580–3 (1787), ii. 129–32 (1793); cf. *Pennsylvania History* (*P.H.*), xxii. 140, and Knox, *Enthusiasm*, pp. 560–1. It is not clear whether there were as yet any Welsh settlers in Kentucky; a reference in Gwallter Mechain (Walter Davies, *General View of the Agriculture of N. Wales*, p. 269) might be taken as indicating their presence there in 1797. It will be shown later that John Rice Jones was in Kentucky in 1786, but only *en route* for further west.

13. Rev. xii. 6; Jenkins, *op. cit.*, i. 399.

14. Hansen, *Atlantic Migration*, p. 53. John Rice Jones (*infra*, p. 27) is an exception. A lawyer in comfortable circumstances, with no known 'whimseys' in politics or religion, he seems to have been attracted solely by the wider opportunities offered by the opening West.

15. D. Williams in *T.C.S.*, 1948, pp. 114–20.

16. *Id.*, pp. 121–46.

17. *Trans. Caerns. Hist. Soc.*, xiii. 49–50; T. Parry, *Hanes Llenyddiaeth Cymraeg* (1944), pp. 242–3; *Y Brython*, Tremadog, i. (1858), p. 37. The account is badly mangled in the reprint of *Y Brython*, which is followed by Mardy Rees in *Notable Welshman*, p. 143.

18. *Cambrian Register*, i. 460, ii. 247–51; *T.C.S.*, 1948, p. 121; *T.C.H.S.*, xiii. 45–6, 54, 57. Actually Jones was a churchwarden and a stout champion of the Church against Methodism; his 'heresies' were in politics only (*Bywgraffiadur Cymreig* (1953) p. 492). Cf. Benjamin Childlaw's father to his young son on America after working there from 1792–9: 'a great and good country beyond the ocean where there is no king, no tithes, and where poor people can get farms and where apples abound' (B. W. Childlaw, *Story of my Life* (Philadelphia, 1890), pp. 18 ff.)

19. *T.C.S.*, 1948, pp. 109, 129–32, 143; J. J. Evans, *M. J. Rhys a'i Amserau* (1935), ch. ii; J. T. Griffith, *M. J. Rhys* (2nd ed., Carmarthen, 1910); *Nat. Lib. of Wales Journ.* (*N.L.W.J.*), ii. (facsimile of prospectus opp. p. 131); *P.H.*, xxii. 134–5 (with plan of Beula); G. A. Williams, 'Morgan Rhees and his Beula', *Welsh History Review*, iii (1967), 441–472.

20. See e.g., quotations in A. H. Dodd, *Industrial Revolution in N. Wales* (1951), pp. 381, 385, and cf. J. Evans, *Tour in S. Wales* (1804), pp. 327–8, Williams, *Wales and America*, pp. 62–3, Evans, *M. J. Rhys*, p. 38.

21. For George Roberts's letters from Cambria (1800–23), see *P.H.* xxii. 136 ff.

22. Evans, *M. J. Rhys*, pp. 37–9; *T.C.H.S.*, xiii. 42–67; Williams, *op. cit.*, pp. 51–71; Dodd, *op. cit.*, pp. 381, 397; Joshua Thomas, *Hanes y Bedyddwyr yng Nghymru*, ed. B. Davies (1885), pp. 281–2; Benedict, *op. cit.*, i. 600; *N.L.W.J.*, ii. 139; David Jones, *Welsh Congregationalists in Pennsylvania* (Utica, N.Y., 1934), ch. 1; D. J. Williams, *One Hundred Years of Calvinistic Methodism in America*, (Phila., 1937), pp. 35–6, 38–9, 42–3.

23. *Cincinnati Miscellany*, i. and ii.; *Ohio Arch. and Hist. Soc. Publications*, xvi. 199 ff; D. J. Williams, *op. cit.*, p. 126.

24. *N.L.W.J.*, ii. 175; W. T. Utter, *Hist. of . . . Ohio*, (1942), ii. 370, 379, 396; Chidlaw, *Yr America* (1840) (trans. in *O.A.H.S.*, xvi. 194–227); D. J. Williams, *op. cit.*, ch. viii.

25. W. Davies, *Agriculture of N. Wales* (1810), p. 443.

26. Hansen, *Atlantic Migration*, pp. 61, 143; Jenkins, *Charles*, ii. 140–1; *N.L.W.J.*, ix. 42–59; *Publications of Historical and Philosophical Society of Ohio*, (*H.P.S.O.*), vi. 28–9; D. J. Williams, pp. 37–70, 77–9; D. Jones, pp. 63–4.

27. I am indebted for this information to Mr. James Dallett, Secretary and Librarian of the Athenaeum, Philadelphia.

28. Three volumes of minutes of this Society (P.W.S.), covering the years 1798–1912, are preserved in Philadelphia at the headquarters of the Pennsylvania Historical Society, through whose courtesy I have been able to use them. See P.W.S., 1, 24 Mar., 24 Apr., 4 June, 3 Dec. 1798, 4 Feb. 1799, 1 Mar. 1809, 2 Sept. 1822. On Samuel Jones cf *T.C.S.*, 1948, pp. 117, 142, Benedict, *op. cit.*, i. 581, Joshua Thomas, *op. cit.*, p. 356 and *n*. 1, Jenkins, *Charles*, ii. 129 ff.

29. Evans, *Tour in S. Wales*, pp. 327–8; Hansen, *op. cit.*, pp. 73–4, 98; *P.H.*, xxii. 145 *n*.

30. Dodd, *op. cit.*, p. 381; P.W.S., 7 June 1802.

31. P.W.S., 1 Sept. 1800, 7 Dec., 1801, 6 Dec. 1802, 2 Dec. 1811, 1 Mar. 1820, 1 Sept. 1823, 1 Mar. 1827.

32. Hansen, p. 108; P.W.S., 1 Mar. 1821, 1 Mar. 1826; cf. Dodd, *op. cit.*, p. 385.

33. P.W.S., 28 Feb. 1818, 1 Mar. 1819, 1 Mar. 1820, 1 Dec. 1823, 1 June 1829, 3 Sept. 1832. These figures, covering only the minority of immigrants actually helped in a single state, make it impossible to accept the official estimate

of an average of 18·5 Welsh settlers per annum to all parts of the States during the decade 1831–40 (Brown and Roucek, *One America*, p. 663).

34. P.W.S., 5 June 1809, 2 June 1828, 7 Sept. 1829, 1 Mar. 1831.

35. *Id.*, 1 Mar., 4 Apr. 1821, 1 Mar., 2 Dec. 1822, 1 Sep. 1823, 1 Mar. 1824 (Pittsburgh), 3 Sep. 1821, 1 June, 1829 (Indiana), 2 Dec. 1822, 7 Dec. 1829 (Ohio), 7 Sep. 1829 (New York).

36. Benedict, *op. cit.*, i., 601; P.W.S., 4 June 1821.

37. Dodd, *Industrial Revolution*, p. 410.

38. *Id.* in *Merioneth Hist. Soc. Journ.*, ii (1956), 249–59.

39. P.W.S., 1 Mar. 1831, *et seq.*; Hansen, *Atlantic Migration*, p. 144; *H.P.S.O.*, vi, 30–1; D. Jones, pp. 24–5, 78–9; D. J. Williams, pp. 89–93.

40. P.W.S., 5 Jan., 1820, 1 Mar., 2 Dec. 1822, 7 Dec., 1829, 6 Dec., 1830, 1 Mar., 1831; Griffith, *M. J. Rhys*, chs. iv and v. The hardships of the voyage and the frequent and formidable epidemics are also illustrated in *N.L.W.J.*, ix. 45–6 (1817) and in *P.H.*, xxii. 136–7 (1801).

41. E.g. Montgomeryshire and Denbighshire, P.W.S. 2 June, 1 Sept., 1 Dec., 1828, 7 Dec. 1829.

42. *T.C.S.*, 1948, p. 117; Cundall and Landman, *Wales, an Economic Geography* (1925), p. 135 *n.*

43. *T.C.H.S.*, xiii. 62–7.

44. *Atlantic Monthly, loc. cit.*; *N.L.W.J.*, ix. 58; *H.P.S.O.*, vi. 27–30; R. G. Thwaites, *Wisconsin* (1908), p. 294; *Wisconsin, a Guide to the Badger State* (1941), pp. 47, 129, 160, 275, 536. The Welsh settlers here were mainly miners and stock breeders; by 1844 they had organized their first *cymanfa* (D. J. Williams, pp. 67–71).

45. D. Williams, *Wales and America*, pp. 69–77.

46. Hansen, *Atlantic Migration*, pp. 143–4; D. Williams, *op. cit.*, pp. 62–5; Dodd, *op. cit.*, pp. 123, 130; B. W. Chidlaw, *Yr. America . . . nodau ar daeth o Ddyffryn Ohio i Gymru . . . Hanes Sefydliadau Cymraeg yn America*, (Llanrwst 1840) and *Story of my Life*. Chidlaw emigrated with his father as a monoglot Welsh lad of nine, and became pastor of the Welsh Chapel at Paddy's Run, Ohio. Cf. recruitment of emigrants for Ohio from Cardiganshire and Montgomeryshire by letters and personal visits from Welsh settlers, 1831–3 (D. J. Williams, pp. 127–8).

47. *T.C.H.S.*, xiii. 58–61; cf. J. J. Evans, *M. J. Rhys*, pp. 130–1.

48. *N.L.W.J.*, ii. 140.

49. Hansen, *The Immigrant*, pp. 131–3, *Atlantic Migration*, pp. 46–9; *Brief State of Pennsylvania* (1755); P.W.S., 6 Dec. 1802, 7 Dec. 1807; D. Williams, *op. cit.*, pp. 56–7.

50. Browning, *Welsh Settlers*, p. 379.

51. P.W.S., 1 Mar. 1831, 1 Mar. 1832.

52. E.g. *id.*, 1 Mar. 1862.

53. *Id.*, 1 Mar. 1819, 1 Dec. 1823. This may be Quaker influence.

54. *Id.*, 7 Dec. 1801, 7 Dec. 1829.

55. *Id.*, 1 Mar., 3 June 1811, 2 June 1824, 2 Dec. 1861. Dr. Ivor Griffith of Philadelphia informs me that the St. David's Society, of which he was president for seventeen years, lasted on till the second world war, still preserving its 'popular' character and fostering Welsh singing.

56. *A View of the Primitive Ages* (Ebensburg, 1834). Cf. *Gent. Mag.*, 1740, pp. 103–5.

57. P.W.S., 1 Mar. 1875.

58. Alan Conway, *The Welsh in America* (Cardiff. 1961).

59. Richards, *Rhestr Eisteddfodau*, p. 33.

60. *O.A.H.S.*, xvi. 202; D. Jones, pp. 10, 79, 250; D. J. Williams, p. 62; Emrys Jones in *T.C.S.*, 1952, pp. 15–41. Cf. B. W. Chidlaw, who knew nothing but Welsh when he first landed, yet eighteen years later could not venture on a Welsh pastorate in Ohio without a prior visit to Wales to brush up the language (*Life*, p. 70).

61. *William and Mary Quarterly*, X. ii. 346; *East Tennessee Hist. Soc. Publications*, xxi. 19–23.

62. *Early Writings of F. J. Turner*, ed. Fulmer Mood (Madison, 1938), p. 217.

63. L. B. Wright, *Colonial Civilisaton of N. America* (1949), pp. 142, 218. But Dr. Wright's assumption that in mid-seventeenth century there were Welsh settlers alongside Scots and Irish, Germans and Scandinavians, in what became New York State, does not appear to be warranted by the authorities he cites.

64. This comes out equally in the letters from New York and Pennsylvania and the denominational histories cited above, in the minutes of the Pennsylvania Welsh Society, in Chidlaw's autobiography and in surveys like that of W. H. Jones in *O.A.H.S.*, xvi. 194–227.

CHAPTER THREE

The Migration of Labour into the Glamorganshire Coalfield (1861-1911)

by Brinley Thomas

(1) THE POST-WAR CONTRACTION

THE phase of the depression experienced in the coal industry in the last three years (1928–30) has been accompanied by an abnormally large mass of unemployment in the coalfields. The Report of the Industrial Transference Board concluded, on the basis of the information available in June 1928, that 'it would be unwise if any figure below 200,000 were taken as the permanent surplus in the industry'.[1] Of this total the south Wales and Monmouthshire coalfield was responsible for 55,000, Durham 40,000 and Scotland 25,000. The Report emphasized the serious fact that the unemployment is ' "frozen" by its close concentration in or about the coalfields in areas of comparatively small extent. Industrial development within these in the past has been highly specialized. In the inland districts many large communities, e.g. the Rhondda in south Wales, with a population of some 162,000, are dependent on one industry only— the coal industry . . . the future of large sections of the population if they remain in these areas is most precarious.'[2]

It is true that the number of workers on the colliery books rose during 1929.[3] Moreover, within its limits, the labour transference scheme has been operating effectively, the number transferred from all the depressed mining areas in 1929 being 32,000;[4] but its significance can well be over-estimated. A solid mass of unemployment still remains,[5] much of which cannot be touched by any transference scheme, and it is probably safe to prophesy that the industry will contract still further before it reaches stability.

It may not be unprofitable to examine the pre-war growth of population in those districts which are now burdened with 'pockets' of surplus labour. This inquiry will be limited to the county of Glamorgan in the period 1861–1911, paying special attention to the volume and direction of the migration.[6]

(2) Distribution of Population in the Iron Period

It has been shown that, in the first half of the nineteenth century 'in general, the evidence for any strong influx into coal-mining is not plentiful. A large part of the new labour required by the expansion of the industry probably came from the natural increase of a notoriously prolific section of the population.'[7] At that time coal was not yet king in south Wales. The latter part of the eighteenth century had seen the establishment of the famous iron-works which soon extended from the locality of Merthyr Tydfil to Blaenavon, along the northern and north-eastern fringe of the coalfield—a development which in its early stages gave rise to a remarkable migration of iron-workers from the Midlands.[8] Between 1830 and 1847 the make of iron in the area increased by 150 per cent[9] and in the latter year south Wales produced over a third of the total British pig-iron output of 1,999,608 tons.[10] Prior to the fifties the working of coal was for the most part a mere subsidiary to the iron, tinplate and copper works.[11] Population had thickened on the 'hills'—the northern and eastern outcrop of the Lower Coal Series—where ample supplies of ironstone, good smelting coal, furnace sandstone and limestone co-existed, and on the sea-board in and around Swansea. Taking Merthyr Tydfil,[12] which was in 1851 the largest town in south Wales and the centre of the iron industry, we find that of the 35,093 persons of twenty years and upwards enumerated there in that year, only 9120 (about 25 per cent) were born within the town, and 4146 in Glamorganshire (beyond the limits of Merthyr Tydfil); 21,827 (or 62 per cent) originated outside the county, and of these 14,189 or about two-thirds came from the four neighbouring Welsh counties of Carmarthen, Brecknock, Pembroke and Cardigan. It is significant that as many as 2330 were of Irish birth, most of whom had been driven from their country by sheer starvation during the great potato famine of the forties. In the second half of the century the export trade in the smokeless steam coal of the valleys was to displace the iron industry as the dominant element in the economic life of Glamorgan. It was in virtue of this phase of its development that the county became one of the most densely populated parts of the country.

Though the population of Glamorgan had grown by 227 per cent (from 70,879 to 231,849) between 1801 and 1851, the density in mid-century was still only 253 persons per square mile, compared with 259 in Cornwall and 289 in Somerset.[13] In the fifty years prior to 1911 its population registered an increase of 253 per cent (from 317,752 to 1,120,910), and that of England and Wales 80 per cent (20,066,224 to 36,070,492). The outstanding factors characterizing the period were the enormous demand for the unrivalled 'Welsh smokeless',[14] consequent upon the great expansion in the use of steam, especially for navigation, the paramount influence of the railway[15] in making the coalfield accessible from all parts of the country, the relative decline of the inland iron industry, the tendency for Siemens steel and tinplate works to localize near the sea-board, and the depression in agriculture.

(3) The Statistical Data and the Method Applied

The accompanying table represents an attempt to estimate, from the birth-place statistics of the censuses, the extent of migration from other counties into Glamorgan during each decade. The method[16] used requires some explanation. The number of natives of each county in England and Wales, of Scotland and of Ireland enumerated in Glamorgan is given for each census year. In order to estimate how many of these entered the county within a given period of ten years, it is necessary to ascertain what proportion of the people enumerated in the first year survived: this is done by using the mean death rate[17] for that decade in the different age-groups in the Registration County of Glamorgan (excluding the wholly rural District of Gower).

The process may best be described by taking as a concrete instance the case of Devonshire. At the beginning of the period, in 1861, there were 6101 people living in Glamorgan who were born in Devon. In order to gauge the proportion who would be alive in 1871, we reduce this total by a percentage (13 per cent) based on the 1861–70 mean annual death rate of the age-group 35–45 (i.e. 13 per 1000). The remainder is substracted from the number of Devonians enumerated in the county in 1871, giving a figure of 400 (to the nearest hundred) newcomers in 1861–71. The next step is to apply the 1871–80 mortality-rate of the age-group 45–55 (i.e. 17 per cent) to those who survived, and that of the age-group 25–35 (i.e. 10 per cent) to the 400 who arrived in the previous decade: the sum of the two lots of survivors is then subtracted from the number of Devon-born people enumerated in 1881 (13,526 − 4410 + 375), and we are given 8700 new arrivals from that county in the years 1871–81. This process is applied for the whole period to every county or group of counties. A rough guess has to be made at the age-composition of those returned in 1861 — the initial figure: the choice of the age-group 35–45 is considered to be least objectionable. The fact that migrants to the coalfield were for the most part young people is held to justify the application

39

of the death-rate of the age-group 25–35 to the newcomers of each decade.

The results afford some indication of the gross movement inwards every ten years. It is fully realized that the method used has

MAP OF ENGLAND AND WALES

showing the origin of the persons born outside the county enumerated in Glamorgan in 1911

(One dot represents 500 persons having originated in the county where it appears)

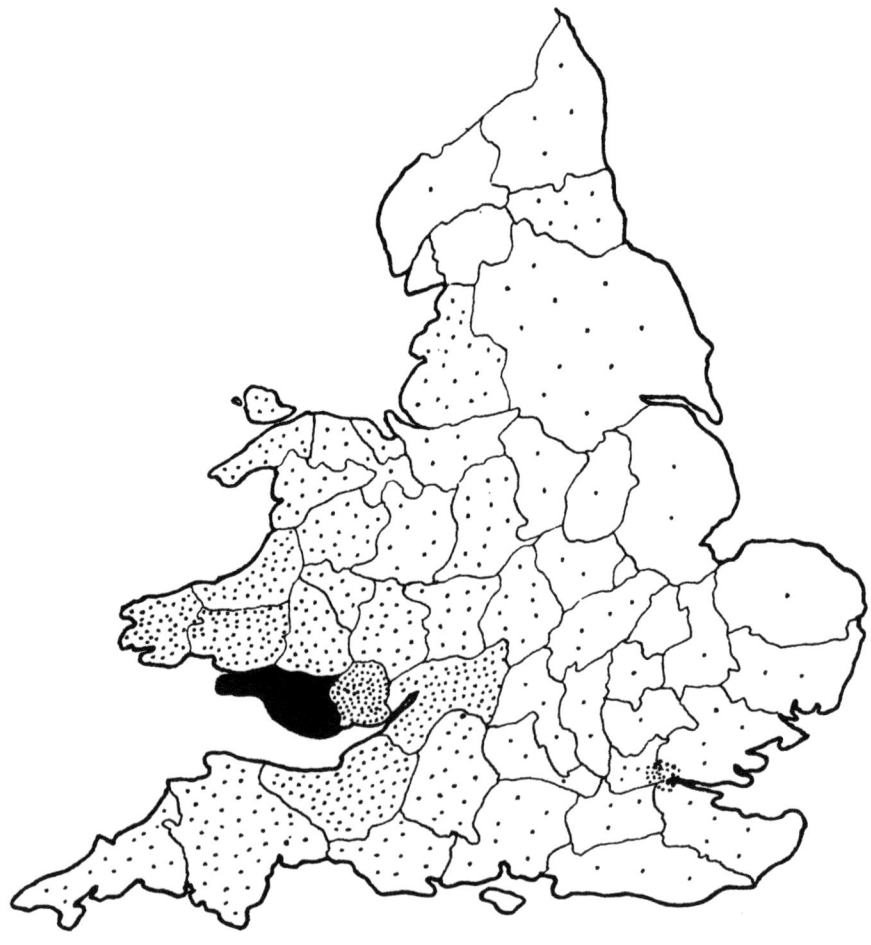

decided limitations; and too much importance must not be attached to the figures as such. But, within these limits, it seems plausible to arrive at some broad conclusions based on the relative trends brought out by the statistics. It is illuminating to note the proportions coming each decade from the five border counties (Carmarthen, Brecknock, Monmouth, Somerset and Devon) and from the non-border or distant counties. The excess of the enumerated over the natural increase in the county is a fairly accurate index of the net gain by migration. Some idea of the movement outwards has been obtained from the figures of Glamorgan-born people returned in other counties in each decennial year, and applying a method similar to that already outlined. This latter computation helps to explain the disparities between the gross immigration and the net gain. Emigration to foreign countries has also to be taken into account; but, unfortunately, separate information for counties is not available.

(4) THE FIRST WAVE OF MIGRATION: THE CHARACTERISTICS OF THE SEVENTIES

It is proposed to analyse the volume and direction of the inward flow of population in relation to the course of various indices reflecting the rate of expansion of the coal industry during the period. The accompanying diagram illustrates, for the period 1871–1911, the growth of the annual output of coal and the number of miners employed in Glamorgan, of the annual coal and bunker exports (including coastwise) from Cardiff and the mean annual f.o.b. price of large coal, together with the fluctuations in the mean annual wage percentage on the 1879 standard.

The amount of migration in 1861–71 was quite moderate compared with later decades, even though the gross estimate of 21,000 may err on the low side. About 70 per cent of the migrants were recruited from the neighbouring Welsh counties of Cardigan, Pembroke, Carmarthen, Brecknock and Monmouth. The output of coal in south Wales (excluding Monmouthshire) advanced swiftly between 1861 and 1866 (6,800,000 to 9,376,000 tons), but for the next five years it remained stagnant.[18] The coal industry was in process of freeing itself from the leading-strings of the iron-trade.

After the seventies the welfare of the coalfield was to become increasingly dependent on forces operating in the international sphere. The period witnessed a phenomenal expansion, the rate of which was periodically retarded by downward reactions in prices. Between 1817 and 1911 the number of coal-miners in Glamorgan rose by 341 per cent (from 34,000[19] to 150,000), the output by 278 per cent

F   41

(from 8,600,000[19] to 33,500,000 tons), and the cargo and bunker (including coastwise) exports of Cardiff by 600 per cent (from 3,000,000 to 21,000,000 tons). The peaks of the upward price movements occurred in the years 1873, 1884, 1891, 1901 and 1908; and more or less acute depressions prevailed in 1875–9, 1885–8, 1892–7, and 1902–6. It is noteworthy that the temporary reductions in the number of employed were few and slight—during 1874–8, 1892–3, and 1895–6. The sliding-scale method of determining wages was in effective operation after 1880 (it was replaced by the Conciliation Board in 1903) so that there is throughout a very close correlation between the variations in the wage percentage and the f.o.b. price of large coal.

	Coal-output in Glamorgan (million tons)	Exports of Coal, etc., from Cardiff (million tons)	Number of mineworkers employed in Glamorgan (1000s)
1871	8·6	3·0	33·5
1881	16·0	6·4	52·4
1891	21·8	11·0	84·4
1901	27·7	18·5	107·2
1911	33·5	21·4	150·1

Sources: Finlay Gibson, *Compilation of Statistics of the Coal Mining Industry* (1922); Annual Reports of the Mines Inspector for the South Wales District; Annual Reports of the Cardiff Chamber of Commerce.

In the ten years following 1871 about three-and-a-half times the number in the previous decade appear to have migrated to Glamorgan; and 50 per cent of them were natives of non-border counties. Only 38 per cent came from the five neighbouring Welsh counties; while the stream from Cornwall, Devon, Somerset and Gloucester amounted to no less than 37 per cent of the total. Miners from the Radstock and Forest of Dean coal districts must have been prominent among those who left the two latter counties.

The boom of 1872–4 was primarily due to the enormous demand for iron.[20] Miners' wages rose to an unheard of level. There are no average rates for the whole coalfield in those years; but the following data of wages paid in some Glamorgan collieries serve to indicate the fluctuations between 1869 and 1878.

AVERAGE WEEKLY EARNINGS IN CERTAIN SOUTH WALES
COLLIERIES

	1869[21]		1873[22]		1878[22] (Feb. to May)	
	s	d	s	d	s	d
Hewers	24	5	48	9	19	1½
Timbermen	25	0	53	4	23	6
Hauliers	20	0	31	6	16	11
Landers	21	0	36	9	18	8½
Labourers	15	0	24	0	14	9½

GLAMORGANSHIRE COAL INDUSTRY
1871–1911

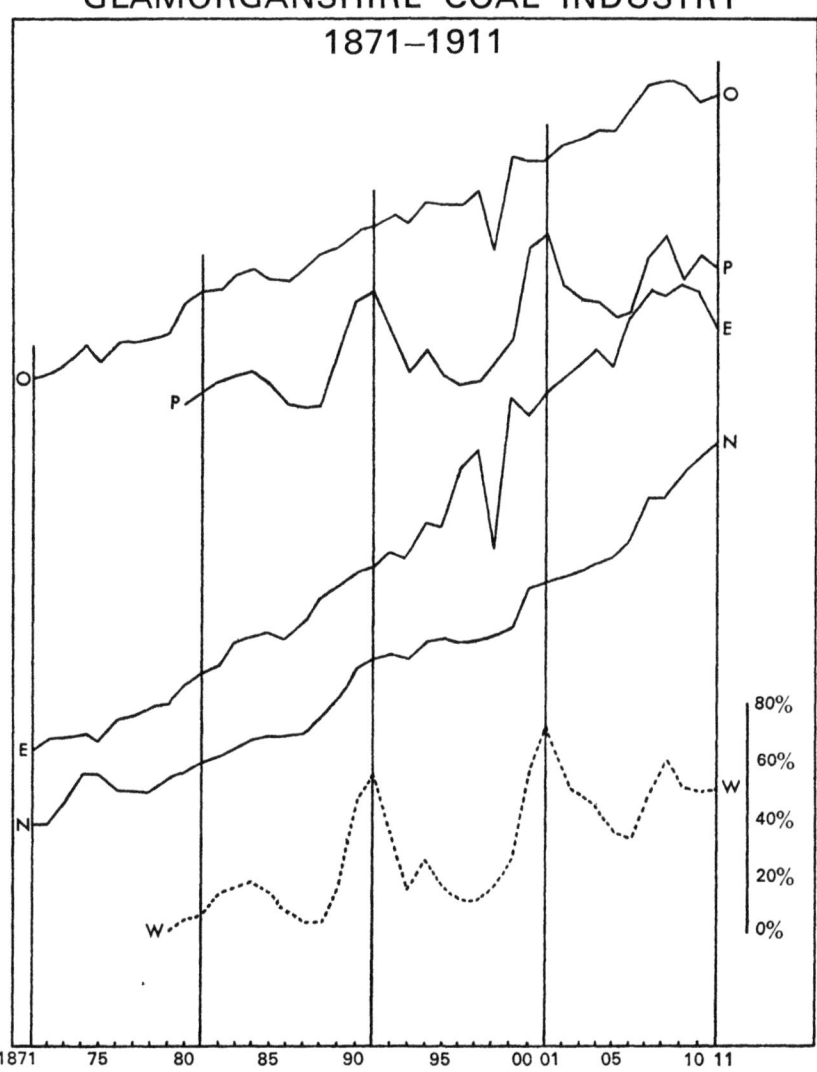

O = Annual Output of Coal
P = Average Annual F.O.B. Price of Large Coal
E = Exports of Coal, Coke, Patent Fuel and Bunkers
   (including Coastwise) from Cardiff
N = Annual Number of Mineworkers employed
W = Mean annual Wages Percentage on 1879
   Standard

⎫
⎬ Mean of 1886–91 = 100
⎭

In the years 1871–3 the labour force in the Glamorgan mines grew from 34,000 to 40,000.[23] Labour was very scarce,[24] and the supply of coal inelastic. It was some time before the abnormally high wage rates could attract sufficient workers from distant places. The fact that the rates paid to hewers and timbermen were doubled between 1869 and 1873 reflects the keen shortage of skilled labour. Up to that time, as we have seen, most of the migrants had been drawn from the surrounding rural districts. The unprecedented boom prices led to the sinking of many new pits, especially in the Rhondda and Aberdare valleys, but these could not begin to operate for four or five years.[25] By the time these mines, manned with the necessary labour, were ready to swell the output, the price had long since dropped and the slump had set in. The number of miners fell from 48,900 in 1874 to 43,500 in 1878 when the depression touched its lowest point.

The decade was thus one of glaring contrasts; the price pendulum swung from one extreme to the other. The sudden burst of prosperity in the first few years made the area very attractive. The severe reaction of 1875–9, no doubt, drove many of the newcomers back to their homes, particularly those who had gone into mines dependent on iron-works.[26] An irretrievable blow was struck at the once supreme inland pig-iron industry. About 15,000 people who had been born in the county moved elsewhere—much of this migration being due to the lean years. A good number probably emigrated abroad, especially to the coalfields of Pennsylvania.[27]

In spite of the steep fall in prices, the output of steam coal and the exports from Cardiff present a remarkably steady upward trend after 1875.[28] Depression in values could not curb the youthful vigour of the steam coal industry; and this growth involved an interesting internal shift of population. The rapidity with which the early exploitation of the steam coal measures proceeded had compelled the 'sale-coal' owners to offer high wages in order to secure labour. Consequently a disparity of as much as 25 per cent grew up between wage-rates in the Rhondda Valley and those in the Merthyr iron-works district.[29] The natural result was a tendency for people to move from one locality to the other, and it was greatly accelerated by the intense hardship experienced in the iron-making centres during the depression. During 1871–81, the Census returns[30] show that the Registration District of Merthyr Tydfil lost 18,800 people by migration and that of Bedwellty (adjoining it in Monmouthshire) 5051, while Pontypridd, where the smokeless steam coal is chiefly mined, absorbed 26,552, and Cardiff, the port and its immediate hinterland, 14,724 persons.

The striking increase in the mobility of rural inhabitants in the seventies compared with the sixties merits further notice. There can be no doubt that new forces began to make themselves felt in the countryside after 1870. The Elementary Education Act of that year had a temporarily disturbing effect on the agricultural labourer's standard of living. 'By restricting juvenile labour and diminishing the aggregate amount of the family earnings',[31] it tended to make him more likely to migrate. Moreover, the clash between the militant Labourers' Union and the masters in the early part of the decade ushered in the era of the 'cash nexus'; and 'the general levelling up of the standard of efficiency pressed hard upon the casual labourers and the "odd men" of the villages'.[32] Another new factor was the union's policy of financially assisting labourers to move to the mining and manufacturing centres[33]: in this way it was hoped that the diminished labour supply on the farms would strengthen the men's bargaining power.[34] The impact of these disturbing influences is a partial explanation of the moderate rural exodus which occurred while agriculture was still prosperous—the great depression did not set in till 1879, the price of wheat in the early seventies being between 55s. and 60s. and the average for the decade about 45s.[35]

(5) THE SECOND WAVE: AGRICULTURAL WAGES AND MIGRATION

From 1881 to 1891 the coalfield passed through a stage of practically unchecked development. It is true that wage rates fell from 17·5 per cent (on the standard) in 1884 to the extremely low level of 2·9 per cent in 1887; but the personnel of the mines did not actually diminish during this slump. There was an addition of 54 per cent during the ten years and we may well infer that this temporary setback did little to mitigate the sustained attractiveness of the area. The figures reveal a second wave of immigration of considerable dimensions, 63 per cent being contributed by non-border counties. The most distant ones were well represented, and the dispersion of people from Somerset and Gloucestershire (many of whom were coal miners) is again an outstanding feature.

Some of the Reports on Agriculture submitted to the Labour Commission (1893) supply corroborative evidence regarding this movement. The Assistant Commissioners for Wales pointed out that the adequacy of the agricultural labour supply depended on the distance at which a district was situated from an industrial or mining centre.[36] Furthermore, 'labourers from Wiltshire, Somerset and Devon, from Hereford and the Cirencester district of Gloucestershire have almost everywhere superseded the indigenous Welsh labourer in the Vale of Glamorgan, excepting, along the seaboard,

45

in parts that are remotest from railway communication. But even the newcomers do not remain very long on the land, for higher wages and shorter hours almost invariably succeed in attracting them to the mineral districts, so that other labourers have to be continually drafted from the same English counties to replace them.'[37] When the demand for coal was brisk, the pits could absorb a large quantity of unskilled labour.[38]

These raw sons of the soil would generally be given the lowest paid jobs on the surface or underground,[39] until they acquired enough experience of the mine to enable them to do more specialized work. It was natural that the 'old hands' should be jealous of their hereditary skill and should strongly resent their occupation being inundated by a miscellaneous crowd of outsiders.

It is difficult to find any consistent relation between the relative trend of agricultural wages and the extent of the loss of labourers in different parts of the country. This kind of explanation was offered for the variations in the percentage decline in the number of labourers during the period 1871–81: some of the counties where the rise in remuneration was least (e.g. Huntingdonshire) underwent a relatively considerable, if not the most marked, diminution in labourers, and vice versa (e.g. York, North Riding).[40] But such a theory of causation is not borne out by an examination of the statistics of all the counties. An advance in the average agricultural wage-rate of a county in a given period may be, on the one hand, a cause of a relatively low volume of migration outward, or, on the other hand, an effect of a scarcity of labour consequent upon a relatively large volume of migration. Nor must we place too much faith in average rates of earnings, for striking differences in remuneration might persist for a generation in villages of the same neighbourhood.[41]

We may generalize by saying that agricultural earnings would be highest within the coalfield, and would tend to be higher in the inner ring of border counties than in the outer. For instance, Mr. Wilson Fox's statistics for 1898 point in this direction.

AVERAGE EARNINGS OF AGRICULTURAL LABOURERS IN 1898[42]
(including value of allowances in kind)

County	Ave. rate s	d	County	Ave. rate s	d	County	Ave. rate s	d
Glamorgan	19	1	Devon	16	7	Montgomery	15	5
Brecon	16	8	Cornwall	16	7	Gloucester	15	1
Monmouth	16	8	Somerset	15	10	Wiltshire	15	0
Radnor	16	8	Hereford	15	10	Cardigan	14	9
Carmarthen	16	7	Pembroke	15	10	Dorset	14	9

46

Not a few of the labourers from distant counties like Cornwall, Dorset, Wiltshire or Montgomery moved a short distance at a time with the general stream directed towards the coalfield. Thus, 'even in the case of "counties of dispersion" which have population to spare for other counties, there takes place an inflow of migrants across the borders, and this inflow is most considerable across that border which lies furthest away from the great centres of absorption'.[43] Apparently, the Welsh agricultural labourer was more mobile than his English prototype, and his natural inclination to migrate was no insignificant factor in the rural depopulation of Wales.[44]

We have seen that during the eighties there was a strong influx into Glamorgan, especially from distant counties. The net absorption amounted to 76,200—two-and-a-half times that of the previous decade. In this connection there seems ground for suggesting that the Minority Report of the Commission on Depression in Trade (1886) had not taken all the facts into account when it stated that 'whilst the amount of labour employed in agriculture has greatly declined during the years 1874–85 . . . there has been no absorption by the textile industries of the labour displaced . . . and we have no evidence to show that it has found employment in any other productive industry'.[45] There can be little doubt, from our analysis of the statistics, that the coalfield which was expanding at a greater rate than any other[46] in the kingdom received some of its labour supply from rural areas in those years, particularly during 1880–5.

(6) THE THIRD WAVE: THE EFFLUX FROM THE COUNTY

The rate of the inward movement was distinctly less during the period 1891–1901. The net addition to the population through migration was lower by 40 per cent than the 1881–91 total. The contraction was most conspicuous in the case of the more distant counties. The state of the coal trade was the chief cause of this retrogression. From 1892 to 1899 the industry was in the trough of an acute price slump, and there was an actual falling off in the number employed in 1892–3 and 1895–6. Wages during these eight years averaged only 18 per cent on the standard, while the net growth of the labour force was only 8800. In the first year of the boom which followed no less than 11,200 workers were added to the colliery books. It is none the less significant that, whereas the staple industry was depressed for so many years, the gross inflow should have been relatively so high.

According to the estimate, about 35,000 Glamorgan-born people migrated elsewhere, more than double the number in the previous decade. It is worthy of note that in the years 1871–81 and 1891–1901, when this 'emigration' assumed comparatively large proportions, there was a clear preponderance of females among those who went to London, the South-west, West-midland and North-west counties. This is brought out by the following figures:

NATIVES OF GLAMORGAN ENUMERATED IN LONDON,
SOUTH-WEST, WEST-MIDLAND AND NORTH-WESTERN COUNTIES

	Males	Females	Total
1871	4,931	5,951	10,882
1881	7,550	9,452	17,002
1891	9,645	11,887	21,532
1901	14,556	16,794	31,350

ESTIMATED NUMBER OF FEMALES MIGRATING FROM
GLAMORGAN TO THE ABOVE COUNTIES

1871–81	1881–91	1891–1901
4,200	3,500	6,500

Most of them probably went into domestic service in the metropolis and the holiday resorts of the other counties. The distress in the mining areas in recent years has had a similar consequence. Depressions in the coalfield seem, at least, to have had one redeeming feature—they have always helped to ease the domestic servant market.

With the abnormal prosperity of 1899–1902[47] the coalfield resumed its role as a powerful magnet attracting population from all parts of the country; there was only a temporary lull in 1902–6. By 1911 the output had reached 33,500,000 tons and the number employed 150,100, the expansion during the decade being 21 per cent and 40 per cent respectively. Seventy-three per cent of the 'immigrants' in 1901–11 were drawn from beyond the border counties; and the net gain was more than double that of the preceding ten years. The total crossing the border from Carmarthenshire was far less numerous than would be expected judging from previous decades. This is due to the fact that the anthracite coal trade developed very rapidly, the number of coal and shale mineworkers enumerated in that county being 10,792 in 1911 compared with 6347 in 1901.

Moreover, the demand for Monmouthshire coals (e.g. the celebrated Black Vein) became very brisk, and the addition to the population of that county in 1901–11 was 30·9 per cent, second only to Middlesex, and 0·4 per cent higher even than that of

Glamorgan.[48] These facts explain the unusually low percentage of migrants from border counties. A large majority of the new migrants into Monmouthshire went from Glamorgan,[49] but the total emigration from the latter county only slightly exceeded that of the previous decade.

Though the volume of this third wave of migration was to some degree checked by the contemporaneous expansion in the coal industry to the east and west, it was greater than either of the previous ones. No doubt it reflected the progress in means of transport and communication, the wide spread of education, which was responsible for more knowledge of and taste for town life,[50] and the shrinkage in the scope for labour in agriculture, as a result of prolonged economic difficulties.[51] The fundamental factor, however, was the remarkable development of the coalfield itself: smokeless steam coal came thoroughly into its own in the era of 'international anarchy'.

(7) Conclusion

From the foregoing analysis we find that the absolute contribution of the border counties was more or less stable from 1871 to 1911 (the unexpected drop in the last ten years has already been explained); the stream from the more distant counties, however, fluctuated directly with the buoyancy of the coal trade. Three considerable waves of migration are clearly distinguishable, and they synchronized with the periodical cycles of prosperity in the mining industry. It generally happened, of course, that these phases coincided with flourishing conditions in the bulk of the country's industries, and thus, at first sight, there would seem no reason why the coal industry should prove so exceptionally attractive.[52] But the fluctuations in the coal industry, enhanced in South Wales by the unsurpassed quality of the commodity, were so extensive that the miners' earnings could easily reach a point at which they were distinctly superior to those of other trades: hence the incursion of such a large body of long-distance migrants.

The addition to the population of Glamorgan through the excess of births over deaths mounted steadily from 61,000 in 1861–70 to 169,000 in 1901–10. The decennial natural increase expressed as a percentage of the actual population at the beginning of each decade actually shows a steady upward tendency, which means that the coalfield, with its notoriously high birth-rate, was providing itself with an increasingly large labour supply.

The social and economic characteristics of these closely packed, one-industry communities offer a wide field of study.[53] Suffice it to mention here the marked preponderance of males in the population, due to the large number of single young men among the migrants and the fact that many married men would go to work in the mines, leaving their families to look after small-holdings in the country, and returning to them for a few weeks every summer. In 1901 the number of husbands not enumerated on the same schedules as their wives was 10,434 in Glamorganshire.[54] The geographical isolation of the valleys, the predominance of one staple industry and the reasonable possibility for a person to be earning a skilled hewer's wage at a fairly early age made it inevitable that coal-mining should absorb a large majority of the juveniles entering the labour market.

The system of wage-determination may, possibly, have had some bearing on the immigration at certain points. For, since the sliding-scale did not take cognizance of the state of the labour market,[55] a glut of workers would not of itself serve to push down the rate of remuneration; a scarcity, on the other hand, would no doubt have the effect of raising it. The average migrant, if not impelled by force of circumstances, would be persuaded to try his luck by the information reaching him regarding money-wages[56] in the coalfield. He was not likely to concern himself very much about the varying rates for degrees of skill or the probable housing conditions; the mere prospect of handling more money was in itself alluring. It is, therefore, conceivable that the rate of wages in the pits in a given year would prove high enough to attract distant outsiders, even though at that particular time there was already a general over-supply of workers. And even this enhanced surplus would not necessarily lower the wage percentage, unless there was a concurrent reduction in the market price of coal.

Furthermore, it must be noted that, for reasons partly economic and partly geographical, falling wages would seldom lead to a substantial migration of miners out of the area. The recurring cycle of prices taught the men to regard a period of low remuneration as an interval to be followed in the nature of things by a span of prosperity. We have already seen that in years of stress the movement out of the coalfield was composed of a large proportion of females, and this suggests that low wages and unemployment tended to force the miner to lighten his family budget as a temporary expedient rather than leave the district. His supreme desire to maintain his standard of living in these depressed periods would also prompt him to intensify his effort, so that, by increasing his output, he could, as a piece worker, to some extent counteract the fall in the *rate* of earnings. In coal-mining a decline in wage-rates is generally accompanied by a rise in the average get per man employed. The geographical position of the south Wales coal-basin isolated, as it is, from other thickly populated regions, would also be a factor impeding the outward flow of labour.

When we realize that the percentage increase of the population of Glamorgan in half a century (1861–1911) was about the same as that of England and Wales in a century (1811–1911), we cannot escape the impression of precocious growth.[57] The dead hand of this hectic past now [1930] weighs heavily on its congested valleys. There is probably a great deal of truth in the suggestion that 'if the coal had not been so valuable the development would have proceeded more slowly, limited by the supply of labour which would have been available at a lower rate'.[58] The conjuncture of peculiarly favourable circumstances gave unusual scope for unbridled enterprise, and a stubborn spirit of individualism was thereby nurtured which has been the bane of the industry in post-war days.

This examination has brought out, particularly over short spaces of time, a degree of labour mobility which is far from negligible. It is a matter of important theoretical interest to what extent the mobility assumption underlying the classical approach to the theory of wages has a valid foundation in actual fact. It is not permissible, perhaps, to generalize from results in a narrow field. Yet experience seems to suggest a vital connection between the rate of a community's natural increase and the amount of internal population movement that can be expected.[59] During 1871–1911 the rate of growth in England and Wales was 59·0 per cent, compared with 79·0 per cent in 1801–41. The increase in the later period was considerable, especially when viewed in the light of present-day tendencies. While recent history, e.g. of the coal industry, may illustrate the wide prevalence of immobility,[60] an era of expansion seems to allow a margin, in short periods and within certain limits, for a fairly effective degree of labour mobility.

TABLE A

ESTIMATED NUMBER OF MIGRANTS ENTERING GLAMORGAN
(Civil County)

Counties of birth	1861–71	1871–81	1881–91	1891–1901	1901–11[66]
I London	200	1,900	3,200	2,800	8,000
II South Eastern[61]	200	1,700	2,700	1,000	4,400
III South Midland[62]	Nil	900	1,500	1,200	3,300
IV Eastern[63]	Nil	500	1,200	400	2,000
V Wiltshire	300	1,700	2,900	1,800	3,400
Dorset	Nil	1,200	1,500	600	2,600
Devon	400	8,700	3,900	4,600	6,200
Cornwall	1,700	2,500	1,500	1,900	2,000

TABLE A—(continued)

	Somerset	Nil	9,900	11,900	8,700	6,000
VI	Gloucester	Nil	6,400	9,400	6,000	19,300
	Hereford	400	1,500	3,400	2,400	3,200
	Shropshire	200	300	1,300	900	1,500
	Staffordshire	300	600	1,600	1,100	2,700
	Worcestershire	200	400	1,400	900	2,600
	Warwickshire	200	500	1,300	700	2,000
VII	North Midland[64]	100	400	1,200	800	1,700
VIII	Cheshire	Nil	200	600	600	800
	Lancashire	200	1,100	2,100	2,000	3,700
IX	Yorkshire	Nil	800	1,700	1,200	2,700
X	Northern[65]	Nil	1,100	1,700	1,300	1,900
	Monmouthshire	2,300	10,100	10,500	13,500	11,600
	Carmarthenshire	5,700	4,900	9,300	11,000	6,800
	Pembrokeshire	3,700	5,800	5,500	7,100	5,500
	Cardiganshire	1,500	4,100	7,600	3,800	2,900
	Brecknockshire	2,100	3,600	4,300	4,200	3,800
	Radnorshire	400	700	1,400	700	1,300
	Montgomeryshire	400	1,400	4,100	1,400	2,200
	Flintshire	Nil	100	400	300	300
	Denbighshire	100	200	700	300	1,100
	Merionethshire	100	200	1,600	1,100	2,500

Counties of birth	1861–71	1871–81	1881–91	1891–1901	1901–11
Carnarvonshire	Nil	300	1,900	1,000	3,900
Anglesey	Nil	Nil	600	400	1,000
SCOTLAND	300	1,000	1,600	1,200	1,800
IRELAND	Nil	Nil	3,000	6,600	3,800
Totals	21,000	74,700	108,500	94,400	128,500

NET GAIN BY MIGRATION
(excess of actual over natural increase in Registration County)[67]

	18,981	30,309	77,417	41,093	92,121

TABLE B

THE DECENNIAL NATURAL INCREASE AS A PERCENTAGE OF THE
POPULATION IN THE FIRST YEAR OF EACH DECADE
(Glamorgan Registration County)

1861–71	1871–81	1881–91	1891–1901	1901–11
18·6%	20·3%	18·8%	19·2%	19·9%
		England and Wales[68]		
13·58%	15·09%	13·97%	12·39%	12·43%

TABLE C

NUMBER OF MIGRANTS FROM BORDER[69] AND NON-BORDER COUNTIES

1871–81		*1881–91*		*1891–1901*		*1901–11*	
Border	Non-border	Border	Non-border	Border	Non-border	Border	Non-border
37,200	37,500	39,900	68,600	42,000	52,400	34,400	94,100
50%	50%	37%	63%	44%	56%	27%	73%

TABLE D

ESTIMATED NUMBER OF PERSONS MIGRATING FROM GLAMORGAN TO
OTHER COUNTIES IN ENGLAND AND WALES

1871–81	*1881–91*	*1891–1901*	*1901–11*
14,600	16,700	35,600	39,000

TABLE E

ENUMERATED POPULATION OF GLAMORGAN (CIVIL COUNTY)

1861	*1871*	*1881*	*1891*	*1901*	*1911*
17,752	397,859	511,433	687,218	859,931	1,120,910
		Total number born outside the County			
116,812	117,904	180,794	260,684	297,833	390,941

Sources: The Population Census of England and Wales, 1861 to 1911; the Decennial Supplements to the Annual Report of the Registrar-General of Births, Deaths and Marriages, 1875 to 1914–16.

NOTES

1. Cmd. 3156, 1928, p. 8.
2. P. 15.
3. The number of wage-earners in the south Wales and Monmouthshire coalfield increased from 169,400 in March 1928 to 180,400 in March 1930. (*Ministry of Labour Gazette*, April 1928 and 1930.)
4. *Report of the Ministry of Labour for 1929* (Cmd. 3579, 1930), p. 16.
5. In the four Labour Exchange areas comprising the Rhondda Urban District the average percentage of unemployed on the registers (Local Unemployment Index figures) for January to May 1930 was 33·8 per cent.
6. For a treatment of the subject mainly from the geographical standpoint see A. E. Trueman, 'Population Changes in the Eastern part of the south Wales Coalfield', *Geographical Journal*, 1919, pp. 410–19, and D. Lleufer Thomas, 'The Geography of the South Wales Coalfield and its Influence on Population' (Paper read at the British Association (Geography Section), Cardiff, 24 August 1920, reprinted in *Welsh Housing and Development Year Book* (Cardiff, 1921).
7. A. Redford, *Labour Migration in England, 1800–50* (1926), p. 49.
8. See T. S. Ashton, *Iron and Steel in the Industrial Revolution* (1924), p. 199.
9. J. H. Clapham, *An Economic History of Modern Britain*, I (1926), p. 426.
10. H. Scrivenor, *A History of the Iron Trade* (1854), pp. 123–7.
11. See H. Stanley Jevons, *The British Coal Trade* (1915), p. 102.
12. See 1851 *Census Returns*, 1852–3, LXXXVIII, Pt. 2, p. 892.

13. See A. Redford, *op. cit.*, p. 12.

14. An interesting account of the early efforts made by one of the pioneers to demonstrate its unique qualities, e.g. to the French Ministry of Marine, is given in J. E. Vincent, *Life of John Nixon* (1900), pp. 131–44.

15. The South Wales Railway was opened between 1850 and 1859. In 1862 the total mileage (including lines worked) of the Great Western and West Midland Railways was 1104. (E. T. MacDermot, *History of the Great Western Railway* (1927), pp. 863–5.)

16. I am indebted to Prof. Bowley for valuable advice regarding the application of this method.

17. The statistics supplied by the Decennial Supplements to the Annual Report of the Registrar-General of Births, Deaths and Marriages: 1875, xviii, Pt. II; 1884–5, xvii; 1895, xxiii, Pt. II; 1905, xviii; 1914–16, viii.
The actual figures are as follows:

GLAMORGAN REGISTRATION COUNTY
(excluding registration district of Gower)
Decennial death-rates in age-groups

Decennium	25–	35–	45–	55–	65–75
		Per 100 of the Mean Population			
1861–70	11	13			
1871–80	10	13	17		
1881–90	8	12	17	34	
1891–1900	8	11	17	35	70
1901–10	6	9	15	34	68

The decennial death-rate represents ten times the mean annual death-rate given in the Registrar-General's Decennial Supplements.

18. *Select Committee on Coal* (1873, X, 313), Appendix No. 3, pp. 324–5.

19. Based on figures given in the Report of the Mines Inspector for the South Wales District (1872), XVI, 653), allowance being made for the inclusion in the latter of Brecknock, Carmarthen and Pembrokeshire.

20. Report of *S.C. on Coal, op. cit.*, p. xi.

21. Sir Thomas Brassey, *Lectures on the Labour Question* (1878), p. 36. (These figures relate to a single colliery.)

22. Sir Thomas Brassey, *Foreign Work and English Wages* (1879), p. 318. (Figures for a group of collieries.)

23. See Annual Reports of the Inspector for the South Wales District.

24. *S.C. on Coal* (1873), *op. cit.*, evidence of T. A. Wales, Inspector for the South Wales District, Q. 1536.

25. *Ibid.*, Q. 1581–2.

26. The iron-making communities suffered chronic distress. See *Return on the Present Condition of the Unions in South Wales and the Measures taken by the Boards of Guardians for dealing with applicants for Relief during the Present Pressure of Distress in that District* (1878, LXV, 7).

27. See E. Abbot, *Historical Aspects of the Immigration Problem* (Chicago U. Press, 1926), p. 208, and *S.C. on Coal, op. cit.*, Q. 1540.

28. See *The Colliery Guardian*, 14 November 1879.

29. A. Dalziel, *The Colliers' Strike in South Wales* (Cardiff, 1827), pp. 15–17. This wide disparity in rates of remuneration for work of similar skill in the same coalfield had a significant bearing on the early stage of the evolution of trade unionism and owners' organization. Geology and the rapidity of expansion go far perhaps to explain the comparatively large crop of stoppages that have been a typical feature

of the south Wales coalfield. A study of the Strikes and Lock-outs Reports bears this out.

30. 1883, LXXIX, p. 669, Table 10.

31. *Report on the Decline of the Agricultural Population in Great Britain*, 1881–1906 (1906, XCVI, 3273), pp. 9–10.

32. *Ibid.*, p. 10.

33. Hasbach, *A History of the English Agricultural Labourer* (1908), p. 280.

34. See Joseph Arch's evidence before the Agricultural Commission (1882, XIV, 3309 (1), Q. 58,433). He admitted that this policy had proved a failure.

35. *Report on Decline of the Agriculture Population of Great Britain, op. cit.*, p. 10.

36. *Royal Commission on Labour, The Agricultural Labourer, Wales.* Reports by D. Lleufer Thomas and C. M. Chapman (1893, XXXVI, 6894 (xiv), p. 8).

37. *Ibid.*

38. The Agent, on behalf of the Aberdare and Merthyr Miners' Association, in his evidence before the Labour Commission, complained that fully 25 per cent of the mining labour in his district was unskilled (1892, XXXIV, 6708 (iv), Q. 3942–9). The same feeling was prevalent in the boom of 1872–3. See J. R. Raynes, *Coal and its Conflicts* (1928), p. 34.

39. Special provision has had to be made for this class of worker by the insertion of 'subsistence-wage' clauses in wage agreements in the 1920s.

40. See S. B. L. Druce, 'The Alteration in the Distribution of the Agricultural Population in England and Wales between the Returns of the Census of 1871 and 1881', *The Journal of the Royal Agricultural Society*, 1885, pp. 96–126.

41. J. Ashby and B. King, 'Statistics of some Midland Villages', *Economic Journal*, 1893, p. 5.

42. *Report on Wages and Earnings of Agricultural Labourers* (1900, LXXXII, Cd. 346), p. 108.

43. E. G. Ravenstein, 'The Laws of Migration', *Statistical Journal*, 1885, p. 191. This paper contains an analysis of the dispersion of Devon-Cornwall natives in 1871–81.

Incidentally, it must be remembered that, when we estimate that so many natives of a certain county, say Wiltshire, entered Glamorgan within a period of ten years, it cannot be assumed that they all travelled the whole distance from Wiltshire during that decade.

44. S. B. L. Druce in the *Journal of the Royal Agricultural Society*, 1885, *op. cit.*, p. 111.

45. The passage is quoted in Hasbach, *A History of the English Agricultural Labourer* (1908), p. 314.

46. The county of Durham presents a striking contrast. In 1851–71 it had a high net immigration of 130,000, but after 1881 it consistently lost population, the total net efflux up to 1911 being about 70,000 (H. A. Mess, *Industrial Tyneside* (1928), pp. 30–33). The labour force in the Durham coalfield was stationary between 1875 and 1887.

47. The chief cause of this boom was 'the demand for steam coal for navigation purposes (assisted no doubt by the requirements of transports for the war in South Africa) coming on top of depleted stores, as a consequence of the prolonged struggle in 1898 in South Wales'. D. A. Thomas, 'The Growth and Direction of our Foreign Trade in Coal, 1850–1900', *Statistical Journal*, 1903, p. 46.

48. See 1911 *Census, General Report* (Cd. 8491, 1917), pp. 47–8.

49. *Ibid.*, pp. 229–30.

50. See *Report on the Decline in the Agricultural Population of Great Britain* (1906), *op. cit.*, p. 15, and the Replies to Questions.

51. *Ibid.*, pp. 12–15.

52. See R. H. Hooker, 'On the Relation between Wages and the Number Employed in the Coal Mining Industry', *Statistical Journal*, 1894, p. 631.

53. A useful survey may be found in the *Commission of Inquiry into Industrial Unrest, Report for Wales including Monmouthshire* (1917–8, XV, 8668), pp. 11–24. Space does not permit an analysis of the *quality* of the migration as distinct from its volume and direction. The whole question of the effect of the movement on age and sex distribution in the coalfield and in the rural districts supplying the migrants merits separate treatment.

54. See D. Lleufer Thomas, 'The Geography of the South Wales Coalfield and its Influence on Population', *op. cit.*

55. See W. Ashley, *The Adjustment of Wages* (1903), p. 55; and A. C. Pigou, *Principles and Methods of Industrial Peace* (1905), p. 104.

56. See R. H. Hooker in the *Statistical Journal* (1894), *op. cit.*, 'It is not as a rule until the man has had experience of the conditions of life in a new district that he appreciates the difference between real and money wages', p. 633.

57. The population of the Rhondda valleys grew from 3857 to 162,717 between 1861 and 1921; the density became no less than 4480 persons per square mile and 23,680 per square mile of the area built upon. (See *Commission of Inquiry into Industrial Unrest, Report on Wales including Monmouthshire* (1917), *op. cit.*, p. 14.)

58. H. S. Jevons, *The British Coal Trade*, *op. cit.*, p. 122.

59. See Professor Robbins, 'Notes on Some Probable Consequences of the Advent of a Stationary Population in Great Britain'. *Economica*, April 1929, pp. 76–8.

60. See Professor Sargant Florence, *Statistical Method in Economics and Political Science* (1929), p. 242.

61. Surrey, Sussex, Kent, Hants, Berks.

62. Middlesex, Herts, Bucks, Oxford, Northants, Hunts, Bedford, Cambridge.

63. Essex, Norfolk, Suffolk.

64. Leicester, Rutland, Lincs, Notts, Derby.

65. Durham, Northumberland, Cumberland, Westmorland.

66. The birthplaces statistics of the 1911 Census are given for administrative counties and their associated county boroughs, whereas in each previous Census the unit was the civil or ancient county. This change introduces a slight element of incomparability over time in the case of the contributions of some counties, but is not sufficiently important to justify leaving out the decade 1901–11. It does not, however, affect the aggregate, for, in 1911, in the case of Glamorgan, the administrative county (with associated county boroughs) actually coincides with the civil county.

The unfortunate omission (in the interests of economy) of the birthplace classification according to county from the 1921 Census returns makes it impossible to carry this analysis beyond 1911.

67. The registration county in 1911 had a population of 1,130,668, and the administrative county (with associated county boroughs) 1,120,910.

68. *Census of England and Wales*, 1911 (1912–13, CXI, Cd. 6258, p. 11, Table E).

69. I.e. Monmouthshire, Brecknockshire, Carmarthenshire, Devonshire and Somersetshire.

PART TWO:
INDUSTRY

CHAPTER FOUR

Anthony Bacon, M.P., An Eighteenth-Century Merchant

by L. B. Namier

M R. CHARLES Wilkins, in his *History of Merthyr Tydfil* (1867), p. 145, describes Anthony Bacon as the chief agent, in the early development of the iron trade in south Wales, the first venturer in it to bring 'into operation great energy, strong influence and capital'. 'Little can be learned', he says, 'of this remarkable man's origin. He was, like the majority of our early iron-masters, of northern extraction, and a successful merchant in London at the time of his becoming connected with our neighbourhood.'

In reality it is possible to trace Bacon's origin. An article in *The American Quarterly Church Review*, for October 1865 describes the Rev. Mr. Thomas Bacon, of Maryland, as 'a native of the Isle of Man', and the comment is added: 'He . . . was of good lineal descent being the brother of Sir Anthony Bacon.' Whatever 'good lineal descent' may mean, the statement about it is based on a rank which Anthony Bacon never held. Mr. Lawrence C. Wroth, in an article on 'A Maryland Merchant and his Friends in 1750', published in *The Maryland Historical Magazine* in September 1911, supplies more accurate information about the two brothers; this article also contains an interesting account of the trade in which Anthony Bacon was engaged in his young years, and with which he remained connected till the outbreak of the American Revolution:

> The Maryland Trade, as it was called, consisted in 1750 chiefly of the exportation of tobacco and the importation of manufactured goods of all sorts—cloth, cotton goods, utensils and tools. . . . The business was in the hands of a few great English merchants such as the Cunliffes, Anthony Bacon, the Hunts, the Hydes, the Gildarts and a few others of less importance. Each of these houses had an agent or factor in one or more of the Maryland ports of entry.

The house of Foster Cunliffe & Sons[1] had its headquarters

and chief factor at Oxford [Maryland], another large store on the Chester River about twelve miles above New Town, as Chestertown was then called, and a smaller store halfway between these at Head of Wye. The other firms were not behind them in the number and strategic positions of their posts. . . . These trading concerns . . . were the foundation of Maryland's commercial greatness, the promoters of which amassed fortunes, acquired titles and left an undying tradition of their enterprise and adventurous spirit in the fields of trade.[2]

Between 1740 and 1750 Robert Morris (whose son, Robert Morris of Philadelphia, was to become the financier of the Revolution) was the chief factor of the Cunliffes at Oxford (Md.); his assistant was Henry Callister, a Manxman, who, though of 'a good armor-bearing family', came out to Maryland as a servant indented for five years, at £20 a year. On 28 July 1745, Callister wrote to one of his brothers in the Isle of Man about the Rev. Mr. Thomas Bacon (whom Mr. Wroth describes as 'that ornament of the colonial clergy, celebrated chiefly as the compiler of . . . Bacon's *Laws of Maryland*'): 'This Mr. Bacon you speak of I suppose is brother to Mr. Anto. Bacon who kept a store on this river[3] and is now a merchant in London, for I heard that one Bacon, a brother of his in Dublin who wrote a Book of Rates,[4] was expected in this country after getting orders in London to be inducted parson of our parish, and that he had another brother in Dublin who kept a coffee house.'[5]

In reality, the other brother, 'who kept a coffee house' in Dublin, was the same, very versatile, Thomas Bacon. Biographical notes of the two brothers, Thomas and Anthony, appear in William Hutchinson's *History of Cumberland* (1794),[6] in connection with Whitehaven, Anthony Bacon's first commercial base:[7] 'Mr. Thomas Bacon's first début in life appears to have been in the care and management of a depot, or bank, of coals in Dublin; to which he was appointed by his townsmen, the ship-owners in Whitehaven. The design was, to promote the dispatch of the coal-ships, by enabling them, in case of a dull market, to land their coals immediately and leave them to be sold at a more favourable opportunity. . . . Whilst he was in this situation, Mr. Bacon became acquainted with a smart widow, who kept a coffee house, whom he married.'[8]

When in 1754, Samuel Richardson accused certain Dublin booksellers of having tried to pirate his novel, *Sir Charles Grandison*, and was, in turn, taxed by them with 'having formerly engaged with a Mr. Bacon, of Dublin, in a scheme which . . . was likely to be very detrimental to the printers and booksellers of Dublin in general', he replied:[9]

> This was the fact: Mr. Bacon, an ingenious man, now, in orders, an Irishman, or one who had always had his connexions with that kingdom,[10] . . . kept a coffee house, of note and credit, in Dublin, at which were frequently held auctions for books and merchandize. He had been concerned with the press as a corrector, and proposed to set up a public paper there, and to take up his freedom of the Company of Stationers in Dublin. He did both. The latter in the month of November 1741. The paper was called *The Gazette*. The advertisements of the Public Offices were printed in it. He set up entirely on the Irish footing, and purposed . . . to avail himself, as other Irish printers and booksellers made it their endeavour to do, of such copies of books published in London as he could procure early and *fairly, by consent of the proprietors.* . . . Mr. Bacon was an absolute stranger to Mr. Richardson, brought to him by Mr. Thomas Osborne,[11] of Gray's-inn.

Richardson agreed to his reprinting *Pamela* at Dublin, but another Irish bookseller clandestinely obtained the sheets.

> [Bacon] was deprived of the intended benefit; and also forestalled in the sale of the genuine edition; 250 of which were sent him, in resentment of such base treatment. . . . Tho' Mr. Bacon's prospects were at that time very favourable; . . . yet Mr. Richardson's concern with him, to Mr. Bacon's great regret, held but one year.[12]
>
> Not succeeding in Dublin [continues Hutchinson], Mr. Bacon was encouraged and assisted by his brother to try his fortune in Maryland; whither he soon after went. . . .
>
> Mr. Bacon was twice married; but never very happily. He was a warm-hearted, benevolent man; but, for want of economy, though he generally was in the receipt of an handsome income, a large portion of his life was spent under difficulties and distress.

And this is the account given of his brother:

> The late Anthony Bacon, Esq., of London, — — — is one instance . . . to shew how a man of good abilities may, by exertion and application, from almost any station, rise to distinction and eminence. When he was more than thirty years of age, with his

great talents, and, we may add, great success, he was still but the master of a vessel employed in the tobacco trade from this port [Whitehaven].

He is described as a man of 'an active, vigorous mind', and although by prosperity thrown off his guard, when in difficulties and danger, rising 'with recruited vigour' and extricating himself. 'Once at least, if not oftner, his creditors were called together and his books shewn; and he has been heard to declare, that several times, even in the apparent zenith of his prosperity, had the same thing then happened to him, he would have been found worse than nothing.'[13]

In his will, drawn up in May 1785, Anthony Bacon describes himself as 'past my sixty-seventh year', and must therefore have been born in 1717 or 1718. His connection with Maryland started most probably through the tobacco trade, for which Whitehaven, the English port nearest to the Isle of Man, was a staple place; Whitehaven's connection with the tobacco trade may have had something to do with the Isle of Man, at that time an excellent entrepôt for smugglers.[14] It is not known how long Anthony Bacon stayed in Maryland, but on 9 November 1759, in the course of an examination before the Board of the Treasury, he is reported to have stated that 'he went to North America and staid there till 22 years of age',[15] which would mean that he left America about 1740; and in a pamphlet published in 1775, he claims to have passed many years of his life 'in one of the colonies, and traded very extensively in them all'.[16] Nor is the precise date at which he settled in London known to me. His name does not appear in the London commercial directories in, or prior to 1744, while none are extant at the British Museum for the years 1745–8; but in 1745 Callister refers to him as 'now a merchant in London'. In the directories for 1749 he is mentioned as a merchant in Threadneedle Street; in 1759, his firm appears as 'Anthony Bacon & Comp., merchants, Copthall Court, Throgmorton Street';[17] the partnership seems to have been dissolved about the year 1773.[18]

For the years which intervened between Bacon's return from Maryland and 1758, nothing is known to me about his business and movements. His first government contract, which I can trace, was concluded in 1758 and was for the victualling of the troops sent 'to garrison the forts lately taken from the French on the River Senegal'. There is nothing to show how Bacon had come to be interested in the West African colonies. But the two staple exports of the Gold Coast were gum, which was used in the printing of linens, calicoes, etc.,[19] and which found a market in Ireland, Scotland, and Lancashire, that is, round Whitehaven, Bacon's original base,[20] and negro slaves, exported to the southern colonies, with which Bacon had long been connected, and to the West Indies. Along either line his business may have extended to the Gold Coast.

Samuel Touchet, subsequently M.P. for Shaftesbury, had been concerned in the equipping of the expedition which effected the capture of Senegal, and in June 1758, proposed terms for the victualling of the troops which seemed 'extravagant' to the Duke of Newcastle and the other Lords of the Treasury. He demanded 10d. a day per man if the troops were to be supplied with the navy rations, which included rum, and 7d. if supplied with the rations of the Gibraltar garrison. There, only 5½d. was paid, but Touchet argued that all charges were heavier in proportion upon a small contract, that the risk of getting the provisions across the bar of the Senegal River could not be insured at less than 5 per cent, and that the freight to Senegal was more than to Gibraltar.[21] Still, even after further examination and discussion the Lords of the Treasury were not convinced, and 'upon consideration of the whole matter . . . ordered that an advertisement should be published, for receiving proposals to supply the said troops with provisions and to remit their pay'.[22]

The advertisement was answered by a number of merchants— Drummond,[23] Touchet, Mackay, Stewart, Dupré & Andrews, Knox, and Bacon. After the various offers had been considered, particularly those of Drummond and Bacon, that of the latter was accepted on 27 July 1758.[24]

On 26 October 1758, a letter from Bacon was read at the Board desiring 'to be informed for what time the 800 men ordered to the coast of Africa are to be victualed, and whether he is not to be paid in case the troops should be ordered away before they have consumed the provisions'. To which the Lords of the Treasury replied that 'he is to victual the troops for six months, and he is to be paid for what may be left by recalling those troops, provided he will take care that in such case his agents shall dispose of the said remaining provisions for the publick benefit, consulting the Commander-in-Chief of His Majesty's said troops upon that subject'.[25]

At the meeting of the Treasury Board on 11 November 1758, an inquiry was read from Bacon 'whether any money is to be sent to Senegal for the pay of the troops'; and when called in, he explained 'that many vessels had gone to the coast of Africa with goods to trade with, and that the soldiers of the garrison may undoubtedly lay out their money in merchandize carried thither, and if necessary, traffick with those goods among the natives for fresh provisions'. The Lords of the Treasury replied that they 'are of opinion there is no other practicable method for the Government to make payment to the soldiers but in money, which rule must be followed till they receive more certain advice to the contrary'. Meantime the Secretary to the Treasury was instructed to 'write to the new Governor of Senegal for particular information on this subject'.

The minutes with regard to the Senegal contracts throw much light on the way in which such business was conducted. While showing the difficulties and deficiencies of the service, they go far to disprove the cherished legend about the negligence and inefficiency of mid-eighteenth-century government boards—Mr. Grenville is said to have 'lost America because he read the American despatches, which none of his predecessors ever did'. In reality the Duke of Newcastle, both as Secretary of State and as First Lord of the Treasury, applied himself with much zeal even to the detail of colonial government and business, and so did Lord Halifax as First Lord for Trade and Plantations.

On account of complaints concerning the provisions and liquors for the Senegal garrison, Bacon and Commodore Keppell appeared before the Board on 15 March, 1759.

Present: the Duke of Newcastle, the Chancellor of the Exchequer, Mr. Nugent, the Earl of Bessborough.

Commodore Keppel being called in says that . . . the fleet carried to Goree four months provisions for 400 men, of which ten weeks are elapsed. Left no provisions there but these when he came away. They can get neither flour or bread but from Europe. Proper goods will supply them with fresh meat. The proper goods are India baft, iron bars, good brandy for trade only, and beads. On his arrival at Senegal they were so near starving that individuals were near shifting for themselves. They had not tasted fresh provisions for some days.

Mr. Bacon called in, and said he had sent bafts, but dyed here and not in India, and guns, and powder, and beads; he is now sending iron bars.

Mr. Bacon produced a letter from his correspondent dated 20th January at Senegal advising him that it is excessive difficult to land provisions, that Commodore Keppell had brought 300 men to Senegal, and there were 400 before. That he victualled there near 900 men, and that the Governour has ordered provisions for 400 negroes. No fresh beef to be had for a fortnight before the date of the letter.

Mr. Bacon says that he had sent provisions from time to time according to his directions from the Lords. His two last ships sailed in December with sufficient provisions to last 800 men 13 months, and he has now a vessel ready to sail with more; the first ships he sent were detained a long while waiting for convoy, the two ships that went in December probably arrived in Africa the end of January.

Eight months provisions for 400 men at Goree are now in the Downs, and have been ready these three weeks.

Mr. Keppell says that Mr. Bacon had supplied Senegal with brandy from the Canaries, which is poison. He adds that there is nothing in Senegal Bay to prevent a privateer of 14 guns taking all the provisions. A vessel may be two months there, and not get over the bar, and therefore there is reason for convoy.

Mr. Bacon is directed to send the ships away directly for Goree, not waiting for convoy for fear of disappointment.

Mr. Bacon said he had received these orders already, and would act accordingly.

Write to Governor Worge an account of the quantities and qualities ordered, and that he is to distribute them according to the necessities of the garrisons of Goree and Senegal, and that my Lords have ordered the contractor to send those species of goods, that are recommended by Commodore Keppel to trade with in the purchase of fresh provisions for the garrisons.

Commodore Keppell says they should always have nine months provisions in store there.

Mr. Bacon says he must be allowed for what shall be spoiled, and that in order to have nine months provisions constantly in store, there must be twelve months afloat.

The Lords agreed.

Vinegar and mustard by Commodore Keppell's advice to be sent, and the value stopt out of the soldiers' pay, and the same prices to be paid to the contractor, as are paid by the Victualling Office. . . .

Ordered that Mr. Bacon do provide for 400 additional men, on account of the supplies ordered by the Governor for the blacks, making in the whole 1600, and that for the future he supply both the garrisons with Vidonia wine, instead of brandy, with which he was formerly directed to furnish the garrison of Senegal.

Read a letter from Mr. Mason, Governor of Senegal, to the same effect that Mr. Keppell's account, as to the badness of Canary brandy, and mentioning that if the Lords had known the circumstances of the place, the soldiers might have been paid in

German dollars, the negroes having been used to that coin, but that they are now too well acquainted with the Spanish dollar.[26]

April 25, 1759.

Read a letter from Mr. Anthony Bacon, stating that he understood red wine to be absolutely necessary for the garrison of Senegal, at such seasons of the year, as are apt to produce fluxes in that part of the world, and Mr. Martin acquainted the Lords, that Major Mason had been with him, and declared red wines to be necessary for the garrisons in Africa, and especially in the rainy seasons.

The Lords are of opinion, that red wines should be furnished, and that Mr. Bacon should immediately propose his terms, and from what country he will supply it, red wine not being included in his contract; and let Major Mason be wrote to, and asked what quantity will be proper to be sent to Goree and Senegal.[27]

The subject of the wine was still to come up several times before the Board, also of arms to be sent to the Governor for distribution 'in presents to the Africans' which Bacon was to supply,[28] various warrants are noted advancing money to Bacon on his contracts; and a complaint is entered from the assistant-surgeon at Senegal that the wine and brandy furnished by the contractors were 'impure and new'. On 12 July 1760, after Bacon had started remitting the silver for the pay of the garrision, a complaint reached the Treasury Board concerning the coin supplied by him. On the 29th the reply was read from Mr. Franklyn, 'partner with Mr. Bacon, the remitter of money to Senegal etc. in answer to a complaint from Goree of the distress occasioned to the garrison by being paid in dollars which had pieces taken out of the middle'. . . . 'The answer is — that the dollars sent by Bacon to Goree were purchased in London, on account of the Lords of the Treasury and charged by the ounce and not in tale.' Whereupon their Lordships observed that this being so, the contractor 'is not chargeable with any fraud'.

A further discussion of how to provide for the garrisons of Senegal and Goree appears in the minutes of the Treasury Board on 21 May 1761:[29]

Read a Memorial of Major Money, lately arrived from Goree enumerating the species and quantities of goods which are necessary to be sent to the garrison of Senegal for presents to the Indian [sic] Cheifs to induce them to permitt supplies of fresh provisions from the natives and recommending a sloop and two boats to be sent to Goree for the supply of the garrision with wood and fresh provisions.

Read a letter from Mr. Bacon undertaking to furnish such sloop as is wanted at £35 a month.

Major Money and Mr. Bacon called in.

Mr. Bacon is directed to procure the boats wanting which are to cost twenty-two pounds each.

My Lords agree to his proposition for the sloop.

Write to the Admiralty to desire that the carpenters of the Men of War on that station may be employed to putt together the several parts of the said two boats which must be framed here and sent to Africa in pieces and also to trim the sloop.

Major Money declares that the troops of the garrison are dying for want of fresh provisions and proposes that the contractor for the garrison shall undertake to procure for their use an herd of cattle to be kept upon the Continent opposite to Goree on condition that he is paid for such as the Governor shall certify to be stolen at the price they cost.

Bacon proposed to provide the cattle and to engage that 'such loss shall not exceed £150', to which the Lords agreed.

The outbreak of the Spanish War on 2 January 1762 made a material change with regard to providing wine and Spanish silver for the African garrisons, and on 3 February Bacon declared that 'he cannot proceed with his contract for remitting dollars on account of the interruption occasioned by the Spanish War', and having been discharged from it, was instructed 'to send them for the future to Senegal upon the best terms, that they can be procured for, being allowed a commission of $2\frac{1}{2}$ per cent'.[30]

In 1762, I find the first tenders from Bacon to supply coal, which in time was to play a main part in his business. On 9 March a letter was read from him concerning 'coals and new bedding' for the garrisons of Senegal and Goree;[31] and under date of 27 May there appears in the Treasury minutes another contract for the supply of coal to Belle Isle.[32]

On 6 May 1763, six months notice was given to Bacon of the termination of his contract for provisioning the two African garrisons,[33] possibly because of a reduction in them on the conclusion of peace. It was in the victualling of some West Indian garrisons and the supplying of negroes for public works that Bacon next found a field for business transactions with the Government. Contracts were due to him now, for in the meantime he had become a Member of Parliament.

In November 1763, Bacon unsuccessfully contested Honiton,[34] a very corrupt Devonshire borough, against Sir George Yonge, whose family, with few interruptions, had represented it since 1654. But on 25 January, 1764 he was returned to Parliament for Aylesbury *vice* John Wilkes, 'expelled the House', and the following, probably much coloured, account was given by Alexander Fall, a London merchant, in a letter to Charles Jenkinson on 29 January: 'They likewise say that Bacon was obligd to get member coast what it would other ways he could not pass his accompts as contractor, he pay'd five guineas a man att Ailsbury and £8,000 it coast him oposeing Young att Honiton.'[35]

Bacon entered Parliament under the wing of George Grenville, then First Lord of the Treasury,[36] with whom he may have got connected through Charles Jenkinson, Secretary to the Treasury; as a Whitehaven merchant he had dealings with Sir James Lowther,[37] the biggest mine owner in Cumberland, on whose interest Jenkinson sat for Cockermouth 1761–6 and for Appleby 1767–72. It was probably in the same way that Bacon first came into touch with John Robinson, Lowther's Member for Westmorland 1764–74, a connection which must have proved most valuable to Bacon, the government contractor, when Robinson, as Secretary to the Treasury, practically ran the Treasury from 1770 till 1782.

At first it was not intended that Bacon should permanently retain the seat at Aylesbury; he was to establish his interest at New Shoreham in Sussex, a corrupt borough which specially welcomed 'such an one, as may have it in his power to promote the trade of building ships, which is the chief object and support of the greatest part of the inhabitants of this place. . . .'[38] And Bacon was a ship-owner and shipping contractor—witness, for example, the representation from the Board of Trade, under date of 9 May 1765,[39] 'on a letter from the Governor of Grenada, showing that Mr. Anthony Bacon, a London merchant, had offered two ships of 700 and 300 tons' at a charge of '5,000 guineas for 1,000 tons for one year, which ships may carry out the officials as well as the stores destined for the islands' (these ships were to remain at the island of Tobago 'as hulks for the accommodation of the Lieut.-Governor and other officers and settlers, until convenient habitations can be erected on shore').[40]

When Lord Rockingham, as First Lord of the Treasury, reinstated Newcastle's adherents who had been removed from their places in the proscriptions of 1762–3, Newcastle, on 11 August, 1765, sent him a list of 'honest sufferers' still awaiting restitution; the following entry was put against Shoreham: 'It is also desired, that Mr. Thomas Snooke of New Shoreham (who was lately discharged from being boatman there and put upon the superannuation, contrary to his will, by Mr. Grenville, in order to support the interest of Mr. Bacon who is now chose for Aylesbury,) may be restored, in the room of John Buckoll, who succeeded Thomas Snooke, at the recommendation of Mr. Bacon, who was set up for that borough by Mr. Grenville.'[41]

A by-election was impending at Shoreham, and Thomas Snook was an important figure in the 'Christian Society', in which some 80 out of 136 Shoreham voters were organized for purposes of electoral corruption, while John Buckoll, though 'well respected at Shoreham' and able to 'command several votes',[42] does not seem to have belonged to that club.[43] On 29 September the Rev. T. Hurdis, Newcastle's secretary, explained to William Michell, one of his Sussex agents, the reason for the delay in 'Mr. Snooke's affair':

> Mr. Bacon has been with my Ld. Rockingham and told his Lp., that he has twenty five votes at Shoreham, to be depended on; that it is true, there is a combination of eighty voters: but not above eight of them, sure; the rest will be for the highest bidder; that some of them have been in town, to look out for candidates, and such as will bid most for them. Now Mr. B. is ready and willing to give up his pretensions; and to assist Admiral Cornish [Newcastle's candidate]; but hopes, he shall not be disgraced; meaning, the affair of Mr. Snooke: and therefore it is proposed for consideration, whether it would not be right, to defer the restoring Mr. Snooke, till after the election, and thereby securing Mr. Bacon's assistance.[44]

Newcastle did not relish this procedure, and feared that 'the tampering with Mr. Bacon, and the delay of Snooke's restitution to his old place, has disobliged some of our friends;'[45] and on 5 October Joseph Hickey, to whom Cornish had 'committed the conduct of his affairs' at Shoreham, thus described the situation:

> The motives of Mr. Bacon's conduct are very obvious and his plan for succeeding in the borough well formed, upon all occasions he has declared his interest to be very great with the late Administration and as a convincing proof of it got Snooke most unjustly superannuated in order to make room for his friend, the greater the exertion of power is, so much the stronger must the interest appear. I was credibly informed that he has been secretly practising every artifice to form an interest in opposition to any other

person, however supported, and finding himself disappointed, is become desirous of making a merit of assisting His Grace's nomination which is not at all wanted. In this he has a double view, to continue his friend and to shew that his influence is not diminished with the present Administration. If Snooke be restored the eyes of the Shoreham electors must be opened and his weakness exposed.[46]

The question of Snooke and Bacon was becoming to Newcastle a cardinal affair of State. 'I hope', he wrote to Rockingham on 6 October, 'your Lordship will not let me have the mortification, to see the application of such a fellow, as Mr. Bacon, be prefer'd to mine, by the Marquess of Rockingham *in my own countrey*.'[47] In reply, Rockingham, on 8 October, expressed his regret that Newcastle, 'after so long an acquaintance', should let himself be persuaded 'to put the *not* dismission of Snook as a personal point between your Grace's weight with me and Mr. Bacon's'; and proceeded to explain:

I saw Mr. Bacon and Mr. Serjeant[48] this evening—they seem to think that a degree of understanding between them and the Admiral might have made all matters easy at Shoreham, but that there are some there who for their own importance try all means to prevent it.

They certainly imagine that they have an interest there and do not mean to neglect it. In all our lists they both are marked plump against us in the House of Commons and I am sure with a little moderation might be changed to plump for us—but I now imagine they are to continue as originally set down.[49]

On 23 December 1765, Admiral Cornish was returned for New Shoreham, everything having been 'conducted with decency and ease to the candidate';[50] and when on 4 January 1766 the 'gentlemen of Shoreham' addressed Newcastle on the subject of candidates for the next general election, they added the following postscript: 'My Lord Duke, we must crave your Graces pardon for our objection to Mr. Bacon in particular, for we are determin'd never to accept him a candidate for this borough or any one in his interest.'[51] Bacon now gave up New Shoreham; he retained his seat at Aylesbury till 1784, having stood election contests in 1774 and 1780.

From 'Local Occurrences' and other authorities [writes Mr. Robert Gibbs in his *History of Aylesbury*[52]] we obtain an insight into the mode of conducting elections at Aylesbury in the latter part of the last century. In January 1768, Mr. Bacon made a present of six guineas to all voters who would accept it; a few days after Mr. Durand[53] made a similar distribution. . . . About Christmas 1780, Mr. Bacon and Mr. Orde[54] gave twelve guineas to such of the electors as would accept that sum, and those who could not prove themselves legal voters, two guineas each. In 1781 the same gentlemen gave the voters ten shillings each at the Bell Inn, and a supper, and it is added, 'a very handsome company there was'. In 1782, a like distribution was made, and doubtless on many other occasions not recorded; indeed . . . with so much certainty were these payments looked forward to, that landlords waited for the rents; tradesmen would give credit on the faith of benevolences, and some of the expectants would even raise loans on the security of their deferred election money.

In time Bacon acquired a considerable following in the borough: in the 'State of Representation and Remarks' drawn up for Lord Shelburne in August 1782, John Robinson speaks of 'Mr. Bacon's popular interest' at Aylesbury,[55] and in the paper compiled in December 1783, while questioning 'whether Mr. Bacon would desire to come in again for Aylesbury', states that he was 'personally lik[ed] there'.[56]

At the time of Bacon's entry into Parliament, American affairs, with which he was intimately acquainted, were under discussion both at the government boards and in Parliament. Like other 'American merchants', he tried to promote the interests of his customers in the Colonies, wherever they were not thought contrary to those of Great Britain and of its commercial community; his name, for instance, is found among the signatories to a Memorial presented, in 1764, by the London merchants trading to America in favour of encouraging the production of naval stores in the Colonies.[57] But on currency questions he naturally opposed the endeavours of the Colonies to give the character of legal tender to depreciated paper currencies in which the colonists would then have paid the heavy debts they owed to British merchants. He was also in 1764 among the signatories to Memorials from the London merchants trading to Virginia and to North Carolina, complaining of such paper currencies; and on 17 April 1764 Charles Garth, agent for South Carolina, wrote to the Committee of Correspondence of that province, saying, 'I have reason to believe we should have heard no more of it [the paper currencies] this year, had it not been for a Mr. Anthony Bacon (a North Carolina merchant) who had mooted that point with us before the Board of Trade [in February

1764]; since that time he has procur'd himself to be elected for Ailesbury, and on the 29th of March started the question in the House'. Garth tried to delay it and provided several Members with arguments against it. But on 4 April Anthony Bacon moved for permission to bring in a bill on that matter, and Mr. Rice, a Commissioner of Trade, seconded him. In the end a compromise was concluded 'that the present Bill should be confin'd to the single points of preventing the Colonies for the future from passing Acts issuing Paper Bills with the clause of legal tender, but not to affect or set a period to any at present subsisting'.[58]

In the same letter Charles Garth wrote at length about the resolutions which were introduced in the House of Commons on 12 March 1764 and were to form the basis for the American Stamp Act. Anthony Bacon, in his pamphlet published in 1775, claims to have opposed it from the very beginning; he 'was favoured with a long, though unsuccessful, conference with the minister then in being, on the subject of the American Stamp Act; in the course of which, all that has since happened, in consequence of that ill-concerted measure, was very nearly predicted'.[59] His objections to the Stamp Act, 'the seed plot of our present misfortunes', had not been based on rights, but on fairness. He considered that the British Parliament had the power to tax the colonies, but no sufficient knowledge to decide of matters concerning their internal taxation. 'The friends ... to both countries have now the satisfaction of reflecting that they did not fail to assure the author of that tax, that it had everything in it, which must render it hateful to the Americans; that it must needs be very oppressive in many instances.'

Whatever the truth may be about Bacon's original opposition to the Stamp Act in 1764–5, at the time of the repeal he came out on the side of the Colonies, as did most merchants trading with America. During Benjamin Franklin's examination before the House of Commons relative to the Stamp Act, in February 1766, Bacon asked him three questions, designed to show how harmful its continuance would be for British trade:

Q. Are there any slitting-mills in America?
A. I think there are three, but I believe only one at present employed. I suppose they will all be set to work, if the interruption of the trade continues.
Q. Are there any fulling mills there?
A. A great many.
Q. Did you never hear that a great quantity of stockings were

contracted for, for the army, during the war, and manufactured in Philadelphia?

A. I have heard so.[60]

On the third reading of the Bill repealing the Stamp Act, Bacon spoke for it,[61] and possibly that issue influenced Bacon and Sargent in their attempts to come to an understanding with Rockingham. That friendship, however, did not outlive Rockingham's resignation, and in lists of the House of Commons, which Sir William Meredith drew up for Newcastle in March 1767,[62] Anthony Bacon is placed among the King's friends. Judging from his pamphlet, Bacon was opposed to the Townshend duties—'a more absurd or insufficient tax was never conceived, both with respect to the Americans and ourselves'—but nothing is known to me about any action of his in that matter. Soon he was once more firmly in the Treasury camp, and even on 25 February 1774, when on Sir Edward Astley's motion for leave to bring in a Bill for making Mr. Grenville's Act respecting controverted elections perpetual, the Government was defeated by 250 votes against 122, Bacon is found among the faithful minority.[63]

To return to Bacon's government contracts: in the Treasury minutes, under date of 4 April 1764 a proposal appears from him for supplying negroes to Grenada and the Neutral Islands,[64] and under date of 17 May for victualling troops in Tobago, St. Vincents and Dominica at $4\frac{3}{4}$d. a day[65] and another, made in conjunction with Edward Lewis,[66] to remit money for the troops at Grenada at 2 per cent commission.[67] He was successful in all these tenders, and in November 1764 a contract was added for the remitting of money to the troops in the Bermuda and Bahama Islands,[68] and in January 1765, one for provisioning 1,500 men in the Island of Grenada.[69] On 5 July 1765 he was further invited to 'make propositions' for provisioning the troops in the Isle of Man[70] —obviously he had maintained business connections with his native island—and his proposals were accepted.[71]

The contract for supplying negroes to the Government in the islands of Grenada, the Grenadines, Tobago, St. Vincents, and Dominica, dated 2 January 1765, is preserved in the Record Office.[72] Anthony Bacon undertook 'to furnish . . . seasoned, able and working negroes', the Treasury to pay him 27s. 6d. a month for every negro thus employed, and further $3\frac{1}{2}$d. a man per day for provisions. Bacon was entitled to employ one woman to every nine men demanded. No deductions were to be made for disablement or illness, but payment was to stop in case of death or desertion. In August

1767, a certain Lewis Chauvet, a London merchant of Huguenot extraction, was joined to Bacon in the contract.[73]

Few difficulties and complaints seem to have arisen out of the contract; but under date of 29 September 1772 there appears the following minute:

> Read Memorial of Messrs. Bacon and Chauvet, contractors for furnishing and maintaining negroes for the service of the Government in the Island of Grenada, the Grenadines etc., stating the impossibility of furnishing seasoned negroes, according to the terms of their contract. That the nature of the service in which the said negroes are now employed, occasions their being sent in small parties to distant parts of the islands, which renders it impossible for them to employ proper persons to superintend and feed them, in such manner as they ought to do; which occasions more frequent desertions than heretofore. Likewise that the prices of provisions are so much increased since their contract was first made that they are considerable losers thereby: and therefore praying that the officers of Government may be directed not to insist on seasoned negroes. That they may be paid for such negroes as desert the service; and have such further allowance for the maintenance of the negroes as my Lords shall think proper.
>
> Write Messrs. Bacon and Chauvet directing them to attend my Lords thereon on this day fortnight.[74]

Chauvet, Bacon, and Franklyn attended on 13 October, 1772 and pleaded 'the increased price of negroes, and the extraordinary difficulty of procuring seasoned negroes, at any price'; also that the price of provisions had 'nearly doubled'. They therefore asked for an allowance of 6d. per day, instead of 3½d., for each negro, and declared that 'if this request be not complied with, they desire that their application may be taken as notice for the determination of their contract'.[75] The consideration of their request was postponed, whilst Mr. Cooper, Secretary to the Treasury, was directed to inquire into the matter; and on 16 November the contractors were informed that no alteration could be made in their contract, except raising the allowance from 3½d. to 5d. a day. Thereupon Chauvet, who alone appeared on that occasion, agreed to continue the contract for six months longer.[76]

In 1773 Bacon seems officially to have withdrawn from the contract for the supply of negroes,[77] and his name no longer appears in the new agreement which the Treasury concluded with Chauvet and two new partners on 26 October 1773, granting them more favourable terms.[78] But, curiously enough, payments for the supply of negroes in the accounts of the Paymaster-General (published in the *Journals of the House of Commons*) even in 1774–6 are marked as made to Bacon and Chauvet. From these accounts an idea can be formed of the size of those contracts: during the years 1768–76 a total of almost £67,000 was paid to Bacon and Chauvet under this heading.[79]

In November 1765, Bacon tendered again for the Senegambia garrison, and a contract was signed on 29 March, 1766 for provisioning 250 men at Fort St. Louis. The ordinary army rations were to be supplied—7lb. of bread or flour a week for every man, 7 lb. of beef or 4 lb. of pork, 3 pints of peas, 1 lb. of cheese or 6 oz. of butter, 1 lb. of flour or rice—and, moreover, 7 pints of white or red wine; and he was paid 4s. 6d. per week for each man.[80] But soon complaints were raised by Governor O'Hara, and Bacon threw up the contract. The following entry appears in the Treasury minutes for 22 April 1767: 'Read letter from Mr. Bacon in answer to the complaint of Governor O'Hara of the want of provisions and money at Senegal, and in vindication of his own and his agents' conduct in the execution of that contract, and desiring that my Lords will take this letter as a notice that he can continue his contract for victualling the troops at Senegambia no longer than he is obliged by the tenor thereof.'[81]

When, however, Bacon's successor in the Senegal contract became bankrupt in 1771, Bacon once more undertook to provision the garrison, and continued till 1778, when he relinquished his contract.[82]

Also the contracts for victualling the troops in the West Indian islands gave rise to complaints and controversy; there was always the difficulty that, unless sufficient reserves were kept in the islands, accidents easily produced a shortage of provisions, but if greater quantities were delivered 'than could be consumed while they were good and fresh', a loss resulted which the contractor was naturally unwilling to bear. The device seems to have been ultimately adopted of establishing central stores in the island of Grenada, from which the smaller garrisons were supplied with provisions; but this added greatly to the expense of distribution. Bacon's complaints that he was a loser apparently were not unfounded, for when in the summer of 1770 he gave up the contract, his successor, John Durand (his colleague in the Parliamentary representation of Aylesbury 1768–74), was allowed £1,000 a year 'for the freight of the provisions from Grenada to the other Islands'.[83] Possibly a contributory

75

cause for his abandoning the contracts for Senegal, the West Indies, and for the supply of slaves is to be found in the transfer of his interest to his Welsh coal mines and ironworks.

It seems reasonable to assume that Anthony Bacon had entered the coal trade at an early date, while Whitehaven was still his commercial base; that he was one of the shipowners for whom his brother Thomas acted as agent at Dublin, or was at least connected with them; and that also as a mining adventurer he started his career in Cumberland. He died possessed of an estate called Banklands, near Workington, with a colliery on it. Hutchinson, in his *History of Cumberland*, writes about Workington thus: 'The coal trade is of the greatest importance. There are two sets of workings almost contiguous to Workington; nine pits belong to Mr. Curwen, and five to Mr. Walker, as agent to the trustees of Anthony Bacon, Esq., M.P. London; they generally ship, on account of both parties, about an hundred and fifty waggon loads per day, (Sunday excepted) of which Mr. Curwen ships near an hundred loads: each waggon contains three English tons of coal.'[85]

It is uncertain what year Bacon first engaged in the Glamorgan coal mines. Mr. B. H. Malkin gives the following succinct and, it seems, fairly reliable account:

> Merthyr Tydvil . . . continued a very inconsiderable village till about the year 1755, when the late Mr. Bacon took more notice of the iron and coal mines, with which this tract of country abounds, than they had before excited. For the very low rent of £200 per annum he obtained a lease of a district, at least eight miles long and four wide, for ninety-nine years. It is to be understood, however, that his right extended only to the iron and coal mines found on the estate, and that he had comparatively a very small portion of the soil on the surface, on which he erected his works for smelting and forging the iron. He possessed in addition some fields for the keep of his horses, and other necessary conveniences. He at first constructed one furnace; and little besides this was done, probably for at least ten years. The next advance was the erection of a forge for working pig into bar iron. About the beginning of the American war, Mr. Bacon contracted with government for casting cannon. Proper founderies were erected for this purpose; and a good turnpike road was made down to the port of Cardiff, along an extent of twenty-six miles. At Cardiff likewise a proper wharf was formed, still called the cannon wharf, whence the cannon were shipped off to Plymouth, Portsmouth, and wherever the service required. These were carried in waggons

down to Cardiff, at a prodigious expense of carriages, horses, and roads.[85]

Mr. Wilkins produces a story of how Bacon 'in the year 1763, entered the valley in a carriage drawn by mules, and put up at the Star Inn. We met an elderly man some years ago whose mother . . . saw him in his mules' carriage.'[86] The mules may be dropped, but, as Wilkins seems to have seen also the rate books of the district and the original contracts, this part of his account deserves reproduction: 'In the year 1765, Mr. Bacon, in conjunction with other gentlemen, and whom from the rate-books, we take to have been Wood, Richardson[87] and others, leased the great tract of mineral property henceforth to be known in greater part as the Cyfarthfa Estate . . . the Cyfarthfa portion from Earl Talbot and Mr. Richards, of Cardiff, and the Plymouth district from Lord Plymouth.' These estates came in time to be 'colloquially known as "Bacon's Mineral Kingdom" '.[88] Mr. Wilkins writes that 'The original lease of Cyfarthfa is as follows:—Date: 29th August, 1765. Lessors: The Right Hon. William, Earl Talbot, and Baron Hensol, Lord Steward of His Majesty's Household; and Michael Richards, of Cardiff, Esquire. Lessees: Anthony Bacon, of the City of London, Esquire; William Brownrigg,[89] of Whitehaven, Esquire. Time: Ninety-nine years, from 25th March, 1765, to 25th March, 1864.'[90]

Mr. Wilkins's further account of Anthony Bacon is, like most of his narrative, diluted with a great mass of quasi-pleasant descriptions and would-be lively stories. I reproduce, however, a few extracts from it, some because they may possibly contain a residuum of fact, others as a warning to those who might feel inclined to treat his book, as so many done done, as a reliable source of information. About 1782, a certain Homfray, owner of the Callcot Works, near Broseley, in Shropshire, and of a forge at Stewponey, near Stourbridge, is stated by Mr. Wilkins to have 'entered into an arrangement with Bacon to erect a forge at Cyfarthfa, where the latter had two furnaces, but only one in blast at the time. The arrangement was that Bacon should supply them with all the Cyfarthfa pig iron to work the forge etc., for which they were to pay him £4. 10s. long weight, and 4s. per ton for coal.'[91] Next follows a romantic description of how one of Homfray's sons brought workmen from the forge at Stewponey, and landed them at Cardiff on 13 May 1782:

Meanwhile the American War was raging, and Bacon, being a man of position in London, succeeded in getting a contract for supplying the cannon to Government. Charcoal iron hammered was found to suit admirably. The foundry built at Cyfarthfa was, like the forge, worked by Homfray. . . . This contract gave a great impulse to the iron trade. The forge was pushed on briskly, and without delay opened amidst general rejoicings. . . . For about two years the new forge was worked energetically. Bacon and the Homfrays prospered.

But to the wealthy iron-master there came at length a reverse. For some time he had manufactured cannon, and shipped them from Cardiff to Portsmouth and Plymouth, at the place still known as Cannon Wharf; but ugly rumours began to get afloat, and the contract was lost. Captain Smith (*Treatise on the Bute Docks*) states that it was alleged against Bacon that he supplied cannon to the American Republicans as well as to his own Government, and this was why he lost the contract, which afterwards fell into the hands of the Carron Company, Scotland. At the expiration of two years from the opening of the forge, the Homfrays began to complain of a falling off in the supply of pig iron.[92]

A row followed, graphically described by Mr. Wilkins, 'and thus ingloriously ended the connexion between the Homfrays and Anthony Bacon, Homfray disposing of his tenure to Mr. Tanner'.

In reality Bacon's contracts 'for supplying the cannon to Government' started in 1773, and not while 'the American War was raging', or much rather was approaching its conclusion, in 1782; while the Carron Company had held such contracts long before Bacon ever obtained any. 'Charcoal iron hammered' had been 'found to suit admirably' ages ago, but Bacon experimented with iron made from coke. The *Treatise on the Bute Docks*, by Captain Smith, is a pamphlet called *Nautical Observations on the Port and Maritime Vicinity of Cardiff*, published in 1840 by Captain W. H. Smyth, R.N.; and the story about Bacon having been caught trading with the enemy is told as a mere report in a footnote,[93] without any evidence being adduced to support it. In reality, this story with regard to gun-founders was as common at that time[94] as the tale about hidden German gun emplacements in 1914; and, as will be seen from documentary evidence, Bacon did not lose his contract, but asked the Board of Ordance to transfer it to Homfray to whom he had leased his works at Penderyn. As to the row with Homfray and his 'disposing of his tenure to Mr. Tanner', Mr. Malkin still found Homfray at Penderyn in 1804, making weekly 'on a moderate average, fifty tons of bar iron and upwards, and . . .

now extending Penderyn and its buildings, which will soon be completed'.[95]

The authentic story of Bacon's contracts with the Board of Ordnance can be gathered from its minute books preserved at the Record Office. The first entry in these books concerning Bacon appears on 6 July 1773.

> Anthony Bacon, Esq., having represented in his letter to the Surveyor-General of the 3rd instant that the best way to give the Board a proof of what metal is the fittest for the purpose of making guns, will be to cast a gun of metal produced from *coke only*, another from metal produced from *charcoal only*, and a third from a mixture made from the judgment of the founder; and having tendered his service to make three such guns and promised to execute the same faithfully upon his reputation, as a man of honour and integrity, as he expects the future favour of the Board;
>
> Ordered that he be desired to cast three guns as proposed, vizt., 18-pounders; and that he send them to Woolwich as soon as possible.[96]

On 2 November Bacon reported that he had executed the order and 'that he has also sent to Woolwich an iron gun cast solid and bored, which he can afford for the addition only of £2 per ton more than the ordinary and afterwards for less'. The Board thereupon ordered as follows:

> That the three 18-pounders be proved by the Proof Masters and if they should stand the proof, that they be delivered to the commanding officer of artillery to make such experiments as he shall think proper, and that the result be reported to the Board with his opinion upon each respectively.
>
> That the gun cast solid be likewise proved, and that such experiments as the commanding officer thinks proper be likewise made with the said gun cast solid notwithstanding the irregularity of the bore, Mr. Bacon having agreed to this at his own expense.[97]

On 9 December General Williamson reported that, after the guns cast by Anthony Bacon had been fired 45 rounds,

> he examined the three guns and found that the metal at the muzzles of them were spread forward on the bore about 2/10

from the real faces of the guns, but that most guns will do so more or less by frequent firing which is easily made even again by the file.

Ordered that a copy of the experiment be sent to Mr. Bacon, and he be acquainted the Board are ready to receive his proposals, and treat with him for casting iron ordnance for His Majesty's service.[98]

Thus Bacon was entered among the gun-founders with whom orders were placed and whose guns were tested and proved at Woolwich.[99] Under date of 21 April 1774, a further order was given for testing one of Bacon's new guns,[100] and on 29 April the report of the experts is quoted 'that casting guns solid in the manner of Mr. Bacon's is infinitely better than in the ordinary way, because it makes the ordnance more compact and consequently more durable than cast upon a newel bar, but that the expence is greater, the exact difference of which they could not ascertain'.[101] Thereupon the Board ordered on 7 June 1774, 'that letters be wrote to acquaint the gun-founders that the Board have agreed with Mr. Bacon for casting iron ordnance and boring them out of the solid at £18 per ton and that they therefore desire to know whether they will engage to provide guns bored out of solid at the same rate in case the Board should prefer those kind of guns to them for which they have already contracted'.[102]

The answer from one firm, Messrs. Jones, is noted in the minutes of 15–16 November: they could not bore guns out of the solid, being 'threatened to be prosecuted by the person who has a patent granted for that service to himself only'.[103] That person was not, however, Anthony Bacon, but the famous inventor and iron-master, John Wilkinson (best known as associate and collaborator of Watt and Boulton) at whose works at Broseley, in Shropshire, the new type of gun was cast for Bacon. It was Wilkinson who, according to Stockdale first 'hit upon a method . . . of boring cannon and cylinders from the centre'.[104] 'It is difficult to overestimate the importance of this invention', writes Mr. H. W. Dickinson.[105] 'It was really the introduction of the guide principle into machine tools.' By casting solid he diminished the danger of blow-holes and by rigid boring facilitated accuracy.

Whether it was John Wilkinson himself who discovered the new method, or 'a man named Robinson in Wilkinson's employ' who 'rediscovered the art of boring cannon',[106] or whether the discovery was merely an adaptation of methods used elsewhere,[107] a patent (No. 1063) was granted to John Wilkinson on 27 January 1774 for

80

A New Method of Casting and Boring Iron Guns or Cannon which he had proved upon repeated tyrals to be a great improvement.

The said iron guns or cannon are cast in a mould without any nowell or core whatever, whereby they are made perfectly solid and entirely free from any cavity. In the boring of them they are placed upon a carriage or frame on which the gun or cannon is turned round . . . by a wheel moved by water or by the application of a fire engine.[108]

That Anthony Bacon's first deliveries of guns of this type were from Wilkinson's works, is proved by several entries in the Ordnance minutes. Thus on 22 November 1774, a copy 'of a letter from his agent at Broseley' is mentioned;[109] and on 1 June 1776 Bacon informed the Board

> that his agreement with Mr. Wilkinson for casting iron ordnance solid and boring them is now at an end, he therefore offered to supply the Board with such a quantity as they shall be pleased to order of solid bored iron ordnance at £18 per ton at his own works, he having made the necessary preparations for the same.
>
> Ordered to be acquainted he will have orders as soon as the Board know what will be wanted.[110]

By that date Wilkinson's patent had been cancelled. For the Board, having received the above-mentioned letter from Messrs. Jones, had ordered its solicitor to inquire into the patent;[111] and on 7 February 1775, 'the Solicitor having pursuant to the Board's order of December 6, 1774, reported his opinion upon the patent obtained by Mr. John Wilkinson for boring iron cannon, . . . Ordered that the said report be sent to the Master-General . . . that such steps may be immediately taken as his Lordship may judge proper for the revocation of the said Patent, which if permitted to remain in force will [not] only be prejudicial to His Majesty's subjects but very detrimental to the public service.'[112]

Nothing more is said in the minutes of the Ordnance Board about these proceedings, but by April 1775, the new method was in general use,[113] and a 'Memoir of John Wilkinson, Esq., Iron-Master of Broseley', published in November 1799, in the *Commercial and Agricultural Magazine* states that he at length furnished the important improvement 'of boring cannon from the solid instead of casting them hollow by means of cores, as formerly. The treatment he experienced in consequence of this, though pretty generally understood, we forbear at present to discant upon.'

Bacon's deliveries started in the summer of 1774 and a rather curious entry appears in the minutes of 29 August. It appears that Crawshay, who, later on, in June 1777, became officially Bacon's partner,[114] was now intriguing against him.

Mr. Niel Campbell, Clerk of the Survey at Woolwich, having represented in his letter of 15 instant that one Crawshay had acquainted him that he had a third share in the guns served into store by Mr. Bacon and that among the 18-pounders now landed at the place which were said to be bored from the solid, fifteen of them were not. He therefore begd leave to acquaint the Board therewith, to give such directions as should be thought proper as they should be at an uncertainty in granting certificates.

Ordered that Mr. Bacon report what guns are bored out of the solid and what are not.[115]

November 1, 1774.

Read a letter from Mr. Bacon dated 14th September last reporting pursuant to order of 29 August, 1774, that he has not offered to the Board one gun but has been bored out of the solid, and that the report made to the Board was not true.

Ordered that a proof of iron ordnance be made at Woolwich on Saturday and Monday next, 5th and 7th instant, and that all persons concerned have notice as usual.[116]

When, in January 1775, a defect was found in the bore of a 32-pounder gun supplied by Bacon, 'occasioned by an incorrect manner of boring, the engine not being steady, the bars too slight or the bores not of the right sort',[117] Bacon replied that 'it was not to be imagined but that some small imperfections should happen in an invention entirely new and which requires such immence force as the cutting a cast gun of so large a calibre as a 32-pounder, not that he wished to have a gun received which does not come up to any standard that the Board shall please to fix, because he has no doubt but he shall come nearer perfection every day'.[118]

On 7 February Bacon tendered a proposal for casting 4000 tons of iron ordnance in the current year at £20 per ton, although the normal price was £18.

February 24, 1775.

Mr. Bacon having in his letter of 21st instant represented that the guns which have hitherto been cast by him and bored out of solid are much superior to those cast in the common way, he therefore hoped the Board would agree to this price of £20 per ton and give him an order for 1,000 tons, that his works may be kept going and his men employed.

Ordered to be acquainted that the Board will give him orders upon the terms of his present contract, but will not increase the price.[119]

On 21 April 1775 the following distribution was made of orders:[120]

Ordered that warrants be made out to the undermentioned persons to cast and bore out of the solid[121] the following number and natures:

Iron Ordnance	Mr. Bacon	Messrs. Harrison & Co.	Messrs. S. Walker & Co.	Messrs. Jones & Co.
32-pounders, 9½ feet	53	75	30	15
24 ,, 9½ ,,	19	19	24	12
18 ,, 9 ,,	78	48	0	0
9 ,, 7½ ,,	17	17	24	12
6 ,, 7 ,,	28	28	31	15
	195	187	109	54

Under 8–9 August 1775, Bacon is found clamouring for further orders;[122] again on 27 January 1776 appears the following entry: 'Mr. Anthony Bacon having represented in his letter of 15 inst. that he has executed all the Boards orders for iron ordnance, he therefore offered to supply the Board with 1,000 tons[123] of iron ordnance of any size the Board may be pleased to order cast solid and receive in payment for the same 4,000 tons of old iron guns of the same size as the new ordnance and in the same proportion.'[124]

The Board accepted his offer, provided 'he will allow £5 per ton for the old metal'[125]—which countered Bacon's attempt, to get, in a round-about manner, at the price of £20 per ton. And when on 28 March, Bacon replied 'that the price of the old gun metal is quite indifferent to him if the Board agree to give him 4,000 tons of old guns for 1,000 tons of new ordnance,' he was told that this would make the price for iron ordnance '£20 per ton, which the Board do not intend to give'.[126]

With the growth of the armies employed in America, the orders from the Board of Ordnance became more numerous and more pressing. Under date of 29 September 1777 there is an order to Bacon for 34 9-pounders, 7 feet long;[127] and on 22 May 1778 for 63 guns, mainly of the larger types.[128] Now that the gun-founders no longer clamoured for orders but the Board of Ordnance for delivery, Bacon felt he could vent his grievances and press his demands.

June 17, 1778.

Anthony Bacon, Esq., having by letter of this date represented the impossibility of continuing to supply guns upon the present terms: on account of the uncertainty whether they may not be rejected before laid down for proof: and when passed proof, the length of time before a bill is made out for payment. Therefore he requested to be paid £20 per ton. But if within one month from the time of landing [at Woolwich] a certificate be given or imprest made out for the amount of one half the value of the guns delivered, he will abate £2 per ton and engage to deliver 25 tons per week or 1300 tons per annum.

Ordered that Mr. Bacon proceed upon such numbers and natures as are most wanted, to the amount of 650 tons. And Mr. Bacon being present and agreeing to take £18 per ton, the Board engaged to grant an imprest bill for one third of what he delivers. And ordered that Mr. Butler deliver to him very exact gauges and drawings.[129]

Two days later an order was given him for 452 guns,[130] and on 21 August for 46 guns; and letters followed urging 'all possible despatch in the delivery of ordnance contracted' and inquiries when it will be delivered. In 1779, there are three orders for guns from Bacon and Crawshay, for 50 on 15 April,[131] for 270 on 18 September,[132] and for 76 on 16 October;[133] the last in response to a letter from them reporting 'that they can keep all their wheels going without retarding the large guns wanted if the Board will give them orders for some small natures'. In addition, Bacon and Crawshay held contracts for the supply of cannon to the East India Company and to the King of Sardinia, as appears from the debits against them for proving such guns at Woolwich.[134]

In August 1779, Bacon and Crawshay started on a new branch of munition contracts. They proposed 'to cast 100 tons per month of round shot at £12 per ton to be paid for every 100 tons of shot, 150 tons of old metal at £6 6s. per ton and the balance by debenture',[135] and during the following years 'warrants of justification' prove that the contract was made.

Early in 1781 a shortage of money becomes apparent at the Board of Ordnance; the gun-founders were informed in 29 March that the Board 'will grant them imprests bearing interest for the third part of what is due on the proving and passing of their respective guns if the Board have not money to pay the same';[136] and an even more explicit statement of its impecunious condition is contained in the following minute of 6 March 1782:

> Messrs. Bacon and Crawshay having by letter of 1st ult°. represented their distress on account of the great arrears of payment, and requested that all their present debentures of twelve months standing may be paid either in cash, or imprest bills at five per cent interest, and to be paid during the war as at present one third of what is due by imprest on interest;
> Ordered to be acquainted that the Board cannot possibly comply with their request.[137]

At the end of 1781 a new partner, a certain William Stephens, was joined to Bacon and Crawshay;[138] and a minute of 2 September 1782, marks the end of Bacon's connection with the Board of Ordnance:

> Mr. Anthony Bacon, one of the gun founders to this office, having signified in his letter of 30 ult. that he has let his works to Mr. Francis Homfray and requested that the Board would be pleased to give their orders in future to Mr. Homfray instead of Bacon and Crawshay,
> Ordered that the warrants granted upon the last order to Messrs. Bacon & Co. be made out to Mr. Homfray.

Bacon was now about sixty-five years old, and obviously had decided to withdraw from business—and it was this, not sinister dealings with the enemy, which put an end to his career of contractor for munitions.

Mr. Malkin gives the following account of Bacon's disposal of his mines and works when he withdrew from active business:

> About the year 1783, he granted leases, I believe for thirty years, but I cannot answer for my own accuracy on this point, of his remaining term, in the following parcels: Cyfarthfa works, the largest portion, to Mr. Crawshay, for £5,000 per annum; Penderyn to Mr. Homfray, at £2,000 per annum; Dowlais Iron Works to Messrs. Lewis and Tate, and a fourth part to Mr. Hill. What the rents of these two portions are, I have not learned from any direct intelligence; but I conclude them to amount in the whole to £3,000, because it is very generally asserted and believed,

85

that the heirs of Mr. Bacon have from all those works a clear annual income of £10,000.[139]

Mr. Wilkins, although he repeats that the works realized £10,000 a year, gives a different account of the leases. 'In 1784 he made arrangements with Mr. Richard Hill, who took the Plymouth Works and agreed to pay 5s. per ton for all the iron he made. For the same price Cyfarthfa was taken by a Mr. Tanner.' And on this follows an inevitable flourish: 'and then, amid the regrets of his workmen and the villagers, Bacon bade adieu to Merthyr'.

When on the outbreak of the Revolution considerable armies were sent to America, Bacon engaged once more in victualling contracts. The agreement concluded on 2 February 1776,[140] by the Treasury with Messrs. Nesbitt, Drummond, and Franks, who in peacetime had had the provisioning of the main body of British troops in America, served as model for those with the new contractors. They agreed to supply the usual army rations[141] at 5¼d. per man a day; beef, pork, butter, and oatmeal to be delivered on board of ships at Cork; flour, bread, peas, and rice at the ports of London, Bristol and Portsmouth. Their contract was for 12,000 men and was to run 'from this time' till 1 May 1777.

Under date of 9 February 1776, the following entry appears in the Treasury Minutes:[142] 'Messrs. Bacon and Mayne attend and are called in . . . ; they propose to furnish provisions for 6,000 men in America; on the same terms as have been agreed to by Messrs. Nesbitt, Drummond and Franks. My Lords agree; contract to be forthwith prepared. . . .'

The further distribution of contracts made on the same day was as follows:

Henniker, Wombwell, Devaynes, and Wheeler, 12,000 men
Amyand,   3,000 ,,
Durand,   3,000 ,,
James, Smith, Baynes and Atkinson (for Canada), 12,000 ,,

Altogether contracts for victualling 48,000 men were given to fifteen merchants; of these eleven sat in Parliament,[143] while the remaining four were all in partnership with Members of Parliament. On 16 January 1777 the same merchants attended the Board of Trade to discuss a renewal of their contracts; the number of troops assigned to each remained unchanged.

My Lords propose to give up the warranting the provisions good by the contractors; further than to the first port of destination; and to give them 5¾d. per ration.

The contractors withdraw.

Major Caldwell is called in and heard.

The contractors are again called in and signify their consent to my Lords proposals.

Prepare contracts accordingly.

Write to the several contractors directing them to prepare three months provisions to be delivered to the commissary at Corke with all possible expedition.[144]

In April 1778 the number of troops victualled by Anthony Bacon was raised to 4000,[145] in November, to 4900,[146] and in August 1779, to 7000;[147] in that year a new clause was added to the agreements, for indemnifying the contractors for possible losses through 'invasion or insurrection' in Ireland. This seems to have been the last American victualling contract in which Anthony Bacon participated.

Since by 1776 Bacon had become one of the leading mining adventurers in Great Britain, he naturally tendered also for the supply of coal for Howe's army; in fact, his mining operations extended even to the other side of the Atlantic, though ultimately the production of his collieries in the Maritime Provinces does not seem to have counted for much.

When by the peace treaty of 1763 Cape Breton was ceded to Great Britain and became part of the province of Nova Scotia, a certain Mr. Guerish drew up a paper on the advantages which would accrue from the development of its coal mines.[148] He calculated that a chaldron of coal in Great Britain cost 7s. 6d. and its transport to the Continent of America 32s. 6d., together 40s.; whereas in Nova Scotia the digging of a chaldron cost 5s. and the transport to the American Continent 20s., which would leave 15s. on the price to be divided between the government, the entrepreneur, and the consumer.

Two applications for the grant of the coal mines at Cape Breton were made to the Government: one by General William Howe, 'on behalf of himself and the several other Officers,whose names are hereunto annexed',[149] and another by Sir Samuel Fludyer, bart., his brother Sir Thomas Fludyer, Adam Drummond, and Anthony Bacon.[150] Howe's Memorial

SHEWETH

THAT your Memorialist and the said other officers having served in America during the late War, stand entitled under your Majesty's most Gracious Proclamation to grants of lands (in certain portions) in your Majesty's Dominions in that part of the world, as a reward for such their services.

THAT your said Memorialists desirious to shew their sense of your Majesty's goodness; by connecting the publick good, with their private interest herein, are desirous to become adventurers in opening coal mines and endeavouring to establish a colliery in the Island of Cape Breton for the better supplying the several Colonys and garrisons on the Continent with fuel.

THAT to enable them to carry this, their design into execution, they humbly pray, to have granted to them as their allotment, a tract of land on the East shore of the aforesaid island, extending from the point on the North side of Mire Bay to the South East side of the entrances into the Labrador, and seven miles inland, to be computed from the point and entrance abovementioned, and suppos'd to contain about 55,000 acres. Which tract your Memorialists will settle with inhabitants in the manner directed by your Majesty's Royal Proclamation.[151]

THAT should this project succeed, the Colonys in generall will not only reap many advantages in being furnish'd with firing on much more reasonable terms than at present, but be enabled to clear and cultivate large parcels of lands now kept in wood for the supply of fuel.

And as your Memorialists are well persuaded, that it will appear most fully to your Majesty, how great risk, difficulty and expence must attend this undertaking in its beginning, and what great advantages all your American Colonys in generall must derive from it; should it happily be brought to perfection, your Memorialists flatter themselves it will meet with a favourable reception to your Majesty in Council.

W^m. Howe.

[here follow the names of the other 'Memorialists']
9th March, 1764.

Ordered by the King in Council to be referred to the Lords of the Committee of Council.

19th March, 1764.

Ordered by the Lords of the Committee to be referred to the Lords Commissioners for Trade and Plantations.

On 11 April Howe amended his proposals in a letter directed to Lord Hillsborough, then President of the Board of Trade:

> In the Memorial referred from the Council which I had lately the honour to deliver to your Lordship, no other besides the usual quit-rent is offered to the Crown; but if the profits on the grant solicited should be thought too great on those terms, the Memorialists beg leave to propose the payment of two shillings on every chaldron coals (London measure) that may be exported: and we flatter ourselves that we shall meet with your Lordship's countenance to this proposition as not inadequate, considering the risks and disadvantages we must unavoidably combat with in an undertaking of this precarious nature, where added to the high price of labour we shall be at the expence of erecting block-houses and of furnishing them for the defence of the colonists, building habitations for the workmen, boats and wharfs, and finding provisions for every person employed in the undertaking with a passage for them from Europe; and when it is further considered that we had the good fortune to serve in the reduction of Cape Breton and most other military operations carried on in America, I humbly beg your Lordship will be induced to represent these conditions as reasonable and fitting in your report on our memorial.[152]

The paper containing the proposals of Bacon and his partners[153] is not dated, but obviously must have been handed in about the same time:

> To the Right Honble the Lords Commissioners of Trade and Plantations.
> The Memorial of Sir Samuel Fludyer, bart., Sir Thomas Fludyer, knight, Adam Drummond and Anthony Bacon, Esqs.
> SHEWETH
> THAT your Memorialists beg leave to propose to your Lordships, that they are ready to treat with you for a lease of all the coals on the Island of Cape Breton on the following or such other terms as your Lordship and they can agree upon; vizt.
> Your Memorialists will engage to send over immediately a sufficient number of men skilled in coal works, and will also erect all such works as are necessary for carrying on the business.
> In consideration of the great expence your Memorialists must immediately be at, they hope your Lordships will think it reasonable, that they have the use of the coal mines——[154] years free of tax; and at the end of which they are willing to pay to

His Majesty the sum of two shillings and sixpence sterling money for every chaldron of coals of thirty-six bushels they ship off from the said Island, for the further term of ten years; and after the said term of ten years are expired, they are willing to engage to pay to His Majesty the sum of three shillings and ninepence sterling money for every chaldron of coals they shall ship off from the Island as aforesaid.

And at the end of the second term of ten years above mentioned, your Memorialists are willing to engage for a further term of ten years, and will engage to raise the duty to His Majesty to the sum of five shillings sterling per chaldron shipped off from the said Island aforesaid, and which your Memorialists believe is a higher rent than is paid to any proprietors of coals in Great Britain where the rentors work the mines at their expence.

And in order to carry this business into as speedy execution as possible, your Memorialists beg leave to be admitted to treat with your Lordships as soon as ever your leisure will permit.

A 'Representation to the King' on these Memorials was made by the Board of Trade on 10 July 1764 and is signed by Lord Hillsborough, George Rice, Bamber Gascoyne, and Jeremiah Dyson.[155] It emphasizes the importance of opening up coal mines at Cape Breton as 'the high price of coals in almost every part of this Kingdom, and especially in this Metropolis, is a cruel burthen upon the poor, and a very great drawback upon every manufacture', and is certain to increase still more with the growing export of coal from Great Britain to America. They agree with the scheme and calculations submitted by Guerish and they now have two applications for the lease of these mines before them. The first is from General the Hon. William Howe 'and his associates, most of them distinguished officers in Your Majesty's army'. By a subsequent letter, General Howe has put forward some proposals of advantage to the Crown, 'but not sufficient to make us consider the proposal in a different light'; it is 'rather to be a petition to Your Majesty for a grant of these coal mines, as a reward for their military services, than a proposal upon terms proportionate to the value of these mines.' If the matter is to be decided on terms other than those of a reward, they recommend the proposal of Fludyer and his associates, with the following amendments: 'The duty or toll upon the coals should continue at the low rate for seven years only'; and to secure the working of these mines, a minimum sum of £1000 a year should be paid during the first seven years, and of £2000 a year during the remainder of the lease.

This Representation was referred to the Lords of the Committee of His Majesty's Privy Council for Plantation Affairs, and on 20 July 1764, they recommended 'that the proposal of Sir Samuel Fludyer and his associates should be accepted as the most advantageous for His Majesty's service'.[156]

It is not clear whether any grant of land accompanied that of the mines; and of their further story nothing is known to me, except that from certain discussions at the Treasury Board in 1777 it appears that Bacon, who among the four partners was the only expert on mining, still held the lease, and that not much had been done in the way of developing the collieries.

The first entry I can find in the Treasury books relating to Bacon's coal contracts during the American Revolution appears under date of 3 December 1776.[157] He transmits an application from owners of the ship *Happy Return*, of Whitehaven, 'chartered by him last year to carry coals to His Majesty's forces in America; which ship was taken by the rebels; demanding payment of the value of the ship pursuant to clause in the charter party'.[158] In this case the coal was probably from his own colliery at Workington, though he is also found acting as a mere intermediary in supplying it.

The following entry appears in the minutes of the Treasury Board on 13 June 1777:[159]

My Lords take into consideration the supply of coal desired by Sir Wm. Howe.

Read estimate of the expence of coal to be sent from hence.

Mr. Bacon attends and is heard hereon: and also on the practicability of supplying the army with coal from the mines near Louisburg.

My Lords desire Mr. Bacon to prepare proposals for supplying the army under Sir William Howe with 20,000 chaldrons of coal from the mines near Louisburg before the 31st October next: and estimates thereon: and to lay them before the Board on Tuesday next.

When, on that day, Bacon appeared before the Board he declared 'that it is impossible at this season of the year to send out colliers and men to get a supply of coal for the army at Louisburg: for in such an undertaking the men, tools and instruments proper to carry on the work ought to be sent out from hence in the month of February'. The Lords thereupon decided to direct Mr. Bacon 'immediately to write to the several ports on the west coast of

England, where coal is usually shipped; and enquire the terms of freight per chaldron on which he can procure ships to carry coal to Sir Wm. Howe in America'.[160]

On 27 June, Bacon was 'directed to contract for 5,000 chaldrons of coal to be delivered at New York free of all charges, and not exceeding £4 per chaldron: for which my Lords will allow him the usual commission'. It is not said what the commission amounted to, but from the numerous entries of payments for coal shipped by him at various dates in 1777 and 1778 it would appear that the total cost of it to the Treasury oscillated round £4 16s. a chaldron.

On 7 August 1778, Samuel Martin, a merchant of Whitehaven, offered to deliver 1000, or upwards, chaldrons of coal at headquarters in America at £4 10s. His offer was accepted, and when John Deane, Bacon's agent, the same day, offered to send 5000 chaldrons on the same terms as during the preceding year, he was told that 'my Lords will agree with Mr. Bacon to send 4000 chaldrons . . . if he will contract therefor on the same terms and conditions as proposed and agreed to by Mr. Martin'.[161]

Two months later appears the last entry which refers to Bacon's deliveries of coal to the armies in America: 'Read letter from Anthony Richardson declining on the part of Mr. Bacon having anything to do in the business of supplying coals for the army at New York on the terms proposed.'[162]

Fisheries were another branch of business with which Bacon seems to have been connected. For these, especially for herring fisheries, Whitehaven and the Isle of Man were an important base in the eighteenth century, and in the minutes of the Treasury Board on 26 March 1772, Bacon is mentioned as appearing before it on behalf of the 'Adventurers in the British White Herring Fishery'.[163] Moreover, in the *Acts of the Privy Council (Colonial)*, under date of 31 August 1763, there is a 'reference to the Board of Trade of the Memorial of Anthony Bacon, Anthony Richardson, Gilbert Franklyn and John Blackburn, merchants of London, for a grant of 2,000 acres at the Magdalene Islands, to enable them to carry on very extensive fishery in the Gulf of St. Lawrence for whales, codfish, sea cows and seals'.[164]

I have not come across any application from Bacon for grants of land in the Colonies (other than may have been implied in the proposals with regard to the coal mines at Cape Breton). But he acquired a few estates in the old Colonies. William Bacon, who in Anthony Bacon's will is described as his half-brother, went out to America in 1762, and 'was appointed Collector of Pocomoke in

Maryland . . . 3 November 1774'[165]—no doubt through Anthony Bacon's influence. He returned as a loyalist refugee in 1780 and petitioned for relief; a 'Schedule of the estate belonging to William Bacon, late of Worcester County, Maryland', preserved among the papers which he placed before the Commissioners for American Claims, specifies 'a tract of land held in fee of Anthony Bacon, Esq., of London, containing 1022 acres on the northern side of Pocomoke River, confiscated by an Act of the General Assembly of the State of Maryland—value £1,000'.[166] The claim was subsequently withdrawn, as the Maryland Assembly restored the land to William Bacon's sons;[167] but Anthony Bacon had other estates in County Edgcumbe in North Carolina, containing 460 and 78 acres, which were confiscated and sold.[168]

However, at the time of writing his will, in June 1785, Anthony Bacon was still possessed of an interest in an American estate—possibly it escaped confiscation by being held jointly with others. He bequeathed it to his half-brother, William; 'I . . . leave him and his heirs male, all my estate in the Province of Virginia which I hold in partnership with sundry gentlemen, called the Dismal Swamp containing I suppose some thirty thousand acres with my share of all the buildings, slaves and stock that may be thereon.'

What was Anthony Bacon's attitude towards the Colonies during the American Revolution? On 25 March 1774 he, the brother of 'that ornament of the colonial clergy', Thomas Bacon of Maryland, spoke in favour of the Boston Port Bill;[169] and the views which he held at that time on the American problem are fully explained in his pamphlet.[170] There is nothing original about them; his past residence in America and long connection with its trade do not impart the least touch of realism to his discourse. The Mother Country and her 'children' are as much personified in a stereotyped manner as if he had never seen any human beings on either side of the Atlantic; and, of course, the Mother Country should be lenient and tender, and the children dutiful and obedient; but if they are ungrateful or obstreperous, it becomes 'necessary (as well for their benefit as for our own honour), to treat them with a little wholesome severity'. The nature of the connection is to him, in commerce, strictly regulated by the Navigation Acts. Internal taxes should not be laid on the Colonies, because their incidence cannot be gauged and properly adjusted at such a distance, and duties should not be placed on exports from this country to the Colonies, because they are bound adversely to affect trade. But duties on luxury articles, if these are 'the growth of foreign countries' (for example, tea), are a suitable source of revenue, and in the past the Americans submitted to taxes of that description, for example, on wines, their present opposition being due merely to 'a seditious spirit' which is 'at the bottom of this mischief'.

Here are a few excerpts summing up Bacon's views on the constitutional problem and on the situation in 1775:

> The legislative authority of Great Britain extends itself to all its dominions without reserve. . . . The contrary opinion was never broached till within a few years; nor could be without the utmost absurdity. For let me ask—are the colonies a part of the British dominions or are they not? If they are, then are they subject to the supreme authority of Great Britain . . . and was there any supreme authority in the world without the power of taxation? [p. 3].

The doctrine 'that representation and taxation were inseparable from each other' was to Bacon 'the most pestilential doctrine that ever was advanced', instilled into the Americans 'by the patriots of the mother country'.

> The colonists complain of a want of representation; and think it an act of tyranny to propose taxes which so nearly affect themselves, while they have no voice in our public councils. In answer to which, I must beg them to observe, that as they are colonies, and not kingdoms, they can be no more than virtually represented; and this they now are, being included in the commons as members of the kingdom of Great Britain. The laws and usages of this kingdom determine what commoners are to elect for all the rest, wherever dispersed. Besides, it would be grateful only to remember, that when taxes really injurious were laid upon them, they found friends enough in the British Parliament to get them repealed [pp. 18–19].
>
> There is a . . . set of men who make it a point to oppose the Ministry; and consider the present dispute only as a battery to be played off against those who are in power, that there may be a change of Ministers [p. 37].
>
> The greatest enemy of the person now at the helm will allow, that he is neither profligate in principle, nor inattentive to the general interest of his country. It will therefore be rational in us to support him in every measure, which may tend to bring back the Americans to their duty [p. 40].

But 'what shall be said or done to satisfy the expectations of the merchants trading to the colonies? Every man of sensibility must be filled with concern for the losses they must necessarily sustain on this occasion.' Still they themselves should not urge temporizing measures which would permanently endanger our trade with America. For if the Colonies deny the power of Great Britain to tax them, 'the consequence will be a virtual repeal of the Act of Navigation; the colonies will become independent separate states, and they will trade with Great Britain just as far as they find it convenient to themselves, and no farther' [p. 30].

Let me entreat all whom it concerns (and whom doth it not concern?) to have no share in bringing such accumulated evils upon themselves, their country and their posterity. Let not the fear of a present suspension of trade with the colonies bias the judgment of those who are engaged with them, to propose or consent to anything, which will prove their utter ruin in the end [p. 35].

Can there be found among the gentlemen connected with one another by the most sacred and interesting ties, a selfish desire of rising on the ruins of their countrymen, and fellow merchants? I would willingly believe that there is no man amongst us so destitute of honour, as to take this opportunity of pointing out to his correspondents in America particular persons, who happen to differ from him, in order to expose them to their resentment, and increase his own trade. But my information leaves me no room to doubt that there are such miscreants. . . . [p. 36].

I have only a few words to add . . . to the manufacturers of this kingdom . . . The manufacturer cannot but know, that there are many laws to protect him from injuries which he might otherwise receive in his commerce with America. Part of the iron which is here manufactured, is imported from thence, and exported thither in a variety of articles, on which the maintenance of thousands, and ten thousands of our industrious poor depends. By laws now subsisting no person in America can set up any flatting, slitting or tilting mill. Without this prohibition they would be able to manufacture iron cheaper than we can. . . . [pp. 38–39].

To the very end of Lord North's Administration Bacon remained his steady, though not disinterested, adherent. Contracts he had held under various Governments; but a truly surprising statement about him appears in a paper prepared by John Robinson, and presented to George III by Lord North, when he wished to prove what a careful steward he had been of the secret service money. It is marked 'Account of Pensions extinguished and not returned' and is endorsed in pencil: 'Query, Whether this should be copied for His Majesty. I think is shewed attention to reduce.'[171] Among the extinguished pensions to Members of Parliament appears the following entry: 'Mr. Anthony Bacon on his having a contract, 600 l.' It is not stated to what time this refers; Bacon's name naturally is not to be found in John Robinson's secret service accounts for the years 1779–82,[172] but this was the heyday of his career as government contractor. The most likely time for the pension is about 1773–4, when he had given up his victualling contracts for Senegambia and the West Indies and for the supply of negroes, and was only starting as gun-founder to the Board of Ordnance. Even so it is strange that it should have been necessary to provide a merchant of Bacon's prominence and wealth with a secret service pension. Perhaps this was done at one of his moments of financial stringency mentioned by Hutchinson, though one would hardly have thought that at a time of crisis in business conducted on a large scale, £600 per annum could have made a material difference.

In the Memorandum drawn up by John Robinson for Lord Shelburne, in August 1782, the remark is placed against Anthony Bacon: 'Mr. Bacon had connections with government, but they are all now put an end to, yet may be hopeful with attention.'[173] On the dissolution of the House of Commons, in March 1784, Anthony Bacon did not stand again for Parliament;[174] and he died at the end of 1785 or early in 1786—his last will was signed by him on 14 June 1785, and it was proved on 25 February, 1786.

About the last years of Bacon's life we have but scant information. Mr. Wilkins relates that after the leasing of his mines and works, his life 'was singularly undecided. He built himself a house at Aberaman (now the seat of Crawshay Bailey, Esq.), intending to develop the mineral wealth of that valley; but this was never done. Unrest again seized him, and he returned to London. . . . He died when his children were young—two sons and a daughter. . . . By the disposition of his will, one son had Cyfarthfa; the other (Thomas Bushby Bacon, died 1861), Plymouth; and a large fortune, in addition, was given to the daughter.' The works were subsequently sold and 'it is understood that the great bulk of the money possessed by one of the family was lost in gambling transactions, but descendants of unspotted honour and great affluence yet remain in various districts in England. At Aberaman House there is a fine portrait of Anthony Bacon.'[175]

In apparent contradiction to this statement about the children of Anthony Bacon stands the information which the anonymous writer of the article on Thomas Bacon in *The American Quarterly Church Review* gives about one of Thomas's daughters. 'Elizabeth, the eldest daughter, at the request of her uncle, Sir Anthony Bacon, of Glamorganshire, Wales, he having no children, went over and lived with him, and inherited from him £10,000 sterling. Before, however, Sir Anthony's death, she had married George Price Watkins, of Breckon in Wales, whose public charities were so magnificently endowed by him.'[176]

This apparent discrepancy is explained by Anthony Bacon's will at Somerset House. A son from his wife, Anthony Richard Bacon, had died on 26 May, 1770,[177] and Anthony Bacon at his death left no children from her, but four (not two) illegitimate sons and one illegitimate daughter from a certain Mary Bushby; he writes thus about them in his will: 'the children hereafter named . . . I acknowledge to be my children'. Whereas the bastards of aristocrats in the eighteenth century almost invariably bore the names of their fathers, this middle-class merchant did not give his name to his illegitimate children. At the time when Anthony Bacon wrote his last will, in May 1785, his eldest son, Anthony Bushby, was 'at school at Gloucester . . . by the name of William Addison', and it was not till 1792 that he assumed the name of Bacon.

To this Anthony Bushby his father bequeathed the lands and royalties he held 'under lease from the late Earl Talbot and the late Michael Richards at Merthyr Tydfil, and the house there, etc., the furnace called Cyfarthfa and the forge at Cyfarthfa now let to Homfray'; to the second son, Thomas Bushby, the Plymouth lease together with the furnace and estate of Trebetha; to the third, Robert Bushby, the furnace at Berwin, together with the royalties of its iron and coal mines. To his daughter, Elizabeth Bushby, who was 'afflicted with lameness' and who he did not expect would marry, he left an annuity of £300 to commence when she was twenty-one—not 'a large fortune' as stated by Wilkins. William, the youngest son, born in March 1785, was to receive the remainder of a fund (though not more than £10,000) to be formed from the surplus of Anthony Bacon's estates after payment of legacies, etc. To his wife, Elizabeth, Bacon left a clear annuity of £700 besides household furniture, etc.; and to Mary Bushby, his mistress, £1000, and for the maintenance of her four youngest children £50 for each so long as they continued with her. The executors appointed by Bacon were the Rev. Dr. Samuel Glassie, to whom he left £1000 'in acknowledgment of the very singular friendship I have received from him and the great affection I bore him'; William Stevens, of Broad Street, London, who had become a partner in his ordnance contracts in 1782; and Thomas Harrison of Whitehaven, who received £500 each; and Richard Hill, Bacon's agent at Cyfarthfa.

The only assets besides the estates in South Wales that are specifically named in the will are as follows: a share in the estate in Virginia, called the Dismal Swamp, mentioned above; debts due to Bacon from Gilbert Franklyn in the island of Tobago; and debts due to him in the 'several Provinces or States of North America'. These he devised to his half-brother, William Bacon, 'desiring him to pay one fourth part of such sums as he may recover to the two daughters of my late brother, the Rev. Thomas Bacon, now living in Maryland'.

NOTES

1. Foster Cunliffe, the son of Ellis Cunliffe, Fellow of Jesus College, Cambridge, was originally intended for the Church 'but evinced a decided preference for commercial pursuits, and he eventually became not only the first man in Liverpool, but was supposed to have a more extended commerce than any merchant in the kingdom' (Joseph Foster, *Lancashire Pedigrees*). He was Mayor of Liverpool in 1716, 1729, and 1735, and in that year unsuccessfully contested Liverpool (see Pink and Beavan, *The Parliamentary Representation of Lancashire*, p. 199). His son, Ellis Cunliffe, represented Liverpool in Parliament from 1755 till his death in 1767, was knighted in 1756, and created a baronet in 1759.

2. *The Maryland Historical Magazine*, vi. 3. 215.

3. The Chesapeake Bay.

4. *A compleat system of the Revenue of Ireland, in its branches of Import, Export and Inland Duties*, in five parts, Dublin, 1737. Later works of his, *Two Sermons preached to Slaves* (1749) and the *Laws of Maryland* (1765), are erroneously entered in the British Museum catalogue as by a different author, bearing the same names.

5. *Maryland Historical Magazine*, vi. 219.

6. Both footnotes are marked '*Biog. Cumb*', but neither in the British Museum catalogue, nor in any Cumberland bibliography have I been able to trace a work bearing that title.

7. Hutchinson describes the two brothers as natives of Whitehaven, but it seems more likely that they were Manxmen who had moved to Whitehaven, the English port nearest to the Isle of Man.

8. Hutchinson, *op. cit.*, ii. 41.

9. 'An Address to the Public', appended to *The History of Sir Charles Grandison*, (second edition, 1754), vi. 431–2.

10. Richardson was in reality quite aware of Bacon not being an Irishman; on p. 417 in the same *Address*, he describes him as 'an English printer of character and integrity, then there [at Dublin]'.

11. A prominent London bookseller.

12. The following account of the transaction appears in Hutchinson (*op. cit.*, ii. 41): 'Some Dublin booksellers found means . . . whilst his Sir Charles Grandison was printing in London, to corrupt one or more of his printers. . . . Mr. Bacon was

very instrumental in detecting and defeating this deep-laid scheme of iniquity; and Mr. Richardson makes honourable mention of him, in a well-written narrative of the transaction, usually annexed to the earlier editions of Sir Charles Grandison.'
Sir Charles Grandison was first published in 1754, long after Thomas Bacon had left Dublin, and even with regard to *Pamela*, he did not succed in defeating the 'deep-laid scheme' of the Dublin booksellers; the 'well-written narrative' was badly read by the author of the biographical note on Thomas Bacon.

13. Hutchinson, *op. cit.*, ii. 87.

14. To put an end to 'the mischiefs arising to the revenue and commerce of Great Britain and Ireland, from the illicit and clandestine trade to and from the Isle of Man, in 1765 the proprietary jurisdiction of the Duke and Duchess of Athol was bought by the Crown for £70,000' (see *Parliamentary History*, xvi, columns 16–34).

15. R. O., T. 29/33, p. 240.

16. *A Short Address to the Government, the Merchants, Manufacturers, and the Colonists in America, and the Sugar Islands, on the present State of Affairs* (London, 1775), p. 2.

17. The partner in Bacon's commercial firm seems to have been Gilbert Franklyn, a West Indian, and their precise address was 12 Copthall Court.

18. In 1772, the '& Comp.' still appears after his name; for 1773 there is no commercial directory in the British Museum, but in 1774 Anthony Bacon alone is mentioned. In 1785, the year before his death, his address is given in *Kent's London Directory* as 26 Thaves-inn, Holborn, and in 1786 his name does not appear in it any more. But as, later on, 26 Thaves-inn appears in these directories as the address of William Bacon, Anthony's half-brother, the entry in 1785 may be due to a mistake in initials.

19. See *A Letter of a Merchant at Bristol; concerning a Petition of S[amuel] T[ouchet], Esq., to the King for the exclusive grant to the trade of the River Senegal. By a Merchant of London. To which is prefixed a copy of the Petition* (London, 1762), p. 38. Also an article on Senegal in *The Gentleman's Magazine*, June 1758, pp. 262–3: 'The most important production of Senegal is the gum so called, of which great consumption is made in the process of several manufacturers here in England, particularly that of printed linnen, which has so increased of late years as to raise that drug to a very high price.'

20. For evidence of Bacon having been engaged in the gum trade, see Minute Books of the Treasury Board in the Record Office T. 29/35, pp. 99–100. Other entires bearing on the subject are under date of 7 October, 1766, T. 29/38, p. 143, which mentions a Memorial from Bacon, praying leave to export twenty tons of gum to Dublin; and of 24 October, 1771, T. 29/41, reproducing a Memorial in which Bacon and others state that the Society of Merchants trading to Africa have received information that considerable quantities of Senegal gum have been exported without payment of the duties imposed by 5 George III, and beg for information of the quantity of such gum imported into, and exported from, Great Britain.

21. T. 29/33, pp. 54–6, minute of 21 June, 1758.

22. *Ibid.*, pp. 60–1, 28 June, 1758. The advertisement, dated 'Whitehall, Treasury Chambers, 29 June, 1758', appeared in *The London Gazette* for 27 June–1 July: 'The Lords Commissioners of His Majesty's Treasury hereby give notice, that they are ready to receive proposals from any person or persons willing to supply the following sorts and quantities of provisions for four hundred men, viz. for each by the week, seven pounds weight of biscuits or soft bread, two pound and half of beef, one pound of pork, four pints of peas, three pints of oatmeal, six ounces of butter, eight ounces of cheese or four ounces of butter in lieu thereof;

[being the allowance to the garrison of Gibraltar]; and likewise such quantities of rum, brandy or Vidonia wine as shall be judged necessary; which provisions and liquors are to be delivered within three calendar months from the date of the contract, at the fort or forts lately taken from the French on the River Senegal in Africa, for the use of His Majesty's troops which shall be put into garrison there. The Lords will be also ready to receive proposals for remitting the pay to the said troops in Spanish silver. Proper security must be given for the performance of the contract; and the said propositions are to be sealed up and directed to their Lordships Secretaries at the said Treasury Chambers, at any time on or before the 12th day of July next.'

23. Drummond's proposals (T. 29/33, p. 75) incidentally show the cost of insuring cargo from London to Senegal:

	%
Goods in a merchantman without convoy	14–15
Silver ,, ,,　　　,,　　　　,,　　,,	13–14
Goods ,, ,,　　　,,　　with convoy	5
Silver ,, ,,　　　,,　　　,,　　,,	4
,, ,, ,, ship of war, 20 guns	2½–3
,, ,, ,, ,, ,, ,, 40 guns and upwards	2

24. T. 29/33, p. 78.

25. *Ibid.*, p. 100: A copy of this minute is also in the Newcastle Papers, Add. Mss. 32885, fols. 99–102. 'They are to be for six months' means not that the troops are to be there six months, but that six months' provisions for the garrison are to be kept in store.

26. T. 29/33, pp. 155–7.

27. *Ibid.*, pp. 172–3.

28. Minutes of the Treasury Board, 9 May, 1759; *ibid.*, p. 177: 'Let Mr. Bacon purchase 300 stands of arms to be delivered to the Governour of Goree, to be by him distributed in presents to the Africans, Mr. Bacon taking care that the arms he purchases be good and safe arms, and let the like number of arms be sent annually for the same purpose.'

In a paper marked 'In Accounts of Extra Services' and docketed 'Presents to Indians &c. Rece'd from Mr. Yates, August 1, 1763' (Liverpool Papers, Add. Mss. 38335, fol. 185) occurs the following entry: '4 December, 1759. To Anthony Bacon, Esq., to be by him laid out for goods &c. to be consigned to the Govr. of Senegal to be disposed of in presents to the Negroe Princes and Chiefs in the neighbourhood of Senegal and Goree 2,000£.'

29. T. 29/34, pp. 78–9.

30. T. 29/34, pp. 216–7.

31. *Ibid.*, p. 240.

32. T. 29/35, p. 92.

33. *Ibid.*, p. 82.

34. Still, Bacon's influence at Honiton must have rested on some solid and enduring foundation, for although he himself never contested it again, the following note was placed against the borough in a paper drawn up by friends of the younger Pitt in December 1783, in anticipation of a general election: 'Send Mr. R[obinson] to see Mr. Bacon . . . for on Mr. Bacon's sending for the proper person *in due time* . . . will depend on bringing in a friend not in opposition to but with Sir George Yonge and make both come easy' (W. T. Laprade, *Parliamentary Papers of John Robinson*, p. 112).

35. Add. Mss. 38202, fol. 67.

36. It had been intended to put up Robert Child, the banker; see a letter from

E. Kynaston, M.P., to C. Jenkinson 26 November, 1763 (Add. Mss. 38201, fol. 266), and from Lord Harcourt, 30 November (*ibid.*, fol. 270). Bacon was a second choice.

37. In 1764, Bacon is found acting with Lowther in a case which arose over certain bankruptcies at Whitehaven; see Add. Mss. 38202, fols. 149, 253, 269, 292–3, 316, 320–1, and Add. Mss. 38337, fols. 264 and 293; also Treasury Minute Books at the Record Office, T. 29/35 (references to be found in the index under Peter How).

38. The 'gentlemen of Shoreham' to the Duke of Newcastle, 4 January 1766; Add. Mss. 32973, fol. 41.

39. *Acts of the Privy Council (Colonial)*, p. 618.

40. *Acts of the Privy Council (Colonial)*, p. 617, under date of 27 January 1765.

41. Add. Mss. 32969, fol. 9. See also paper marked 'Sussex, and other Mems.' 5 September 1765, *ibid.*, fol. 304, in which it is stated that a petition on behalf of Snook had been signed by himself and above 60 other New Shoreham men.

42. Add. Mss. 32970, fol. 194.

43. For a list of its members see Add. Mss. 32977, fol. 163; there are four among them of the name of Snook (they themselves spelled it without an 'e' at the end).

44. Add. Mss. 32970, fol. 95.

45. Newcastle to Rockingham, 3 October 1765; *ibid.*, fol. 149.

46. *Ibid.*, fols. 179–80.

47. *Ibid.*, fol. 198. See also his letter to George Onslow, a Lord of the Treasury, on 7 October: 'I don't hear, but that Mr. Bacon's application, a Hackney contractor, is still prefer'd to mine, in my own county' (*ibid.*, f. 209); and Hickey's letter to Hurdis the same day; 'The point in my humble opinion is, who shall be considered at Shoreham to have the most weight with the Administration, His—— [Grace] or Mr. B.' (*ibid.*, fol. 224).

48. John Sargent (1715–91) of May Place, and afterwards of Halsted Place, Kent, a London merchant, M.P. for Midhurst 1754–61 and for West Looe 1765–8. He had been connected with Henry Pelham and subsequently with Newcastle, but, on being left out in the cold at the general election of 1761, turned to Bute and Grenville. He was engaged in the American trade, and De Berdt, the agent for Massachusetts, wrote about him to Stephen Sayre on 29 July 1766: 'I wrote last to New York to apprize you there is a party pretty strong for making Mr. Ray (you remember him), Agent or at least joint Agent with Mr. Sergeant, a draper to whom they have voted a piece of plate for his services, so greatly are people imposed upon in America, you know the neutral part he acted untill the division of the House discovered which side the strength lay and Mr. J. tells me he was introduced into Parliament by Mr. G.-s interest, this is setting the fox to watch the geese that it will be necessary without delay to go to New York and trye our interest' (*Publications of the Colonial Society of Massachusetts*, xiii. 318).

Sargent was a friend of Benjamin Franklin's, and was concerned with him in the negotiations for the Ohio grant in 1770 (see *Writings of Benjamin Franklin*, ed. by A. H. Smyth, v. 467); early in 1775 took Franklin to Lord Stanhope, with whom Franklin went to see Chatham at Hayes (*ibid.*, vi. 321); and in June 1775 was asked by Franklin to take charge of his property in England (*ibid.*, vi. 406–7).

49. Add. Mss. 32970, fols. 226–8.

50. Harry Bridger, Newcastle's Shoreham agent, to Newcastle, 30 December 1765; Add. Mss. 32972, fol. 376.

51. Add. Mss. 32973, fol. 41.

52. P. 245.

53. John Durand of Carshalton, Surrey (1719–78), was a captain in the service of the East India Company, acquired a large fortune, and became a London

merchant and government contractor. He represented Aylesbury 1768–74, when he was defeated by John Aubrey.

54. Thomas Orde (1746–1807), M.P. for Aylesbury 1780–4 and for Harwich 1784–96; he married, in 1778, the illegitimate daughter and ultimately heiress of the fifth Duke of Bolton, and in 1797 was created Lord Bolton.

55. Laprade, *op. cit.*, p. 45.

56. *Ibid.*, p. 71.

57. See *Acts of the Privy Council (Colonial) 1745–66*, pp. 646–8.

58. Copies of Charles Garth's Letter Books are in the possession of Mr. William Godsal, of Haines Hill, Berks., a descendent of Garth; I am much indebted to him for his kind permission to use them.

59. *A Short Address to the Government*, etc. (1775), pp. 2–3.

60. The text of the questions and answers is given in A. H. Smyth's edition of Franklin's *Writings*, iv. 434–5; the identity of the person who asked them is shown by Franklin's 'Memorandum,' reprinted in x. 232.

61. See *The Correspondence of King George III*, ed. by Sir John Fortescue, i. 277.

62. Add. Mss. 33002, fols. 470–3.

63. *The Correspondence of King George III*, ed. by Sir John Fortescue, iii. 71.

64. T. 29/35, p. 350.

65. *Ibid.*, p. 394; see also Add. Mss. 38203, fol. 39.

66. A London merchant, M.P. for Radnor, where he was put up as Tory candidate by Lord Oxford and supported by Lord Bute; on this election see my book on *The Structure of Politics at the Accession of George III*, pp. 332–44. Lewis withdrew from the contract on 25 November 1765 (see T. 29/37, p. 234).

67. T. 29/35, p. 397.

68. T. 29/36, p. 145.

69. T. 29/36, p. 241; for the terms of the Grenada contract of 16 October 1767, see T. 64/133 (a collection of the original contracts).

70. T. 29/37, p. 57.

71. For his proposals see *ibid.*, pp. 69 and 80. It appears from the accounts of 'Extraordinary Services' in the *Journals of the House of Commons* that Bacon continued for several years contractor for the troops in the Isle of Man.

72. T. 64/133.

73. T. 29/38, p. 455.

74. T. 29/42, pp. 229–30.

75. T. 29/42, pp. 250–1.

76. *Ibid.*, p. 313.

77. There is an entry under date of 17 June 1773 to the effect that 'as Mr. Bacon has now no concern in the contract', Bacon and Chauvet pray that 'a new contract may be made out in the name of Mr. Chauvet to commence on the 1st July next' (*ibid.*, p. 82).

78. *Ibid.*, pp. 197, 206–7, and 223.

79. See *Journals of the House of Commons*, xxxii. 284 and 652–3; xxxiii. 171 and 571; xxxiv. 254 and 719; xxxv. 264–5 and 614; and xxvi. 172. Because of certain irregularities in the manner of closing the accounts, two payments to Anthony Bacon, arising from the contracts for provisioning the forces in the Isle of Man, and for negroes employed in the Ceded Islands, were inquired into, in 1783, by the Commissioners 'appointed to examine, take, and state the Public Accounts of the Kingdom'; see *Journals of the House of Commons*, xxxix. 527–8 and 655–6.

80. T. 64/133.

81. T. 29/38, p. 355.

82. His new proposals were accepted as the lowest on 19 June 1778 (T. 29/47,

p. 195); but on 2 July he asked permission to relinquish his contract to Mr. George Browne, to which the Treasury agreed (*ibid.*, pp. 222–3).

83. T. 29/40, p. 318. In 1777, in consequence of a petition from Bacon that the same be given to him for the time when he was contractor for these islands, £750 were allowed (T. 29/46, p. 308); apparently only then, seven years after the contract had expired, were the accounts for the freight of provisions passed by the auditors.

84. Vol. ii. 139–40.

85. *The Scenery, Antiquities and Biography of South Wales* (1804), p. 174.

86. *The History of Merthyr Tydfil* (1867), p. 145.

87. Anthony Richardson, a London merchant, a relative of Bacon's to whom in his will he bequeathed 'all the debt which may be due to him from Gilbert Franklyn, Esq., in the Island of Tobago except £1200' which Franklyn owed on a bond entered into by Bacon and paid to a Mr. Appleton. Also, a Rev. Mr. Thomas Richardson is mentioned in the will. Samual Richardson, the novelist, does not seem to have been connected with this family as in the account of his transactions with Thomas Bacon he states that the latter was an 'absolute stranger' to him until introduced by Osborne (see above, p. 61).

88. R. L. Galloway, *Annals of Coal Mining* (1898), p. 360.

89. This may have been the famous physician and chemist, born in Cumberland, who practiced at Whitehaven, the first scientist to investigate gases in coal mines; about him see *Dictionary of National Biography*. Anthony Bacon, in his last will, left £100 'to my cousin, Mary Brownrigg'.

90. Wilkins, *op. cit.*, p. 146.

91. *Ibid.*, p. 156.

92. *Ibid.*, p. 157.

93. P. 8: 'This contract was forfeited, it is said, from proof presumptive that the enemy procured a supply of great guns from the same source.'

94. The same story was told also about John Wilkinson, the famous Broseley iron-master. John Randall, in his book on *The Wilkinsons* (1872), pp. 15–17, alleges that Wilkinson did a regular trade with enemy countries, and that guns were smuggled out of the country as water pipes or ship's ballast till the British Government finally stopped this 'pipe making'. No date is named and the entire tale is so confused that one cannot guess whether it refers to the American Revolution or the French Wars, or perhaps to deliveries made to France while no war was proceeding and such trade was perfectly legitimate.

95. *The Scenery, Antiquities and Biography of South Wales*, p. 176.

96. W. O., 47/82, p. 14.

97. *Ibid.*, pp. 208–9.

98. *Ibid.*, p. 318.

99. See minute of 2 April 1774, W. O., 47/83, p. 174, for the formal notification to that effect, and minute of 3 June 1774, *ibid.*, p. 319, about the premature action on the part of Bacon who, on the Board having accepted his tender to cast 300 tons of iron ordnance at £18 per ton, had ordered his works to continue making guns from the drawings he had in hand without waiting for further specifications from the Board. The Board replied that they 'are surprised at his casting 18-pounders without orders, they having no occasion for any of that nature, but they may be landed at Woolwich and disposed of as he thinks proper', while the Board 'desire he will compleat the 300 tons according to the natures that are ordered'.

100. *Ibid.*, p. 213.

101. *Ibid.*, pp. 240–1.

102. *Ibid.*, pp. 327–8.

103. W. O., 47/84, p. 180.

104. *Annales Caermoelenses* (1872), pp. 213-4.

105. *John Wilkinson, Iron Master* (1914), pp. 21-2.

106. *Byegones*, February 1877, p. 189, quoting Jones's *History of Wrexham.*

107. Fave in his *Etude sur l'Artillerie* (1862) describes the work done in France by Griveauval of boring cannon out of the solid but adds (vol. ii, p. 152): 'Maritz, fondeur genevois, avait apporté en France dès 1740, le nouveau mode de fabrication des cannons, qui consistait à les couler plein et à les forer entièrement après le refroidissement, à l'aide des machines perfectionées. Griveauval avait seulement adopté et généralisé ce mode de fabrication.' I am not in a position to judge to what extent Wilkinson's improvements marked fundamental change in these methods adopted at an earlier date in France.

108. See H. W. Dickinson, *op. cit.*, appendix B.

109. W. O., 47/84, p. 190.

110. Minute of 5 June, 1776, W. O., 47/87, p. 484.

111. W. O., 47/84, pp. 194 and 211.

112. W. O., 47/85, p. 88.

113. See p. 82.

114. See minute of 24-25 June 1777 (W. O., 47/89, p. 734), granting Bacon's request that Crawshay's name should in future be joined with his in contracts for casting guns.

115. W. O., 47/84, pp. 79-80.

116. W. O., 47/84, p. 142.

117. Minute of 27 January 1775; W. O., 47/85, pp. 55-6.

118. Minute of 31 January 1775; *ibid.*, p. 69.

119. *Ibid.*, p. 145.

120. *Ibid.*, p. 310; see also W. O., 55/5.

121. Obviously by this time Wilkinson's patent was cancelled; and on 3 May 1775 (W. O., 47/85, p. 345), the Board is found refusing the offer of 35 18-pounders 'of excellent metal' because they 'have come to a resolution not to order any more guns but what are cast out of the solid'.

122. W. O., 47/86, p. 76; '. . . that he has completed the Board's last order for iron ordnance, he therefore requested another order for any quantity the Board may think proper'.

123. By a clerical mistake it appears in the minutes as '100 tons'; see, however, W. O., 47/87, p. 225.

124. W. O., 47/87, p. 42.

125. *Ibid.*, p. 255.

126. Minute of 29 March 1776; *ibid.*, p. 281. A new order to Bacon for iron ordnance appears under date of 19 July 1776 (W. O., 47/88, p. 41):

9-pounders, 8½ feet		25
7½		25
6-pounders, 7 feet		25
6		50
3-pounders, 4½ feet		50

127. W. O., 47/90, p. 326.

128. W. O., 47/91, p. 455; see further entry of 12 June 1778, pp. 529-30.

129. *Ibid.*, p. 551.

130. W. O., 47/91, p. 564.

131. W. O., 47/93, p. 293.

132. W. O., 47/94, p. 178.

133. *Ibid.*, p. 258.

134. Thus on 19 January 1779, among the persons who are to pay 'the sums against their names expressed being the value of powder, shot etc. expended in proving their brass and iron ordnance at Woolwich between 30 June and 30 September, 1778' appears 'Mr. Anthony Bacon, for the King of Sardinia, £16 9s. 11¾d.' (W. O., 47/93, pp. 41–2); and another entry of a similar kind for tests made on 5 December, 1778 (W. O., 47/94, p. 156). About testing for the East India Company, see W. O., 47/94, p. 302 and 47/100, p. 595. For correspondence about some defective guns supplied by Bacon to the Government, see W. O., 47/93, pp. 194 and 219–20.

135. W. O., 47/94, p. 140.

136. W. O., 47/97, p. 352.

137. W. O., 47/99, p. 203.

138. See minute of 1 January 1782; *ibid.*, p. 4.

139. *The Scenery, Antiquities and Biography of South Wales* (1804), p. 175.

140. T. 29/45, pp. 28–31.

141. See p. 75.

142. T., 29/45, pp. 39–40.

143. Arnold Nesbitt, M.P. for Cricklade; Adam Drummond, for St. Ives; John Henniker, for Dover; George Wombwell, for Huntingdon; William Devaynes, for Barnstaple; John Amyand, for Camelford; John Durand, for Plympton; Anthony Bacon, for Aylesbury; Robert Mayne, for Gatton; William James, for West Looe; and Abel Smith, for Aldborough (Yorks).

144. T. 29/46, p. 19.

145. See T. 29/47, p. 75.

146. For the contract see 'Report Books', A. O. 17/53, pp. 16–19; for the distribution of the contracts for victualling a total of 76,381 men during the year 1778–9, see T. 29/48, p. 334.

147. *Ibid.*, p. 439.

148. 'Copy of Mr. Guerish's scheme for improving the coal mines in Nova Scotia', n.d.; in the Liverpool Papers, Add. Mss. 38337, fols. 285–6.

149. Add. Mss. 38337, fols. 225–6; Howe's associates were one brigadier-general, one colonel, three lieutenant-colonels and six captains, and Messrs. Wier and Porter, army 'commissaries' who were obviously the 'men of business' behind the group.

150. Samuel Fludyer, a clothier (but also a general merchant), was at that time M.P. for Chippenham; Thomas Fludyer had unsuccessfully nibbled at Devizes in 1761, and was a few years later returned for Great Bedwin; Adam Drummond sat for Lymington, and Bacon for Aylesbury.

151. The terms on which land was granted in Nova Scotia appear from an entry in the *Acts of the Privy Council (Colonial)*, 1745–66, p. 611: 'Within ten years it is to be settled with one white person for every hundred acres; if one third of the grant is not settled with Protestants in the above proportion within three years, the grant shall be void; such part as is not settled in the required proportion at the end of ten years is to revert to His Majesty; after the expiry of ten years a quitrent of two shillings shall be paid for every hundred acres.' Gold and silver mines and lands marked out as proper for fortifications, public quays, beach for the fishery, roads and other public uses are reserved; 'at the end of three years the grantee must plant and continue to cultivate six acres with hemp and flax'.

152. Add. Mss. 38337, fol. 287.

153. Add. Mss. 38337, fol. 284.

154. The blank is not filled in in the copy in the Liverpool Papers.

155. Add. Mss. 38338, fols. 24–7.

156. *Acts of the Privy Council (Colonial)*, iv (1745–66), 661.

157. T. 29/45, p. 408.

158. He was accorded a compensation of £1700 on 26 June 1777. See T. 29/46, pp. 197–8.

159. T. 29/46, pp. 169–70.

160. *Ibid.*, pp. 173–4.

161. T. 29/47, pp. 312–313.

162. *Ibid.*, p. 366.

163. T. 29/42, p. 12.

164. Vol. iv, p. 551.

165. Loyalist Papers at the Record Office, A. O., 13/60, 7 March 1787, 'Evidence'.

166. Loyalist Papers at the Record Office, A. O., 13/60, 7 March 1787, 'Evidence'.

167. *Ibid.;* see also letter from W. Bacon to D. P. Coke, M.P., 20 June 1785, A. O., 13/39.

168. A. O., 12/91, pp. 31–2.

169. See *The Correspondence of George III*, iii. 85.

170. *A Short Address to the Government, the Merchants, Manufacturers, and the Colonists in America, and the Sugar Islands, on the present State of Affairs.* By a member of Parliament; 1775.

171. Laprade, *The Parliamentary Papers of John Robinson*, p. 49.

172. Add. Mss. 37836, fols 61–140.

173. Laprade, *op. cit.*, p. 45.

174. Mr. Gibbs in his *Worthies of Bucks* (1888) states that 'Mr Bacon contested Great Marlow at the general election of 1802 but was unsuccessful'. But this was his illegitimate son, Anthony Bacon Bushby, who assumed the name of Bacon in 1792, not the Anthony Bacon of the *Worthies*.

175. *The History of Merthyr Tydfil* (1867), p. 159.

176. October 1865, p. 430. The statement about the marriage of Elizabeth Bacon is correct but not the date (she married after the death of Anthony Bacon), nor the sum bequeathed to her. The following notice appears in the *Gentleman's Magazine*, 1787, ii. 638: Marriages: 20 July 1787: 'At St. Martin's Church, Price Watkin, Esq.; to Miss Bacon, of Hanwell, Middlesex.' In Burke's *Landed Gentry* (1846), iii. 1533, he is described as 'George Price Watkins, of Tenby, co. Pembroke', and she as 'Elizabeth, niece of Anthony Bacon, Esq., of Cyfarthfa, co. Glamorgan', The sum left her by Anthony Bacon was £5000.

177. See *The Gentleman's Magazine*, xi. 239.

CHAPTER FIVE

The Tinplate Maker and Technical Change

by W. E. Minchinton

'A WELSH tinplate mill', declared a writer in 1915, 'seems as un-
alterable as the laws of the Medes and Persians. Hanbury, or
from whomsoever's brain it evolved, like Archimedes, appears to
have hit upon the one and only way, for all time, of doing the work
contemplated, by a sort of inspiration, for no decisive improvements
have been brought about since.'[1] The accuracy of this observation
is beyond dispute. As a result of the work of John Hanbury at the
beginning of the eighteenth century, rolling replaced hammering
as the method by which plates were produced. Although various
modifications of the individual processes took place, the manufacture of tinplate underwent no major technical change from that
time until the development of the strip-mill method of manufacture
in the U.S.A. in the nineteen-twenties.[2] Thus, following the early
important development, no further radical change took place for
more than two centuries. The tinplate industry was not technically
reorganized during the classical period of the Industrial Revolution
but at a much later date. The object of this article is to assess to
what extent the tinplate maker, the business man who made policy
decisions in the industry, was responsible for the slowness of technical development. Particular attention will be focused on the history
of the British tinplate industry since 1870, from which date production expanded more rapidly.

I

The history of the industry in these years may be briefly stated.
Although tinplate was made in Germany, France and Austria, these
European industries were too small to meet any but domestic needs
and the British industry, located mainly in south Wales, was the
sole exporter of tinplate. Until the 1890s the U.S.A. was the main
export market for British tinplate, and the expansion of American

demand, particularly for petrol containers and food cans, provided the main stimulus for the expansion of the British industry. Between 1871 and 1891 its output quadrupled, rising from about 150,000 tons in 1871 to 600,000 tons in 1891. Throughout these years about three-quarters of British production was exported to the U.S.A. This market was lost when, under the protective umbrella of the McKinley tariff, tinplate manufacture was established in the U.S.A. As a result the ouput of the British industry shrank by a quarter to 450,000 tons in 1896. Not until 1904 was the 1891 figure exceeded, but thereafter production expanded to reach a peak of 850,000 tons in 1912, a figure which was seldom approached and only twice exceeded during the inter-war period. In 1929, 880,000 tons were produced and in 1937, 958,000 tons.

Meantime production in the U.S.A. expanded from 300,000 tons in 1900 to 878,000 tons in 1912, 1·8 million tons in 1929 and 2·4 million tons in 1937. World production, to which Great Britain and the U.S.A. made the main contributions, rose from 900,000 tons in 1900 to 4·4 million tons in 1937. In 1900 British production was more than twice the American; in 1937, American production was more than twice the British. While American production expanded in the inter-war years, the output of the British industry virtually stagnated. Moreover, directly the U.S.A. began to make tinplate, improvements in the processes of manufacture were introduced there and experiments were made to transform the methods used in a radical manner. These led to the development of the strip-mill process which was quickly adopted in the U.S.A. By 1939 three-quarters of American tinplate was made by this process, whereas the entire British output was produced by the old method. Only in 1939 did Ebbw Vale, the first British strip mill, begin production.[3] Thus the absence of radical innovation and the slowness of technical change was not due merely to the nature of the industry but to factors which specifically affected the British industry.

II

It was scarcely to be expected that Great Britain could retain a virtual monopoly of the manufacture of tinplate since this monopoly was based not on permanent advantages, such as the possession of localized supplies of essential raw materials, but on purely temporary advantages, the skill of the labour force and comparatively easy access to export markets. When other countries began to produce tinplate, it was inevitable that the British share of world production and world trade should decline. Nor was rapid adaptation to the new conditions or speedy modernization of plant to be expected. Yet need the British industry have lost ground so fast, need innovation have been so long delayed?[4]

Part of the explanation is no doubt to be found in the relationships of costs and receipts and in the relative costs of the various factors of production, in terms of marginal analysis. But, as P. W. S. Andrews among others has pointed out, the decisions of industrialists are not always amenable to analysis in rational economic terms.[5] They are explicable only if other factors are considered. The course of development of an industry is affected not only by cost considerations but, amongst other factors, by the character of its industrialists, its policy makers. In this particular case, what part did the tinplate maker play, to what extent was he responsible for the course of events? Any such consideration of human behaviour in descriptive terms must necessarily be interim and tentative, the exposition of an hypothesis rather than the statement of the proof of a theorem.

From about 1870, the British tinplate industry was highly localized in south Wales, most of the works being within fifteen miles of Swansea. As the majority of the tinplate makers were drawn from this area they formed a fairly homogeneous group. Their outlook and behaviour were therefore largely determined by three influences: (a) the nature of the industry; (b) the method of recruitment of the tinplate makers; and (c) the nature of the local society in which they lived.

Towards the end of the nineteenth century, the British tinplate industry was in a state approaching perfect competition. The product was virtually homogeneous, the unit of production—the mill— was small and the duplication of units was easy. Although the output of a mill increased in the course of the nineteenth century, the main means of expanding output, in the absence of radical technical developments, was by the construction of additional mills.[6]

Because there were no significant indivisibilities or economies of scale, works remained small, only a few having more than four mills. Further, because of the highly localized character of the industry, no firm had any marked advantage in obtaining raw materials or in disposing of its products. Production was therefore possible on a small scale; entry into the industry was easy.

Entry into the industry was easy also because the financial resources required to build and operate a tinplate works were small. For this there were three reasons. First, the industry was labour rather than capital intensive, about sixty workers being required to operate a mill. Second, the capital cost of a tinplate works was small. Up to the end of the nineteenth century, a tinplate mill cost about £3,000 to construct. And, third, the running of a works could be largely financed on a credit basis. The U.S. Consul in Bristol commented in 1894:

> The trade presents some peculiarities. It may be carried on in a reasonably prosperous time with a capital very small in proportion to output and annual turnover. The plant required is limited, and the steel and the tin may be bought by the custom of the trade, on long credit—sometimes nine months, or, with steel a year. The sales of tinplate are 'spot cash', and hence the manufacturer is money in hand long before his bills mature.

A subsidiary factor was the limited liability legislation of 1856 and 1862 which facilitated the mobilization of capital. Due to these Acts, stated Thomas Phillips, a trade union leader, 'butchers, bakers and drapers who had £5 rushed with it and placed it at one time in a tinplate works with the result that so many small works and weak companies had been built'.[8] Since for financial and technical reasons, entry into the tinplate industry was easy and manufacture could be conducted on a small scale, the tinplate makers were a numerous body. While the history of the copper industry in the Swansea area of south Wales can be written in terms of a few names, the Vivians, the Grenfells, the Morrises and the Dillwyns, as a study of oligopoly, the history of the south Wales tinplate industry cannot be so written.

The conditions so far described helped to determine the way in which tinplate makers were recruited. Numerically the most important group was the small tradesman. Although a manager was usually appointed to supervise the technical aspects of manufacture, the butcher, the baker and the candlestick-maker took an active part in the running of works and ownership and control were not separated. These investors brought with them not a spirit of enterprise but the outlook of the small property owner. They looked on the works as security for capital and as a steady source of income rather than as a means to increased profits. One or two works are even said to have been established more for the custom the employees would bring to the local shops than as a direct source of profit,[9] while the truck shop or company shop (Siop y Gwaith) survived till the late nineteenth century despite all the legislation intended to end this abuse. Even later, workers at certain factories found that it was politic to shop with particular retailers if they wanted to retain their jobs. As late as 1935 this attitude to the work as a source of income rather than of profit found expression in the words of H. Spence Thomas, the most outspoken of the small tin-plate makers. 'For generations', he stated, 'the tinplate trade has been characterized by and developed upon strong individualism but latterly, for good or ill, the portals of the trade have been opened wide to welcome "big business" and high finance, with the accompanying desire for immediate dividends.'[10] Such an attitude to business was clearly anathema to the common run of tinplate makers.

In consequence of this outlook little provision was made for depreciation or for future development. In July 1928, *Iron and Steel* stated that 'to a close observer, one of the reasons why the Welsh tinplate trade has not made bigger strides in the past is the fact that during the past twenty to twenty-five years the profits have been freely distributed rather than substantial reserves created with a view to further development and improvement of plant and at the same time writing down capital'. As a result the industry lacked adequate financial resources when radical change became necessary.

Besides the shopkeepers and local tradesmen, tinplate makers were recruited from the suppliers of raw materials such as coal, tin, and sulphuric acid and from the manufacturers of tinplate equipment. The Tregonings were originally Cornish tin smelters, the Gibbins sulphuric acid manufacturers, and there were a number of colliery owners who had interests in tinplate manufacture, while the Glanmor Foundry (Llanelly) was but one of the engineering firms which invested in the industry. Almost all of them were local men whose attitude to business differed little from the tradesmen. For this second group tinplate-making was a subsidiary activity. As the scale of operation was too small and the rate of expansion too slow to attract the large iron and steel firms, few of the tinplate works in the later nineteenth century were linked with firms engaged in iron and steel manufacture. Thus to the comparative geographical isolation of the tinplate industry in south Wales was added a structural isolation from the rest of the iron and steel industry. Even when some tinplate firms invested in steelmaking in the 1900s the financial link did not lead to integrated working.

Three other avenues of recruitment existed: recruitment from the sons of tinplate makers, from the employees in tinplate works, and from the tinplate merchants. Once tinplate firms were established, patrimony—the succession of father by son—provided a convenient but not very stimulating form of recruitment.[11] Several families, like the Tregonings, the Gibbins and the Gilbertsons remained in control of tinplate firms for several generations. From within the industry some clerks and managers rose to ownership and control. Some of the more enterprising tinplate makers entered the industry in this way—Sir John Jones Jenkins (later Lord Glantawe), William Williams of Morriston and Richard Thomas, the founder of the large combine which today bears his name. Lastly, there were the tinplate merchants. In the early years of the history of the industry, the tinplate merchants played an important part in the expansion of tinplate manufacture, the most prominent being the London merchant firm of Miers & Co. In the 1870s Phelps, James & Co. (the English branch of Phelps, Dodge & Co.) did much to encourage the application of Siemens steel to tinplate manufacture. And it was by this route that Sir William Firth, the only innovating entrepreneur of whom the industry can boast, came into tinplate manufacture. He came from outside the local society from which most of the tinplate makers were drawn. The nature of this society of south Wales and its attitude to economic activity is the third factor which must be considered.

In the later nineteenth century, the tinplate area of south Wales was comparatively isolated and self-contained. The Welsh were predominantly a peasant people and the commercial and industrial middle class was—and still is—relatively small. Further, the predominance of the Welsh language was a factor which helped to set west Wales apart from the more anglicized mining area of the east. The large landowners—the Duke of Beaufort and the Earl of Jersey —were English and absentee, there were few small landowners or other industrialists of importance in the late nineteenth century, and the local society was egalitarian in temper. It was also one in which the rationale of capitalism had not yet been fully accepted; the unrestrained pursuit of profit was not generally recognized as the end of human endeavour. West Wales was not in any true sense an acquisitive society. In such a social context, the tinplate maker had little incentive to pursue wealth. With a modest sum it was comparatively easy to become a prominent member of local society and to enjoy a comfortable standard of living.[12] Moreover, the fiat of the chapel which formed the focus of local society was inimical to conspicuous consumption and a deterrent to competitive emulation.[13]

Representative of the Welsh tinplate maker was F. W. Gibbins of the Melyn Works, Neath. Of him, Dr. Thomas Jones wrote:[14]

> He was a properous maker of tinplate in the Neath valley, a County Councillor, a Justice of the Peace, a Treasurer of the National Memorial, and in all offices a man of few but emphatic words, 'rampantly honest' Henry Jones called him. For a short period he represented Mid-Glamorgan in Parliament but quickly tired and would have preferred, as he put it, to pay his office boy

to walk through the Lobbies . . . Gibbins was willing to pay high wages so long as dividends were kept at a satisfactory level and that meant throughout the period of his management an average of 20 per cent free of income tax. At last after 31 years in the business he decided to sell out in 1921. He put up to J. C. Davies, the managing director of Baldwins, a memorandum running to about six lines. There were 144 shares at a paid up price of £250. Gibbins asked Davies for £1,000 per share making £144,000. After visiting the works, Davies suggested knocking off £10,000. Gibbins agreed and sold each share for £900 odd.

Although he was still in his early fifties, Gibbins chose to withdraw from active participation in tinplate manufacture rather than meet the challenge posed by the more difficult trading conditions of the immediate post-war years. In so doing he set an example which other small independent tinplate makers were to follow in the early 1920s. Their action was largely conditioned by the outlook of the local society. They were easily satisfied and had little incentive to expand production or to attain leadership in the industry. Almost without exception, they lacked the narrowness, single-mindedness and aggressiveness of the typically successful businessman, the Carnegie or the Nuffield.[15] Makers were prepared to withdraw from production rather than reorganize and re-equip. As a local newspaper noted in 1891: 'The tinplate industry is peculiar in this respect, in no other do we find such repugnance to the principle of the survival of the fittest.'[16] Part of the explanation for the trend of events in the British tinplate industry, particularly after 1891 when the U.S.A. began to produce tinplate, lies in the fact that the British tinplate maker was unadventurous, highly individualistic, not markedly adaptable, conservative and easily satisfied.[17]

III

In what way did the character and outlook of the tinplate maker affect the technical development of the industry? This question can best be considered under two heads: first, the attitude to the improvement of the pack-mill process and, second, the attitude to radical change, to the introduction of the strip-mill. Between 1913 and 1922 the South Wales Institute of Engineers devoted a series of meetings to papers dealing with some of the problems of tinplate manufacture.[18] To the discussions which followed, a large number of tinplate makers contributed, speaking frankly about technical questions. From these statements their attitude to technical change clearly emerges.

First, 'the trade was, as regards new departures, a very conservative business indeed, anything new was looked upon with such a degree of distrust that it was practically a waste of time to introduce anything which was not in accordance with established usage'.[19] When John Player invented an improved tinning pot he found tinplate makers 'backward in adopting labour-saving machinery'. As F. W. Gilbertson explained, 'the economy of $\frac{1}{2}$d. or the fraction of a penny per box by the adoption of some new device was not, in their opinion, very often worth so much trouble as a careful buying and selling, a careful watching of manufacture, the prevention of waste &c.'[20] And another tinplate maker added, 'generally speaking, when anything new is introduced into any works if it is not right away a success out it goes'.[21] The typical response to any suggestion that new methods should be adopted was 'has any other fool tried it yet?'[22] And unwillingness to adopt improved machinery was sometimes allied with a refusal to believe that improvement was possible. 'They will never succeed', said E. V. John of the attempts to invent a system for the continuous manufacture of tinplate.[23]

Such improvements in the process of tinplate manufacture as took place in the late nineteenth century were carried out within individual works by makers who endeavoured to keep the developments secret. As late as 1915, S. R. Cound, one of the few forward-looking men in the trade, declared, 'I am afraid that in the tinplate trade today there is a fear that one is giving something away in writing papers and the discussion on same: that there is an imparting of special knowledge to the ignorant'.[24] Manufacturers took pride in declaring that nearly all the inventions in the past had come from within the industry, continuing to believe that 'the tinplate trade possessed within itself men of sufficient grit, determination, knowledge and inventive genius to overcome all difficulties'.[25] While processes were improved by minor engineering alterations the technical competence of those within the industry might be accounted sufficient; but reliance on such skill severely restricted the prospect of more radical changes.

But the tinplate maker did not welcome expert advice, and the engineer, the chemist and the metallurgist were long denied recognition. 'The average tinplate manufacturer was rather suspicious of engineers.'[26] 'Those expensive fellows' was the general opinion.[27] And a large number of examples could be cited to document these general statements. 'In a tinplate works the experienced layman is better than a man who is simply and solely an engineer', said John

Williams.[28] What was needed, said E. V. John, was 'practical men who were in sympathy with their rolls and everything else. They could do a lot with machinery if they were in sympathy with it.'[29] And F. W. Gilbertson spoke of 'the luxury of an engineering and analytical staff'.[30] Only a few were aware that 'if progress were to come at all, it must come from the engineers'.[31]

Accordingly there was reluctance to use methods of scientific control. Though the control of heat was important in both the annealing and tinning processes, the methods followed were haphazard. No one knew exactly what the temperatures in the annealing furnace or the tinpot were and until the replacement of coal and coke furnaces by oil or gas the heat provided was irregular and erratic. Yet the introduction of pyrometers was long resisted and discussions of their value continued until recent times. Some makers complained that they had been unable to find 'an accurate pyrometer sufficiently robust to stand rough works usage'.[32] For whatever reason, such aids to improved manufacture were introduced only slowly.

Eventually the engineer won recognition, but an even longer time elapsed before the chemist and the metallurgist came to be recognized as valuable partners in the process of manufacture. Something was known about the machinery but nothing was known about the chemistry of tinplate manufacture, about the quality of tin coatings, about porosity and discontinuity, about the interaction of steel and tin. Not till after 1919 were research establishments developed. The University College of Swansea, with departments of engineering and metallurgy, was founded, the Tin Research Institute, financed by the tin producers, began its work and the government Department of Scientific and Industrial Research (D.S.I.R.) and the British Iron and Steel Industry Research Association also carried out research on problems connected with tinplate manufacture. Not till 1932—and then only as a result of the complaints about the poor quality of some British tinplate—did the industry itself set up a research committee 'authorized to deal with the various processes of tinplate making and their possible improvement with special reference to a consideration of their influence on the quality of the finished product'. As the Industries Group of Political and Economic Planning (P.E.P.) reported in 1933, 'the tinplate industry is one which has had the benefit of very little carefully organized research. Such [pack] mills as are efficient (and it is not suggested that the industry is behind other countries in this respect) work rather on tradition and experience than on scientifically developed technique. . . . A representative research committee makes a small annual grant . . . for research on tinplate problems but this is virtually all that is done by an industry with a normal annual output valued at £15,000,000.'[33]

For long the tinplate industry had relied on the research resources of the steel industry, meagre though they were.[34] It is said that when plates were returned to a tinplate maker as faulty he would say the cause was the steel base and pass the complaint on to the steel-maker.[35] In self-defence the steelmaker was forced to attempt to dis-cover the cause of the trouble. Certainly when the possibility of the improvement of tinplate manufacture was discussed, the question of steel was given prominence. 'I have not seen striking economies effected as a result of the calling in of the engineer,' said H. D. Rees. 'As a manager I would prefer to appeal to the steelworkers to come to the assistance of the tinplate makers and give them a good cheap [steel] bar.'[36] And a tinplate maker who visited the U.S.A. in 1927 to see wide sheet manufacture by the strip mill re-ported on his return 'there seems to be nothing vitally wrong with our tinplate works. Our steel works are too antique to produce a bar comparable with the American bar.' But gradually other factors were recognized as important; a few years later a steel-maker could state that 'he was interested to find that the tinplate manufacturer was abandoning slightly the opinion he had held for so long, namely, that the steel base was the cause of his troubles'.[37]

In general, 'discontent was far too scarce, not sufficiently preva-lent'.[38] In good times modest profits were easy to come by, in bad times makers closed their mills since, with little fixed capital, stand-ing charges were low. Precise accounting methods were not em-ployed and makers paid little attention to marginal increments of cost. As the owner of one works put it, 'I do not attach much im-portance to the saving of a threepenny bit'.[39] Thus the tinplate maker was unreceptive to proposals for the improvement of proces-ses. He must therefore bear some responsibility for the slowness and piecemeal character of technical change during the pack-mill period of tinplate manufacture.

IV

Now the attitude of the British tinplate makers to the strip-mill must be considered. After a number of experiments, the first continuous strip mill to produce commercially was laid down at Ashland, Kentucky, in 1925. Then, in 1929, the cold reduction process was developed which made the hot-rolled steel strip suitable for tinplate production. By these two inventions the manufacture of tinplate was radically transformed. Because of the large automobile demand for steel strip and the growing internal market for canned goods, the strip mill method of manufacture was quickly adopted in the U.S.A. By 1939 75 per cent of the tinplate produced there was made by the cold reduction process. In that year the first British strip mill at Ebbw Vale began production.

The history of the construction of this plant is a history of opposition and delay. Although aware of the developments in the U.S.A. most of the tinplate makers in south Wales were not prepared to build a strip mill. Some were sceptical of the success of the new process. John Williams of Pontardawe poured scorn on the notion that the strip mill would revolutionize the tinplate trade, arguing that similar scares had proved groundless in the past. W. Robson Brown (Old Castle Works, Llanelly) suggested in 1935 that the intelligent conversion of existing works to the mass-production of tinplate by the sheet principle was to be preferred to the erection of a strip mill.[40] And H. D. Rees of Briton Ferry prophesied as late as 1937 that 'in the not distant future the tinplate trade of Wales will revolt against mechanization'.[41]

Allied with doubts about the technique of tinplate manufacture by the strip mill method was an unwillingness to face the problems of reorganization which its adoption would involve. What was needed, as Sir William Firth stated, was 'the sinking of personal rivalries in the desire for a more rational organization of the trade' but, like other British industrialists, the tinplate maker preferred 'to retain personal control of a small, relatively inefficient works rather than pool his brains and capital to the ultimate advantage of the industry'.[42] The result was that, while some tinplate makers, as Sir Charles Wright stated in 1931, were 'alive to the possibilities of certain technical developments and modern methods, schemes of reorganization which are highly desirable are arrested because the reconstruction involved is too large to pursue at this moment in view of the present state of the capital market and the multiplicity of small firms engaging in the trade'.[43] But as important as the practical difficulties was the lack of men with the right qualities of mind to embrace the new methods. As D. L. Burn has written of the British steel industry as a whole 'when changes were proposed, the "man of judgment" was the man who suspended judgment, who in effect adopted traditional methods, shaped his investment policy according to the shortness of his views, and adopted novelties after the cream had been skimmed'.[44]

Technical backwardness would have persisted in the British tinplate industry but for one man, Sir William Firth, chairman of Richard Thomas & Co. For a year in the early thirties he tried to secure the co-operation of other tinplate makers, but personal interests and shrinkage from additional responsibilities and risks barred the way. Undeterred when negotiations failed, he decided to go ahead on his own without the support of the other tinplate makers or the approval of the British Iron and Steel Federation. His firm, Richard Thomas & Co., built a strip mill at Ebbw Vale, thus radically transforming, albeit by a mature, developed technique imported from the United States, the manufacture of tinplate in Great Britain. Alone of the British tinplate makers, Firth had the vision, energy and drive to bring this about. And he had not grown up in the industry nor was he drawn from the local society of the tinplate area of south Wales. He was the 'deviant person' the industry required, the man who could speed technical innovation.

To explain fully the course of events in the British tinplate industry account must be taken of many other factors. This article has endeavoured to demonstrate that the business man, the tinplate maker, was, at least to some degree, responsible for the pace and character of technical change in the industry.

NOTES

1. John Williams, *Proceedings of the South Wales Institute of Engineers*, XXXI (1915), 151.

2. The long-established method—the pack-mill or hand-mill process—consisted of a series of largely manual operations: the strip-mill process is a highly mechanized process. Technical descriptions of these processes can be found in W. E. Hoare and E. S. Hedges, *Tinplate* (London, 1945).

3. The history of tinplate manufacture in Great Britain is discussed in more detail in W. E. Minchinton, *The British Tinplate Industry* (Oxford, 1957).

4. Speaking generally of the loss of industrial leadership by Britain, Alfred Marshall stated in 1903, 'It was not inevitable that she should lose as much of it as she has done'. Section L, *Memorandum on Fiscal Policy of International Trade*, H. of C. No. 321, November 1908.

5. *Manufacturing Business* (London, 1949).

6. A mill produced 500 boxes per week (25 tons) in 1870 and 750 boxes (37½ tons) in 1913: in 1870 there were 170 mills, in 1913 there were 525.

7. 'Manufacture of tinplate abroad', *United States Government*, 3402 (1895), 59–103.

8. *South Wales Daily News*, 23 January 1899.

9. The Cilfrew Works, Neath, is an example.

10. *Western Mail, Trade Supplement*, 7 January 1935.

11. Alfred Marshall commented in 1903 that 'many of the sons of manufacturers [were] content to follow mechanically the lead given by their fathers. They worked shorter hours, and they exerted themselves less to obtain new practical ideas than their fathers had done.' Section L of *Memorandum on Fiscal Policy of International Trade*.

12. Compare W. Miller's dictum about the U.S. Steel Corporation whose

trouble is 'to find a president of ability who does not need all his time to spend his salary properly', *Men in Business* (Harvard UP, 1952), p. 293.

13. A more detailed social study of this area of south Wales is to be found in T. Brennan, E. W. Cooney and H. Pollins, *Social Change in South-West Wales* (London, 1954).

14. *Welsh Broth* (London, 1951), p. 130.

15. See W. R. Maclaurin, 'The process of technological innovation' in *American Economic Review*, XL (1950).

16. *Western Mail*, 28 May 1891.

17. Compare the description of French conditions by J. E. Sawyer, 'The entrepreneur and the social order', in W. Miller (ed.), *Men in Business* pp. 7–22.

18. H. Spence Thomas, 'The tinplate trade: Developments', *Proc. S. Wales Institute of Engineers* XXIX (1913), 36–102, 202–42; F. J. Taylor and H. Spence Thomas, 'Tinplate Trade: some notes advocating standardization of plant', *Ibid.*, XXX (1914), 233–80; J. Williams and S. R. Cound, 'How to improve Welsh tinplate rolling with practice', *Ibid.*, XXXI (1915), 149–244; H. Spence Thomas, 'The tinplate trade: modern machinery', *Ibid.*, XXXVIII (1922), 669–721. See also Sir Charles Wright, Presidential Address. *Journal of the Iron and Steel Institute* CXXIII, (1931).

19. F. J. Taylor, *Ibid.*, XXIX (1913), 224. See also J. R. Davies, *Ibid.*, XXXVIII (1922). 690.

20. *Proc. S. Wales Inst. Engineers*, XXIX (1913), 92.

21. *Ibid.*, XXX (1914), 252.

22. *Ibid.*, XXXI (1915), 224.

23. *Ibid.*, XXXI (1915), 231.

25. *Ibid.*, 236. 'Why should I give my ideas away to others?' was the attitude of some tinplate makers. *Ibid.*, XXX (1914), 238.

25. *Ibid.*, XXIX (1913), 236.

26. *Ibid.*, 206.

27. *Ibid.*, XXXI (1915), 222.

28. *Ibid.*, XXIX (1913), 210.

29. *Ibid.*, XXXI (1915), 231.

30. *Ibid.*, XXIX (1913), 92.

31. *Ibid.*, 206.

32. *Ibid.*, XXIX (1913), 59. In this matter the conservatism of the employers was reinforced by the conservatism of the workers. The workmen, it was said, do not take kindly to innovation. *Ibid.*, 207.

33. Political and Economic Planning, *Report on the British Iron and Steel Industry* (London, 1933), p. 25.

34. See D. L. Burn, *Economic History of Steelmaking* (Cambridge, 1939), pp. 293 ff.

35. H. Spence Thomas commented, 'The microscope, so largely used in steel making and other great industries, is practically absent from our trade.' *Proc. S. Wales Inst. Engineers*, XXIX (1913), 59.

38. *Ibid.*, XXIX (1913), 217. See *Ibid.*, XXXVIII (1922), 698.

37. *J. Iron and Steel Inst.* CXXIII (1931).

38. *Proc. S. Wales Inst. Engineers*, XXIX (1913), 206.

39. *Ibid.*, XXXI (1915), 225.

40. *Llanelly Mercury*, 7 November 1935. Brown experimented with a system of single-sheet normalizing with no conspicuous success.

41. *Western Mail, Trade Supplement*, 11 January 1937.

42. *Report of the Departmental Committee of the Board of Trade to consider the position*

of the iron and steel trades after the war. Cd. 9035 (1919) p. 11. Col. Bevan, the chairman of the Briton Ferry Steel Co. stated in 1947, 'it was felt that it would be in the best interest of our Company . . . [not to] invest our liquid funds in a minority equity shareholding in another Company', *The Times*, 17 July 1947.

43. *J. Iron and Steel Institute*, CXXIII (1931), 45.

44. *Economic History of Steelmaking*, p. 297.

CHAPTER SIX

The Development and Decline of the Non-Ferrous Metal Smelting Industries in South Wales

by R. O. Roberts

THE coastal region between Kidwelly and Port Talbot was for a considerable time the main centre of British non-ferrous metal production, and the economic and social life of the area was—and still is—largely based upon metallurgy. Some 90 per cent of Britain's copper smelting capacity was to be found there from the close of the eighteenth century to the late nineteenth century, and during the first world war the area had three-quarters of the zinc producing capacity. Though there have been in all over fifty non-ferrous metal smelting works, only the Swansea Vale Spelter Works now remains: it has about 800 employees. Within the region also, at Clydach in the Tawe Valley, about 1,200 persons are employed in refining nickel. Copper smelting came to an end in 1924 after a century of struggle with new smelting establishments in the mining regions overseas. The smelting works had a considerable effect on the social development of the area—providing work directly or indirectly for a large proportion of its growing population; causing the erection of houses and some schools and churches; and giving the area numerous contacts with other places both inside and outside Britain. These industries provided much scope for inventiveness, and it is interesting that 97 out of 147 patents that came to Wales in the period 1757–1852 were obtained by the people of Swansea and Neath and their surrounding industrial area.[1] The smelting enterprises have left behind not only ruined works and slag tips (some of which have been removed during the last few years) and the names of streets and inns, but they have also left metallurgical traditions and skills which are still a considerable asset—for example, in the non-ferrous metal processing works of the region.

The following essay is an attempt to deal with some aspects of the history of the non-ferrous metal smelting industries in south Wales in the light of recent knowledge. An account of the growth of these industries in Britain as a whole is followed by a discussion of the reasons for their concentration in the western areas of the south Wales coalfield. The paper seeks to show the importance of the industries for the region and considers the reasons for their decline. It does not cover the large subjects of the supply of the various factors of production to the industries and the marketing of the metals.

Non-ferrous metals, and more especially the baser ones, were not extensively produced in Europe in the Middle Ages. They came into greater prominence, however, from the sixteenth century onwards when mercantilist policies, with their emphasis on military strength, encouraged the acquisition not only of 'Treasure', but also of the base metals, copper and lead, for military and other uses. In Great Britain, as elsewhere of course, development of the smelting of these metals was due to the new and expanding uses which were found for them and to the availability of the requisite factors of production: these demand and supply aspects will be surveyed in the next few paragraphs.

Copper, which is the metal with which this paper will be mainly concerned, was used increasingly at the close of the seventeenth and eighteenth century—in cake and pig form—for the manufacture by battering or 'battery' of a wide range of goods; and it was of course a constituent of brass whose output grew from the close of the seventeenth century. (Brass, like 'yellow metal', is a copper-zinc alloy; bronze is a copper-tin alloy, though the word has also come to mean 'superior' alloys such as silicon bronze or aluminium bronze which actually do not contain tin.) There was a growing demand, both from within and from outside Britain, for a wide range of copper and brass products such as coins, kitchen utensils, buttons and buckles, harness parts, guns and other armour. By the 1780s the brass-using trades of the Birmingham area consumed about 1000 tons of copper annually. Military demand for copper undoubtedly stimulated its production in peace-time as well as in periods of war.[2] The metal was used from the later decades of the eighteenth century for sheathing naval and merchant vessels, and during the Napoleonic wars the use of sheet copper for military purposes offset the contraction in the demand for it from the 'Birmingham trades'. In the nineteenth century there were new demands which resulted mainly from technical advances and industrialization; copper boilers and tubes were needed for steam engines; copper vats for brewing, distilling, and dyeing; copper rollers for printing on textiles; and copper wires and plates for telegraph and telephone equipment.

Lead was required in considerable quantities for roofing; and zinc or spelter, smelted commercially from 1740 onwards, was largely utilized for coating iron sheets which were mainly used for roofing purposes. Tin was used for tinplating (which now absorbs about half the world output of tin), for alloys and for solders. Nickel and aluminium also went largely into alloys; but other uses of these metals—of nickel for plating purposes and of aluminium for domestic utensils, for light reflectors, for electric cables, and as foil—are well known.

On the supply side, ores, fuel, labour, and both capital and the willingness to risk it became available in increasing quantities in Britain. Technical backwardness, the virtual monopoly of mining for metal enjoyed under charter since 1568 by the Mines Royal Society and the disturbances of the Civil War had hindered the development of mining and smelting until the late seventeenth century when a large number of factors contributed to a spectacular advance. By Acts of Parliament of 1689 and 1693 the restrictive rights of the Mines Royal Society were abolished, and thereafter entrepreneurs from outside that group could participate more freely in producing copper and lead by new methods evolved during the 1680s. Already in the 1580s a reverberatory furnace (of the type introduced in Germany by 1540) was possibly being used, under German management and for the first time in Britain, at Aberdulais; and certainly coal was being used, along with charcoal, in the charge for the furnace there.[3] Experimentation in the use of coal and of reverberatory furnaces for the production of both ferrous and non-ferrous metals continued in the seventeenth century, and by 1684, at a Bristol lead works, Sir John Clerke and John Coster appear to have been successful in 'adapting the reverberatory furnace to burning coal'.[4] A patent for a new method of smelting copper and tin by the use of sea coal or pit coal was granted to Henry Howard and Richard Bret in 1684[5] but nothing seems to be known of its outcome. Their activities in Bristol having been stopped in 1686, Sir John Clerke succeeded in producing copper by the new methods in London by 1688, and Robert Coster may have similarly succeeded at Upper Redbrook, Gloucestershire, by 1689. The exact nature of the improvements—whether they were due to the use of more suitable coals or more adequate draughts[6]—is still not known, just as the nature of the similar method of smelting iron evolved at Coalbrookdale by Abraham Darby in 1709 was, until recently, surrounded by mystery.[7] Abraham Darby had been a partner in a brass and iron works at Bristol from 1699 until 1707,[8] and this probably provided him with opportunities of learning about the new smelting methods used in that area.

Specialist workmen from Germany and Sweden were induced to operate in British copper works immediately after 1688, just as skilled foreigners had worked in the metal-producing enterprises of the sixteenth and early seventeenth centuries: in producing lead, British workers were more independent of outside assistance.[9] At that time additional ore resources came to be tapped. Copper lodes were found below the upper veins of tin in Cornish workings, and Dr. Rowe states that 'vastly increased exploitation of deep tin itself explains why copper production began in Cornwall in the closing years of the seventeenth century and not earlier'.[10] Gunpowder, which had been used by Staffordshire miners in the 1670s, came to be used in Cornish mines in the 1680s,[11] and there was to be a further stimulus to production from the application of steam pumps in the early eighteenth century. As a result of all these advances it became possible for Britain to produce copper competitively instead of depending entirely upon imports of that metal, mainly from Sweden,[21] as she had done for about two decades before 1685.

Iron and copper accounted respectively for 50 and 30 per cent of the average value of Swedish exports during the seventeenth century, and 75 and 10 per cent of the value in 1730.[13] In the early 1690s, according to Erik Odelstierna, Sweden still supplied about half the European consumption of copper[14] and most of Britain's consumption.[15] In view of the importance of metal exports for their country's economy the Swedes were naturally worried by metallurgical developments in Britain, and they were undoubtedly more concerned because 'in 1687 the excessive and predatory exploitation led to a terrible cave-in in the mines [of Stora Kopparberg, Falun]; and despite rapid recovery, the old levels of output were never regained'.[16]

Many Swedes came to Britain in the seventeenth and eighteenth centuries—for relationships between the people of Sweden and Britain had expanded from the commercial sphere to cover most aspects of life and thought[17]—but none came with a more urgent mission than those who arrived here, as in other parts of Europe, between 1690 and 1760 to investigate the newly-established enterprises for producing copper.[18] Some of the Swedes, indeed, at the beginning of the eighteenth century were prepared to go to great lengths to hinder the growth of mining and smelting in Britain, and their activities were part of the economic warfare between the two countries which became most acute in 1717 and 1718.[19] Already by 1712 Britain was believed by Count Gyllenborg to be producing half as much copper as Sweden, though in his opinion it was of inferior quality;[20] and by that time, largely as a result of protective duties, hardly any Swedish copper entered Britain. Swab, who provided Count Gyllenborg with much of his information, believed that the only way of damaging the British copper trade was for Swedes to purchase British ores and even mines, and drive up prices to unprofitable levels. In a letter from London in 1712 he said that he raised to £200 his bid for a quarter share in a mine at Coniston, which he had been offered for £125—adding that he 'willingly should pay if I were in pounds, or had been supplied with a power to buy it'. He also sought to prove that British ores thus bought could be shipped to Sweden and smelted there and at profit—a policy which could have been carried out with great effectiveness in the 1680s.[21] By the nineteenth century, however, the wheel had turned a full circle, for in December 1827 there was Swedish ore at Swansea in bond and awaiting smelting.[22]

As it turned out, for the reasons and from the beginnings just described, the British copper industry grew rapidly. Output increased from rather less than 1,000 tons in 1712,[23] to some 7000 tons at the beginning,[24] and about 22,000 tons in the middle of the nineteenth century;[25] and it reached its zenith in the late 1880s and early 1890s.

The smelting of non-ferrous metals in Britain has been largely concentrated in the western part of the south Wales coalfield. Copper was the metal mainly smelted in the area; but lead silver, tin, spelter, and more recently nickel and aluminium have also been produced. By 1750 'the Swansea area' already produced 50 per cent of the copper made in Britain;[26] and as stated earlier, from the end of the eighteenth century until the late 1880s (when the industry reached its peak output)[27] south Wales had about 90 per cent of Britain's copper smelting capacity.[28] The decline of copper production from the 1880s was offset by a growth in the smelting of zinc; and the zinc industry experienced a boom during the war of 1914–18, when south Wales produced about 75 per cent of the total British output.

There have been sixty non-ferrous metal smelting works (apart from testing furnaces) in south Wales, the first being established in 1584 at Aberdulais near Neath[29] where copper was smelted under German supervision by a subsidiary company of the Mines Royal Society. The works at Aberdulais had a number of links with metallurgical enterprises in other parts of Britain, including the large mining and smelting establishments near Keswick where a colony of some 4000 workers, largely foreign, were employed.[30]

There followed short-lived lead smelting plants in the Cwmsymlog area of Cardiganshire in the late 1630s. From 1695—immediately following the technical improvements and the freeing of enterprise described above—furnaces were built at Neath; and works were established from 1717 onwards in the Tawe (or Swansea) Valley, and from the 1770s around the Burry estuary.[31] The reasons for this localization will now be considered.

In 1696 one of the Swedish visitors, Thomas Cletscher, explained succinctly the advantages of Bristol as a metallurgical centre. In his opinion it was 'the most convenient place in the whole country' for copper smelting: both copper ores and coal, he said, were available there near the works, exportation of the finished products was easy and the nearby market was large—for 'they find purchasers enough at Bristol'.[32] However, although it had such advantages and although at the beginning of the modern period of copper smelting the most important technical developments took place there, Bristol did not survive for long the competition of south Wales in this field. It did not grow as a smelting centre, and no significant amount of copper was produced there after the eighteenth century.[33]

The advantages of south Wales as a smelting area were realized quite early. In 1727, Robert Morris, of the family that soon afterwards gave its name to Morriston, estimated that copper smelting could be conducted in the parish of Llangyfelach near Swansea at least 40 per cent more cheaply than at Hayle in Cornwall—where there was a short-lived smelting works in the 1720s and a more enduring, but barely successful, one from 1759 until 1806.[34] People concerned in the early Bristol enterprises soon came to see 'that the ports of the South Wales coast in the neighbourhood of Swansea were better placed for smelting'; indeed, Thomas Coster of the Bristol Brass Company took a lease of works at Neath in 1730,[35] and it is significant that his brother, Robert Coster, who from his own experience believed that smelting in Cornwall was economic,[36] also joined the venture. By the 1770s, with the low profits at Hayle as a warning, entrepreneurs would not risk further smelting attempts in Cornwall, despite propaganda from the mines adventurers;[37] but it must be added that the enterprise at Hayle after 1759 was hindered in its early stages by joint opposition from the existing firms, which, 'using every expedient to mortify the spirit of this arduous undertaking, alternately raised the price of Copper Ores and lowered the value of fine copper'.[38]

Placing smelting works on a coalfield was clearly advantageous in the early eighteenth century, for smelting a ton of non-ferrous metal ore then required about three times that weight of coal. If smelting had been conducted in an ore mining area lacking coal (like Cornwall or Anglesey) vessels carrying coal to it would probably have had to return in ballast. It had long been known too that there were advantages to be gained from mixing various types and grades of ore;[39] and, therefore, other things being equal, it was better not to smelt by itself the ouput of a single mine—as, for example, the early Cornish enterprises tended to do. The south Wales coalfield was a comparatively short voyage away from Cornwall, which was the main early source of ore; and Kahlmeter observed that ore could be carried from St. Ives to Swansea and, Neath for five shillings a ton, against ten shillings to Liverpool.[40] The Flintshire and the Lancashire and Cheshire coalfields and, given cheap inland transport, the Staffordshire coalfield, enjoyed a similar advantage for ores from Cumberland, Wicklow, and Anglesey. Flintshire also had its own calamine and lead mines, and lead and zinc smelting works were still being operated there in the late nineteenth century. Copper works existed in south Lancashire and in Staffordshire until the second half of the nineteenth century.[41]

The localization of smelting works on a coalfield provided return cargoes in the vessels which brought the ores, and loads in the ore-mining areas for the packhorses and vehicles returning after carrying ores to the coast. If this coal, carried as a return cargo, could be used wholly, or in part, for a preliminary reduction of the ores at the places where they were mined then a further transport economy would be gained. Coal was thus used in Anglesey for roasting copper ore,[42] but this did not happen in Cornwall[43] where the industrial demand for coal was greater: there the coal was consumed on a large scale by steam engines, used in the copper and tin mines, and also by the tin smelting houses.

Given then that it was more economic to set up smelting works on coalfields, why did the south Wales field eventually gain precedence over the others? A writer in 1769 stated that the smelting industries were established in the Swansea area 'on account of the cheapness of coals and labour there'[44] and useful evidence exists about the comparative costs of these factors. Robert Morris, of the Llangyfelach or Landore works, in 1727 gave the price of coal at Holywell, Flintshire (in the vicinity of which lead was then mined and smelted), as 'three times as much as at Langevelach'.[45] There is a reference a little later to Patten's 'Small copper and Brass works just by Warrington, where Coale is almost Double the price as at Neath'.[46] Wyndham stated of the Swansea district in 1775 that 'the plenty of coals . . . and the convenience of exportation have induced the copper companies to prefer this spot to all others'.[47] Again, in 1792-3 it was said that the firm of William Roe and Co. were contemplating the removal of their works from Liverpool to Neath 'on account of the scarcity and dearness' of coal in Liverpool: one of the partners, however, had reason to complain of the quality and deficient measure of coal at Neath in 1797, and undoubtedly this explains why the firm bought a share in a local colliery in 1803.[48] A number of the south Wales smelting firms—for example, Morris and Lockwood, Vivian and Sons, and Nevill and Co.—had their own coal mines.[49] Roe's works, however, being in Liverpool, were not on the Lancashire coalfield and were, therefore, in a considerably weaker position than the Ravenhead and Stanley Works (belonging to the Anglesey mining interests) in the St. Helens district. Though it has not so far been possible to make an exact comparison of the price of coal at St. Helens and at Swansea, coal probably was cheaper at the former in the 1780s. It was said in April 1783 'That the Price of Coal in Lancashire, where the [Anglesey] Ore is sent to be smelted is 5s. or 5s. 6d. at the Delivery at the Works, and on Ship-board at Swansea 4s. 3d. per Ton'.[50] Dr. J. R. Harris, however, has pointed out that the Lancashire ton was 30 cwts.; so that, as it stands, this price comparison 'is probably invalid'.[51] In fact, the ton at Swansea and Neath towards the end of the eighteenth century must have been only 20 cwts., since the chaldron there 'was then regarded as equivalent to 27-32 hundredweights but conmmonly taken as 1½ tons'.[52] That being so, coal was cheaper on the Lancashire coalfield than in Swansea in 1783. In 1812, however, Pascoe Grenfell chose Swansea rather than St. Helens for establishing new smelting works because coal was considerably cheaper there.[53]

How much cheaper labour was in south Wales than in other parts of Britain is not clear. Labour costs were given by Messrs. Roe and Company as a further reason for moving their smelting works from Liverpool to Neath; and the lower wages they paid at the latter place were, nevertheless, more generous than those ruling in the area, for in 1798 the men at the Mines Royal Works at Neath went on strike with a complaint that 'they do now work for less money than Roe & Co's men'.[54] In Liverpool and its hinterland at the close of the eighteenth century there was an especially strong demand for labour, largely due to the rapid developments in the textile industries and in the overseas trade of the port.

Since even finished metals are costly to move, places for smelting accessible to metal-using works or other markets would be at an advantage—as indicated by Thomas Cletscher in his account, mentioned above, of the advantage of Bristol in the 1690s, and 'the convenience of exportation' from Neath referred to by Wyndham.[55] Clearly, on ground of transport costs, there was a great benefit to be gained by the concentration of all processes in a region a small as possible. In this way the Cornwall, Swansea, and Bristol triangle was a fairly satisfactory area. For example, in the eighteenth and early nineteenth centuries, Cornish copper ore was smelted near Swansea at the White Rock Works of John Freeman and Copper Company, and 'the copper cakes and ingots were sent to Bristol for conversion into sheets, etc., in battery and rolling mills at Woolard, Publow, Pensford and Swinford'.[56] And the triangle of course operated much more cheaply because so much of the transport within it was relatively cheap sea transport. The extent of this advantage is shown by the fact that to convey copper ore from the 'Asselwood' (? Hazelwood) mine near Buckfastleigh in Devon to a ship at Dartmouth—a distance of no more than ten miles, with the possibility of river transport for much of it—cost 9s. 4d. per ton in 1725, whereas freight from Dartmouth to Neath cost only 6s.[57]

Some of the south Wales works extended their plants for manufacturing from copper and brass, thus securing the advantages of integrated production;[58] and the bolts, nails, boilers, etc., produced could be despatched from the nearby port. These works later came to supply important equipment to other industries—copper stools for casting large steel ingots and, after their metallurgists had evolved copper suitable for welding, improved fire-boxes for locomotives and larger and better containers for the chemical industry.[59] (It is interesting to speculate why so few works for processing non-ferrous metals were set up near the smelting establishments. For example, was it the operation of the law of comparative advantages or was it lack of enterprise that hindered the development in west Glamorganshire of a galvanizing industry? The managing partner of a galvanizing works in Staffordshire at the close of the nineteenth century wrote a book 'more especially for the perusal of the manufacturers of south Wales' showing the advantages of the latter region— in terms of costs of materials and labour and facilities for shipment— for such an industry.)[60] Proximity to a market for metals, however, was a much less important factor in the localization of a smelting works than was an abundant supply of suitable coal. This is shown by the experience of Messrs Roe and Company of Liverpool (before their move to Neath about 1793), who found that their advantage from being near the slave-trading copper market and the ship-building yards, where there was a demand for copper sheathing, was more than offset by their distance from a coalfield. In order to retain some of the marketing advantages, however, Messrs Roe kept a warehouse at Liverpool during the whole of their period of operation at Neath.[61]

Of some importance in the localization of non-ferrous metal smelting plants was the availability of good and cheap clay for making firebricks for the furnaces. A supply of such clay was provided for in the lease of land in 1779 to the Parys Mine Company for their Ravenhead Works at St. Helens; and, after some years of experience there, Michael Hughes of Sutton, in 1812, rated it very highly among the locational advantages of the two works at St. Helens. He said those establishments were 'situated most advantageously for being regularly supplied with coals at a low rate—superior fireclay for the construction of furnaces together with other indispensable requisites for the smelting of ores'.[62]

On the coalfields, clay and fireclay was largely a by-product of coalmining;[63] and it appears that in the western districts of the south Wales coalfield fireclay came to be produced in appreciable amounts only when the coal workings became fairly deep.[64] This local supply of fireclay thus became available only at a fairly late stage in the history of the non-ferrous metal industries. A 'superior kind of fire-brick . . . made out of silica', said to be the first of its kind to be made in Great Britain, was produced at Dinas near Neath from 1822 onwards;[65] and in 1869 W. Fairley wrote of the Llanmorlais colliery, west of Penclawdd, that 'The Fireclay . . . appears to be of excellent quality, and has . . . not been observed till the present'.[66] Firebrick works were also established 'at Morriston, Clydach, Glais, Llanelly, Llangennech and Pwll' and, though firebricks still came in from outside the area, these local works supplied much of the requirements of the smelting enterprises in the second half of the nineteenth century.[67]

It was a great advantage that fireclay and firebricks could be brought by sea to the smelting area in south Wales. Already in the late seventeenth century, and probably earlier, these materials were transported over long distances in and around Britain, for the inner linings of furnaces in the Bristol Smelting Works in 1696 were built of a brick, superior to its French counterpart, 'which is made of fireproof earth and comes from Windsor just along Eten (sic)'.[68] In 1705 the Mackworth lead and copper works at Melincryddan, Neath, wanted '100 tuns of Stourbridge clay',[69] and in 1778 the author of *Mineralogia Cornubiensis* stated that Grouan clay from Cornwall 'always answered for bricks to build fire places and furnaces with, equal to Stourbridge and other Clays; insomuch that plenty of it has been sent to Bristol and the

Welch Copper Works . . . besides that famous yellow clay in the parish of Lannant which has produced such an handsome income every year to Humphry Mackworth Praed, Esq'.[70] Vessels arrived at Penclawdd with clay from Hayle at the beginning of the nineteenth century.[71] In the second half of the eighteenth and the beginning of the nineteenth centuries firebricks came to south Wales from Flintshire, where they are still produced.[72]

It has been shown in the last paragraphs why the south Wales coalfield gained precedence over other British fields in smelting non-ferrous metals but, though some of the reasons have been touched upon, it remains to show more fully why development was concentrated at the western end of that coalfield. That region, in west Glamorgan and south-east Carmarthenshire was the most favourable place for four main reasons: the coal measures reach down to the sea only in the area between Port Talbot and Llanelly, and coal was available there—and, because it outcropped, available early and relatively cheaply—near the harbours where the ores could be disembarked; those harbours, and especially Swansea,[73] were suitable for the ore trade; and the navigable waters of the Tawe, Nedd, and Llwchwr rivers facilitated the movement of ores to the immediate vicinity of the coal mines and provided water for processing and for power. Finally, the coals of the western districts of the coalfield were suitable for smelting purposes.

The nature of the supply of coal for the non-ferrous metal industries is a complicated subject,[74] but it is clear that locating the smelting works in the western, coastal areas of the south Wales coalfield was favoured by the wide range of coals—anthracite, sub-bituminous, coking, and gas—which were available there.[75] The historical evidence points to the wide range of coal used by the smelting firms. In 1810 Charles Nevill of the Llanelly Works 'advised using the best Coal at Hafod[76] till the men get accustomed to it, so different from Penclawdd that they will poke it all out, much less binding'.[77] Again 'Mr. N. [Nevill] says that the Mines Royal get their Coal (many years to run) at 37/- the inferior & 45/- the binding. Average 39/- to 40/-'.[78] The earlier processes of the famous Welsh method of copper smelting used 'the coking and non-coking coals . . . available in the Swansea Valley . . . mixed in the proportion of one part of coking to two parts of free-burning' and in refining (which was the sixth and final operation of the Welsh method) 'anthracite or free-burning coal' was used to cover the charge.[79] The three types of coal consumed at the Hafod Works about 1850 were a gas coal of 87 per cent and coking coals of 90 and 91 per cent carbon content.[80] Though these coals would not produce as long a flame as the bituminous coals of the eastern part of the coalfield or the Midlands or Lancashire they were suitable for heating reverberatory furnaces, since they produced a good flame and burned uniformly. Indeed, basing his statement on an article in *The Philosophical Magazine* in 1852, Professor A. H. John has written that 'the free burning coals of the Swansea area were specially suited to the needs of the reverberatory furnaces; for, burning with a good flame, they were neither bituminous enough to clog the bars nor sufficiently friable to fall half-burnt between them. Their tendency to form large cinders, which enabled the furnace-men to reduce the number of firebars and by management of the cinders control the strength of the draught, was an important factor in the economic management of the furnaces'.[81] And, though they were then hampered by serious difficulties in obtaining cheap supplies of ores, the British smelters in the middle of the nineteenth century were held to have 'the advantage . . . of the cheapest and best fuel in the world'.[82] That it was to be found at the western end of the coalfield, which now produces mainly anthracite and sub-bituminous coals of over 92 per cent carbon content, was due to the wide range of types of coal available in the area, as already mentioned, and possibly the fact that the early surface workings yielded more coking and free-burning varieties.

An industrial localization, once established, of course tends to perpetuate itself. Skills, servicing trades, and suitable social capital develop and induce further expansion of the group of industries concerned in the original locality rather than elsewhere. Thus in the region with which we are concerned there were workers who knew secret metallurgical techniques or who possessed rare skills—indeed, the desire to keep processes secret seems to have been one reason for establishing the first smelting works, in the sixteenth century, in such a secluded place as Aberdulais[83]—and these workers might be bound, by the articles of their contract with their employers, not to impart their knowledge except to their own sons.[84] The region in fact evolved 'the Welsh process of copper smelting' already mentioned, which was praised by an American Professor of Metallurgy at the beginning of this century as 'one of the most scientific and beautiful of metallurgical processes'. He added that 'if Swansea had given us nothing else—whereas she has solved a large proportion of the practical problems of treating difficult silver- and gold-bearing copper ores—the blister process alone would be sufficient to distinguish her name'.[85] Dr. J. Percy, F.R.S., Professor of Metallurgy at the Royal School of Mines, had been more guarded in his comments in the 1860s, but he stated that some south Wales smelting works were 'quite as economical with fuel as were the works on the Continent.[86] The availability of highly specialized skills in particular districts may largely explain such 'spot localizations' as the group of spelter works which existed in the region of the present Swansea Vale Works. And the existence of a 'supply of experienced labour' and the 'world-known . . . skill of the Welsh smelters' was given by D. Owen Evans as the main reason for establishing the Mond nickel refinery at Clydach.[87]

The localization was undoubtedly strengthened because some of the firms gained exclusive rights to exploit certain inventions, as the Cheadle Company at Neath and Messrs Vivian at Hafod did for W. E. Sheffield's improved method of smelting after 1811,[88] and as the Muntz Patent Metal Company Ltd. did for the production of yellow metal between 1838 and 1842 at the Upper Bank Works. On the other hand the enterprises might have been dispersed if the campaigns against copper smoke had resulted in legal decisions more adverse to the smelting firms. Smoke from the works was regarded as a nuisance at nearby mansions or townships and held to injure farming in the adjacent countryside,[89] but the resulting actions in the Courts did not lead, in south Wales, to works being moved as those of Roe and Company had to move in the Liverpool area in the 1770s.[90]

The non-ferrous metal smelting industries of south Wales had only a small number of employees by comparison with the main industries of the region—coal-mining, iron and steel-making, tin-plate manufacture, and agriculture. During the first four decades of the eighteenth century the number of workers in the non-ferrous metal smelting works could hardly have reached 200;[91] but the numbers more than doubled between 1740 and 1770. A member of the 'Society of Gentlemen' who surveyed British industries in 1769 gave the number working in the copper, lead, and tin works of the Swansea 'area' as more than 500,[92] and Arthur Young, in 1772, gave the same figure for the non-ferrous metal works of Swansea and Neath.[93]

For comparison with the 200 or less non-ferrous metal smelters of south Wales in the early eighteenth century, there are the employers' figures for the connected industries in England, showing 'a total of 21,350 families distributed over the various branches of the copper and brass industries in the following way: about 12,350 families were constantly employed in raising copper ore in Cornwall and Devon and in transporting it to the coast: 2500 families in digging, calcining and preparing calamine, in smelting copper ore, in raising coal, in digging and transporting 300 tons of Stourbridge clay to the brass works, and in making brass; and finally 6500 families in manufacturing brass into finished goods'.[94] When J. Latimer, in his *Annals of Bristol*, stated that in 1712 the English brass trade employed 21,000 persons he was obviously writing of the group of connected industries.[95] And whereas the south Wales non-ferrous metal smelting works around 1770 had about 500 workers, the Cornish mines in 1787 had 7000.[96] In Wales, the other main centres of non-ferrous metal works were at Amlwch, Anglesey, where 1200 miners and about 90 smelters were employed in 1797;[97] in Cardiganshire and in Holywell, Flintshire, a town which at the end of the eighteenth century had about 600 workers in its copper and brass works, and was surrounded by a number of lead and calamine mines.[98]

In the century after 1750 the non-ferrous metal industries of south Wales grew about tenfold, so that according to the census of 1851 they employed over 2000 workers. (In the same period the industries of coal-mining, iron, and tinplate in south Wales had so grown that together they employed 68,000 persons.)[99] In the early 1830s it was reckoned that families totalling 60 to 70,000 persons obtained their livelihood from the copper mines of Cornwall, and 80,000 from the copper mines of the whole of Britain. Some 20,000 people in Britain must have depended in some way on smelting copper, if it was correct that there were '100,000 souls who compose the population dependent on the Copper Mines and copper works'.[100] By 1851 the non-ferrous metal smelting works of Bristol had disappeared and, apart from the fifteen south Wales smelting works, there were only 'two small establishments at St. Helens near Liverpool, one at Amlwch in Anglesey, and one in Staffordshire'.[101]

The *Census of Population* figures of the numbers employed in non-ferrous metal manufacture[102] in south Wales (including Monmouthshire) after 1850 are as follows:

Year	Copper	Lead	Zinc	Total
1851	2,148	73	32	2,253
1861	2,876	463[102]	—	3,339
1871	2,253[102]	561[103]	517	3,331
1881	2,381	282	607	3,270
1891	2,400	220	454	3,074
1901	2,386	130	624	3,140
1911	2,676	119	974	3,769

The total number employed clearly remained very stable from 1861 until 1911; and it is surprising, in view of the decline in the imports of copper ores and regulus to the United Kingdom and to Swansea after about 1888,[104] that the numbers of copper workers were maintained after 1881, and even increased by 1911. In the *Census* of 1921 metal workers for each of the south Wales counties are described according to the nature of their work, rather than according to the metal which they produced or processed.

Unofficial estimates gave larger figures than did the Censuses for the number of copper manufacturers in the middle of the nineteenth century. According to two sources there were some 3500 workers employed in 'smelting and manufacturing' copper in the Swansea area in 1850.[105] An estimate published in 1857 stated that there were 4000 workers on 600 furnaces 'in the Swansea district'.[106] These estimates undoubtedly referred to the whole area from Llanelly to Port Talbot: within the borough boundaries of Swansea in 1851 the number of copper workmen was 1214 and at the end of the century there were 1051 copper and 496 zinc workers.[107] In 1922 there were said to be some 2000 workers in the six spelter works of the Swansea valley.[108]

Though the total number of workers in the non-ferrous metal works of South Wales never reached 4000, those works were not an unimportant element in the economy of the area. Their employment figure, indeed, was about 1000 higher than the numbers employed in south Wales in 1939 by the enterprises established in the 1930s under the Special Areas policy. The contribution of the non-ferrous metal works in providing employment and income and in inducing further activity, and their diversifying effect on economic life were significant in the western part of the coalfield. The smelting works were 'the great support' of Swansea in 1756, according to Dr. Richard Pococke;[109] and over a century later it was said that, 'What coal is to Newcastle, chemicals to St. Helens, silk to Lyons, and wheat to Milwaukee, copper is to Swansea'.[110]

Some writers sought to emphasize the significance of the non-ferrous metal industries by giving the gross value of their output. The copper works, it was said in 1842, 'do not derive their importance so much from the number of hands they employ as the aggregate value of the metal they produce'.[111] Though too much reliance should not be placed on the figures, the value of the output of copper in the Swansea region in 1858 was given as £3½ million;[112] and in 1910, when the value of the copper produced was given as £2 million, gold, silver, and lead to the value of £250,000 were produced, and the output of zinc was 'nearly that of the entire kingdom, the annual value being given at £500,000'.[113] More important, of course, than gross values were the values added to the raw materials by the smelting processes, and, as mentioned, the favourable effects of the works on employment in the area.

The importance of the works in the latter respect was realized throughout the nineteenth century. For example, it was believed in 1823 'that the smelting establishments on the Swansea river alone, with the collieries and shipping dependent on them support a population of from 8 to 10,000 souls, and cause a circulation in their vicinity of from 2 to £3000 weekly'.[114] The current expenditure of the copper works of south Wales in 1833 was given as £300,000 annually, exclusive of the cost of ores; and about the same time the copper works 'of the Swansea River' were said to be spending on wages and coal £115,000, 'which is principally if not wholly expended in the Town of Swansea and its immediate neighbourhood'.[115] In 1863 the current expenditure in south Wales of works for smelting non-ferrous metals was given as not less than £200,000 a year;[116] but it was stated in 1857 that the copper works of 'the Swansea district' paid almost £4000 a week in wages alone.[117]

Apart from enlarging in this way the total number employed in the area, the non-ferrous metal industries were held to increase the stability of employment. In the early 1830s it was said that 'the comparative stability' of the copper mining districts of England and Wales had been 'the subject of much remark and congratulation'.[118] *The Merthyr Chronicle* in 1837 deplored the over-dependence of its area on an iron industry which was 'subject to the ebb and flow of a very uncertain trade';[119] and thirty years later Dr. Thomas Rees was writing that, 'The copper trade has always been less fluctuating than the iron trade, and consequently the populations dependent upon it are less exposed to privations and unfavourable changes, than those of the iron districts'.[120] It would be wrong, however, to deduce from these statements that the non-ferrous metal trades rarely experienced slumps; for they suffered depression at the beginning of each of the decades from 1820 to 1850. The copper trade was depressed in 1822–3;[121] in June 1832 it was reported that the Llanelly copper works of Daniell, Nevill and Company was closed and that 'the Town sustained a serious shock by the stoppages about six months ago';[122] and ten years later R. J. Nevill referred to 'the total suspension of profit from our copper trade for the last 12 mo. and the apprehension . . . that this must continue for some considerable time'.[123] It does seem, nevertheless, that the demand for copper even in periods of

depression did not fall catastrophically; and the successive developments of new types of copper products and new markets[124] prevented
the depressions of the industry from being very deep.

The total amount of coal used annually for smelting copper and
manufacturing from it in South Wales in the 1850s was about
400,000 tons.[125] According to the, clearly biased, statement of the
lawyer who defended Pascoe Grenfell and Son, in the copper smoke
action of the early 1830s, 'Bituminous coal in the Swansea Mineral
Basin is not of that quality which would entitle it to a sale without
the auxiliary aid of copper works; these works consume in fact
the refuse coal or that portion of the coal worked which could not
be sold or disposed of but by smelting works established in the
neighbourhood'.[126] The copper smelters, as we have seen, came to
mix different types of coal in well-established proportions in
charging their furnaces; but they may have taken some poor or
unmarketable coals such as were more recently used up by
steam-raising plants at the collieries.[127] Apart from their direct
consumption, however the smelting industries caused a large
further demand for coal because, as stated earlier, the vessels
carrying copper and other ores to Swansea and neighbouring ports
took coal and culm as return cargoes. Thus the ships which carried
15,000 tons of ore from Portreath in Cornwall in 1805 could convey
5600 weys of coal to that port;[128] and, though we do not know
whether these were Llanelly weys of 5 tons or Swansea and Neath
weys of 10 tons,[120] or were of some other weight, it is clear that
such shipments of coal were considerable. Indeed, it was said that
80 per cent of the coal shipped from Swansea in the early 1820s
left in the copper ore boats,[130] and in 1837 some 17 per cent of the
coal exports of Neath, Swansea, and Llanelly went to the steam
engines of the copper mines.[131] This coal trade was assisted by the
suspension of duties on sea-borne coal used in steam engines,
a suspension which Cornwall obtained in 1741, as it had for coal for
smelting in 1710,[132] and as Anglesey gained in 1786, after a decade
of petitioning.[133] The advocate defending Pascoe Grenfell's copper
works in the early 1830s averred that 'were the copper works
annihilated this shipping would not come to Swansea in ballast,
as they must then, the Coal not being of that quality to induce
a demand nor would it stand in competition with Coal produced
in other parts of the Kingdom, consequently the Collieries which
are now a source of wealth and yielding employment to thousands
of industrious workmen would instantly cease to exist'.[134]

The *Swansea Tide Table* of 1827 showed that 110 vessels, of which
thirty-four were registered in Swansea, were engaged in the port's

copper and coal trades[135]—which, as we have seen, were closely integrated. The smelting works of the Swansea 'district' were said to keep 150 vessels, and perhaps 750 seamen, employed in the conveyance of ores about 1830;[136] and another source stated that at that time 120,000 tons (gross?) of shipping, at a cost of between £25,000 and £30,000 annually, were needed for the smelting industries.[137] It was added that 'The importance of this trade as a nursery for Seamen must be evident, especially as there is no coasting trade in which the number of Apprentices is greater'.[138] The canal and railway companies (of which smelting entrepreneurs were among the shareholders) also derived much business from the smelting concerns; thus, the South Wales Railway Company in 1848 expected to get £7400 annually from mineral traffic between Swansea and Loughor, including £600 from Messrs. Schneider's fairly small Spitty Works.[139]

Though his figures might be questioned, the importance of the non-ferrous metal smelting industries as described in the above paragraphs was well summarized around 1830 by Dr. Paris. 'When we learn', he said, 'that the amount of wages paid by the proprietors of the smelting works in this district exceeds 50,000 l. per annum; that 12,000 persons at least derive their support from the smelting establishments; that a sum of not less than 200,000 l. sterling is annually circulated in Glamorgan and the adjoining countries in consequence of their existence; that they pay to the collieries no less than from 100,000 l. to 200,000 l. per annum for coal; that 150 vessels are employed in the conveyance of ore; and, supposing each to be manned by five seamen, that they give occupation to 750 mariners; a more serious calamity can scarcely be imagined than the stoppage of such works.'[140] Because of all this it was a considerable loss to the western areas of the south Wales coalfield when smelting ceased in so many of the works soon after the first world war. Those areas thereby became much more vulnerable to the effects of recession in the production and processing of iron and steel and in coal-mining.

It must be stated, however, against the smelting industries, that work in them was very unhealthy. The descriptions still current among older people in the Swansea area of the effects of inhaling poisonous fumes coming from the furnaces, especially those of the spelter works, recall Dr. Maton's account of conditions in the tin-smelting houses of Cornwall over a century ago. 'So dreadfully deleterious are the fumes', he said, 'and so profuse is the perspiration occasioned by the heat of the furnaces, that those who have been employed at them but a few months become most emaciated figures, and in the course of a few years are generally laid in their graves.'[141]

The industries reducing non-ferrous metal ores have disappeared in Britain, apart from the smelting of zinc at Llansamlet near Swansea and at Avonmouth, and the production of aluminium in the Highlands of Scotland. (Plants for the production of aluminium need coal for the reduction of bauxite to alumina and, even more, electric power for reducing the alumina to aluminium. There were a number of short-lived aluminium works in England during the second half of the nineteenth century, but since 1896 the industry has become localized mainly in the Scottish Highlands where hydro-electric power is available. Alumina is produced in Fifeshire and in Country Antrim; and from 1937 until the end of the war there were alumina works in a number of other places, including Newport, Monmouthshire, and Rheola near Neath.)[142] The reasons for the disappearance of the smelting of copper and lead are complicated, and much less attention has been given to them than to the various aspects of the growth of the smelting industries.

The causes of the decline of lead mining and smelting in Britain during the last hundred years have been summarized by Professor A. H. John in a valuable introduction to his edition of the business papers of the Walker family of Rotherham. 'Although increasing quantities of Spanish ore were imported from the forties onwards', he writes, 'it was the fall in lead prices after 1875, together with increased costs of production and the falling silver content of British ores which started the decline in lead-mining in this country. At the same time, the establishment of smelting and refining works in Spain gravely affected the smelters as is shown in the later years of the journal.'[143] Within Britain the Greenside Mine in Cumberland has been recently the most important source of the metal,[144] which has long ceased to be smelted in south Wales. Before the first world war lead ores from Algeria and Chile were imported to Swansea and Llanelly,[145] but further development of smelting in the main mining countries brought this trade to an end.[146] Copper smelting, however, was a much more important industry in south Wales than the smelting of lead; and the following paragraphs give a tentative account of its decline and disappearance.

Though the output of British copper ores expanded until the middle of the nineteenth century it failed to keep pace after about 1825 with a demand which was growing even more rapidly.[147] Indeed, from the middle of the nineteenth century, Europe as a whole 'had to rely increasingly on North America, Chile and the Belgian Congo' and by 1929 it 'consumed a third of the world's copper but produced only a fifteenth of it'.[148] The insufficiency of the supply of British copper ores was partly due to deterioration in their quality as poorer lodes and veins came to be exploited. Transporting and working ores of low metal content was of course most costly, and it was natural for the smelters to encourage the mining of richer ores available overseas. Those ores were even better than the early produce of Cornwall and Anglesey. It was written of the mines of Cobre, Cuba, in 1840 that 'the ordinary average produce is not more than 27 per cent, but even that proportion is so great as to ensure enormous profits to the proprietors in competing with the produce of our native mines of Cornwall, where 10, and even 8 per cent, are considered sufficient to afford a remunerating return. The competition with Cornwall, probably, could not be maintained if the produce of the Cuba mines did not reach 18, or at least 16, per cent in consequence of the expense attending the working of mines in a tropical climate, together with the heavy charges of freight, commission and insurance.'[149] Some of the Australian ores reaching Britain in 1843-6 yielded 40 per cent copper and those of Chile from 20 to 60 per cent.[150]

The developments abroad in copper mining were, of course, part of the opening up of the 'new' countries, and British people and capital had a prominent part in them. For example, 'Trevithick discovered or re-discovered the copper deposits of northern Chili'[151] and 'it was by British loans . . . that the Chileans were able to raise the ore'.[152] 'The challenge of Chile to Cornish supremacy', says Dr. Rowe, 'resulted from the speculative boom of 1823. By the end of 1823 the agents of three English mining companies— the Anglo-Chilean, the Chilean, and the Chilean-Peruvian Mining Association—had been sent to Coquimbo. Among the directors of the Chilean Mining Association were George C. Fox and Alfred Fox of Falmouth, and John and William Williams of Truro, whilst Pascoe Grenfell, besides his interest in the Cuban Cobre mines was a director of the Columbian Mining Association, founded in December 1824.[153] The collapse of the boom had brought hardships and losses to these Companies, but they had led the way for the large-scale exploitation of American copper resources.'[154] Nearly everywhere in the Latin American countries it was the British who pioneered in the use of steam engines in mining; but later, in the introduction of 'industrial railways and tramways, steam shovels, electricity and the cyanide and flotation processes in smelting, citizens of the United States often shared the honours with the British'.[155] In 1876 the total amount of British capital in Chilean metal mines was

£3 millions—about 2 per cent of Britain's aggregate investment in Chile.[156]

The modern period of copper mining had begun in Cuba in 1817, and in Chile in the 1820s, but it could be argued that the 1840s was the crucial decade in the history of copper production in the 'new' countries. In that decade the output of ore increased greatly, and important developments in smelting took place in Cuba and Chile. The Kapunda and Burra Burra mines in Australia and the Cliff mines near Lake Superior came into production in the same decade.[157] The 1850s saw a development of mining in all those areas: around 1860 important mines in Spain and Portugal were opened; and in 1883 the great Anaconda mine in Montana was discovered.[158] After the first world war very large copper fields were found in Northern Rhodesia and the Belgian Congo.

Most of the increase in copper smelting capacity in the nineteenth century was in the countries where the ores were found. In the 1820s there were charcoal-using furnaces in Chile, and R. J. Nevill, in 1830, wrote of the difficulty then experienced by rolling mills in the United States 'of getting adequate supplies of Cake Cor. from So. America'.[159] In 1842 Charles Lambert (who had copper smelting works at Port Tennant, Swansea from 1852 onwards) introduced coal-using reverberatory furnaces at Coquimbo, Chile, with such success that 'in a short time their use was general throughout the country'.[160] Between 1842 and 1847 there was a five-fold increase in smelting in South America[161] and by 1872 there were a hundred smelting works in Chile.[162] In Australia in the 1850s the English and Australian Company (which smelted at the Spitty Works in Loughor in 1852–56)[163] opened smelting enterprises at Port Adelaide and Waratah near Newcastle, New South Wales; and Schneider and Company (who operated in a portion of the Spitty Works in 1847–56[164]) were smelting near the Burra Burra mines.[165] The early struggles between alternative locations in Australia— places having advantages in coal, charcoal, and nearness to copper mines—is an interesting subject; Newcastle, N.S.W., where coal was plentiful, was held in 1847 to have more in its favour as a smelting centre than anywhere in England and Wales.[166] Further works were established in South Australia in the 1860s and in New South Wales in the 1870s.[167] In the United States a smelting works at Tainston, Maine, opened in 1836, was followed in the middle 1840s by the setting up of two works, one at Baltimore and the other at Boston.[168] The establishment at Boston used reverberatory furnaces and has been regarded as marking 'the real beginning of the American copper industry'. From 1848 came works (at

Pittsburg, Cleveland, and Detroit) built away from the eastern seaboard. The United States is credited with the most important contributions to smelting techniques: 'To the older smelting methods have been added blast furnaces, water-jacket furnaces, Bessemer converters, pyritic smelting and enlarged reverberatory furnaces, while an entirely new type of refining has been introduced by the electrolytic method.'[169] Electrolytic refining was pioneered by Elkington at Pembrey, Carmarthen, after 1869; and the Bessemer process was first developed in Britain, from 1856 onwards, for producing steel. It was later applied in other countries to the production of non-ferrous metals (thus reversing the sequence after 1684), and the south Wales copper firms might have arrested the decline of their business if they had adapted the Bessemer converter as was done successfully in the United States from the 1880s.[170]

By the close of the nineteenth century the U.S.A was the largest producer of copper; output in Chile was almost stationary and had been exceeded by the produce of Rio Tinto in Spain.[171] From 1895 until 1927 the United States 'yielded more copper than the combined production of the rest of the world';[172] but thereafter, though it remained the largest producer, its lead was reduced by exploitation of new ore resources and new methods of large scale production in Africa, Canada and Chile.[173]

It is well known how an industry in Britain could enjoy the advantages of early technical progress, but fall back in the economic race when other countries developed their industries. This story has often repeated itself, but always with twists given to it by the special circumstances of each particular case. And so it was with the British copper industry, for there were many special factors contributing to the development of smelting in the 'new' countries rather than sending ore or concentrates to the older smelting countries.

The early enterprises for smelting in the 'new' countries could be the result of any of a number of causes. It was usual for ores to be 'picked' and 'dressed' before despatch to a port *en route* for Europe, and, especially in the case of poorer ores,[174] there was a strong incentive for rough reduction at the mines in order to lower transport costs. Thus concentrates and blister copper came to south Wales in increasing quantities from the 1850s until the 1890s.[175] Freight charges on the copper ore ships were kept down because they carried coal on their outward runs from south Wales, and much of this coal was used for concentrating ores in the copper-mining countries just as Lancashire coal had been used for reducing the produce of Anglesey mines in the eighteenth century.

And there were, in a number of places in the new countries, incentives to go beyond reduction and undertake full smelting—so that, indeed, in most countries other than Britain in the nineteenth century 'smelting was carried on as an adjunct to the mine'.[176] Some of the early mines were so remote that, if charcoal was available, smelting in their immediate vicinity and even on a small scale was worthwhile; and in parts of the semi-desert mineral region of North Chile and in South Australia there was a good supply of it in the early nineteenth century. 'Charcoal', said *The Mining Journal*, 'may be considered to do the work of three times its weight of ordinary coal; and it is said that it could be supplied from the neighbouring woods [in South Australia] for 5d per bushel, or 2 l. per ton, and 1 ton would operate on 3 tons of the ores in question'.[177] When coal was found in regions sufficiently near the copper mines of the coastal districts of northern Chile, the produce of those mines could be sent there as copper and lead silver ores; and regulus from areas further inland was moved to the southern provinces of the country, where coal was obtained from 1870 onwards,[178] and where (unlike the United States) there was also a good supply of fireclay.[179] Most favourable for smelting, of course, were those situations where ores and coal became available together, as they did in New South Wales and near the Great Lakes.[180]

One merchant with twenty years' experience of trade with Chile and Peru suggested in 1847 that the Chileans would smelt more in their own country and send a greater quantity of ore to places other than Great Britain as soon as they had completed 'the tedious operation' of repaying British loans by large exportation of ores to Britain (as in 1843 and 1844). He added that: 'The authorities in Chile were giving every encouragement to the smelting of copper; they admitted coal free of duty; they had altered their laws in order to admit British vessels for the importation of coal and the exportation of copper . . . He was bound also to say that South America was giving every encouragement to the trade with England.'[181]

Technical improvement in the expanding smelting industries of the 'new' countries has already been mentioned, and people from the smelting localities in south Wales played an important part in those advances. This was not unnatural, for the largest group in Britain of persons skilled in copper smelting was in west Glamorgan and south-east Carmarthenshire, and many of them found remunerative openings in countries where the premium on their skill was very high. Thus reverberatory furnaces in the

United States in the 1840s were operated by Welsh smelters, and among the first smelting establishments in New South Wales was that of Lewis Lloyd around 1870.[182] In 1883 there was a Swansea Smelters' Works at Clear Creek near Georgetown, Montana, for reducing Anaconda ores.[183] About the same time, and in the same region, great improvements took place in reverberatory furnace smelting, and Professor Peters stated that 'justice compels us to credit a Swansea-bred metallurgist—Richard Pearce—with the inception of many of the improvements which have so thoroughly revolutionized this process. The Butte smelters followed his lead, but also struck out a line of their own, which has lately culminated in the Great Anaconda reverberatories.'[184]

As early as 1846 some saw the developments abroad as a challenge to technical improvements in copper smelting 'as decided as the hot blast in the smelting of iron ores'.[185] The outflow of skill and enterprise undoubtedly impoverished the Llanelly-Swansea-Port Talbot area; and there are two opinions about the methods and attitudes of those who continued in the smelting industries there. According to one view, the competitive strength of the industries was greatly reduced by a refusal to scrap old techniques and equipment. Some of the smelting entrepreneurs, indeed, were described as 'metallurgically unprogressive',[186] and they may well have been in the mind of Professor James Douglas who, about 1900, attacked 'the ridiculous secrecy maintained at so many of the metallurgical works, especially in Europe', and who added that 'people who will contribute nothing to the information of the world or their co-workers in any art, are not those who are generally most progressive in their own practice'.[187] The other view is that 'the Swansea smelters developed great skill in the construction and management of the reverberatory, and found it peculiarly suitable to the great variety of finely pulverized ores of every conceivable composition, which reached their port from all parts of the world'.[188] The Welsh processes, it has been said, were 'perfected'[189] and formed 'some of the finest examples of skilled metallurgical art with which we are acquainted, especially when the times and working conditions are borne in mind'.[190] Whatever metallurgists might decide as between these views there is no denying the evidence that, at certain times when expansion was rapid in other countries, the Welsh copper firms displayed an 'indifference about taking orders'[191] which undoubtedly injured their prospects. This indifference was an aspect of the monopolistic policy of a group of the firms and will be described below in that context.

It emerges from the above paragraphs that smelting copper in the countries that are now the main producers of the metal was made almost inevitable by discoveries of ores and coal in adjoining areas, and by the need to work ores of low metal content at the places where they were mined. There were, however, certain features of the commercial policy of the British Government and of the attitudes of the smelting entrepreneurs that tended to hasten the development of smelting in the 'new' countries during the middle decades of the nineteenth century. These were the customs duties on copper ore imports and the Navigation Laws, on the one hand, and, on the other, the monopolistic arrangements of the smelting firms in south Wales.

The production of copper and other non-ferrous metals in the eighteenth and early nineteenth centuries was protected by customs duties and these, though reduced in 1825,[192] remained until 1842 at the considerable rates of £27 per ton on 'smelted but unwrought' copper, and £12 per ton on copper ores.[193] These rates, virtually prohibited imports of these commodities for use in Britain, but foreign ores could be brought into the country and smelted in bond for re-exportation as 'Tough' and 'Tile' copper[194] (as undoubtedly happened to the Swedish ores mentioned earlier).[195] Thus 'in some measure the detrimental consequence which the high and prohibitory duties would otherwise have exerted on our foreign trade was avoided'.[196] Ores from Chile and Cuba were smelted in bond in Britain and the metal made from them was sold on the Continent at highly competitive prices. Under that system, indeed, British smelters had gained the French market which had formerly taken 6000 tons of Russian copper every year.[197] It is true that the situation before 1842 did not then satisfy all the smelters. R. J. Nevill wanted a change, not by a new Act of Parliament, but by 'an order from the Treasury to the Commrs. of Customs authorizing them to instruct their officers to allow Bonds to be canceld by the Shipt. of Manufactured Copper equally as by the Export of Tough and Tile Copper as at present.'[198] He held that 'the French and Dutch are exclusively the gainers by a restriction which gives them virtually a Monopoly of 7000 Tons of Copper annually the greatest portion of which ought to be manufactured in British Rolling Mills'.[199] And he discussed the best way of approaching the Government on the subject of tariff revision, without incuring further 'the odium' of the Cornish 'Mining Interests and . . . their would be Organ the Mining Journal'. Finally he concluded that there should be a joint campaign by the smelters and the more influential purchasers of their copper.[200] The Cornish mining interests, both before and after 1842, supported the import duties: and their policy was described as short-sighted in so far as the duties were crippling the British smelters, and encouraging smelting overseas.[201]

Changes in the system of import duties in 1842, however, made the situation of the smelters so much worse that later they longed for a return to the previous system. In 1842 the duties on foreign ores were reduced to rates from £3 to £6 a ton, depending on the quality, and the duties on imports of unwrought copper were brought down to £8 15s.[202] But these developments, favourable to British consumption of the imported commodities, were accompanied by the abolition of duty-free smelting in bond, and this proved very harmful to the output and export trade of British smelters. It was proposed by the Chancellor of the Exchequer in 1848 to reduce the duties to a nominal rate on ores of 1s. 0d., and on copper cake of 2s. 6d. a ton, but it was not until 1853 that the duties were finally removed[203]—and long before then it was argued that the harm of stimulating smelting abroad had been done. The suspension of the system of duty-free smelting in bond was said to have ended importation of foreign copper ores, except to the extent required for mixing with low-grade British ores;[204] but the figures for imports from South America between 1839 and 1846 show that this was an exaggeration.[205] The duties levied on all imports of ore to Britain after 1842 gave advantage and encouragement to the works then established in Chile and the United States and in Hamburg, France, Sweden, and other places in Europe.[206] The amount of ore imported to Hamburg increased from 60,000 tons in 1846 to 407,000 tons in 1847,[207] and the French market was being lost to the new works on the Continent.[208] The smelters on the Continent operated under the disadvantage *vis-à-vis* American smelters of heavy freight charges averaging £3 10s. 0d. per ton of ore;[209] but the cost of taking ores to Britain from the 'new' countries was greater.[210] The South Wales smelters had cheaper fuel, though British coal was cheaper in Hamburg than in London.[211]

It was undoubtedly a fear of the developments in smelting in North and South America that led R. J. Nevill, in 1845, to 'recommend that the Cuba and Pennsylvania Ores . . . be taken generally or they will I fear go at an unreasonably low Standard which seems to me anything but advisable'.[212] The same developments led the smelting interests in Britain to campaign vigorously against the new system of import duties. A delegation of them called on Sir Robert Peel in 1846, and H. Hussey Vivian, M.P. of Swansea, and William Keates of St. Helens drew his attention to the fact that the new establishments in the United States obtained the superior ores of South America unencumbered by import duties. W. R. Lloyd, on behalf of brass producers and merchants in Birmingham, said that traders there 'had often felt the inconvenience lately of having remittances from Cuba, by bills on New York, and other circuitous routes, all so much to the prejudice of their profits on their own shipments'. Other gentlemen in the same delegation explained 'the dangers of forcing into existence unnaturally a trade which, however we might afterwards regret and endeavour to reverse our restrictive measure, would thus have obtained a footing abroad, and ultimately supersede us in one of the most important branches of national industry'.[213] Before the Select Committee on the Copper Trade in 1847 Mr. Brownell, who was engaged in the Liverpool and American trade, stated that he regarded the import duties as being more harmful than the navigation laws, and he too emphasized 'that, as the Americans had commenced the practice of smelting and as they would probably continue it, every day [under the new system of duties] added to the difficulty of the subject'.[214] Similarly, E. Budd, of the firm of Vivian and Sons, while wanting the repeal of both import duties and navigation laws, would 'certainly prefer the removal of the duty', and he believed that 'if the former state of the law were restored, with the exception of greater facilities being given to the manufacture of copper bolts and copper sheathing from foreign ores . . . the copper smelters would be satisfied'.[215] And an anonymous letter to *The Cambrian* expressed surprise that whilst exertions against the duties were being made in Liverpool and Birmingham and in Manchester, by the Chamber of Commerce and the 'not less influential' Commercial Association there, Swansea was inactive in the matter—though it had a new Chamber of Commerce and was 'the town, of all others, that will most assuredly suffer most if these duties are persisted in'. He did not want to overstate the case against them and was 'not an alarmist', but he would refer his Swansea readers 'to either of the Establishments connected with the trade near your town'. He argued further that the yield of the duties was 'inconsiderable, and becoming less every quarter, by the conversion, to a considerable extent, of these ores into copper on the spot, or elsewhere abroad.'[216]

The change in the system of import duties in 1842 brought the navigation laws to bear on the importation of copper ore, and this also seems to have harmed the copper smelting industry in Britain. Until 1842 the copper brought duty-free from abroad for smelting in bond could be carried in the ships of any country. Thus, before that date, ten out of eleven vessels chartered for importing copper ore in one year by a Liverpool firm of merchants were foreign; and E. Budd, of the firm of Vivian and Sons, Swansea, 'had himself imported, under the former state of the law, copper ore in ships of almost all nations; and he did not think that those ships would all have been built for the special purpose of importing copper ores'.[217] When the system of duty-free importation ended, however, so also did the immunity from the navigation regulations. Imports of copper ore were brought under Huskisson's Navigation Act of 1823 whereby non-European produce 'might . . . come either in British ships or in ships of the country from which the goods were the produce *and* from which they were imported'.[218] Since the total tonnage of the shipping of the new countries was small, the Act compelled ores to be carried to Britain in British ships whereas, for example, 'in France and in the United States copper ore could be imported in ships of any countries'.[219] The Act remained in force until 1849.

Owing to certain circumstances the navigation laws raised the freight charges, on copper ores imported to Britain from South America, to levels both higher than they otherwise would have been, and higher than were paid for shipping the ores to other countries. Essentially this was because the total tonnage of British shipping calling in the western ports of South America was insufficient to carry the copper ore available there for shipment to Britain, whereas vessels belonging to other countries were short of cargoes at those ports. British manufactured goods—and, as we have seen, coal also—went to Latin America 'chiefly . . . in British bottoms; but the tonnage so employed must be insufficient to bring home the copper ore' and, before 1842, 'not only did all British ships get return cargoes, but foreign vessels were also employed'. Under the navigation system this tended to drive up the rates which British vessels would charge on cargoes to Britain; and there was a clash of interests between ship-owners and importers. Again the large shipments of guano from the Chilean coast after 1836 also 'to some extent diminished the supply of vessels for importing copper ore and to that extent raised the freights'. The guano brought to Britain, before and after 1842, had of course to be carried in British ships. E. Budd complained, not only of the cost, but also of the quality of the services provided by British vessels. 'English captains', he said, 'frequently overloaded their vessels, and had to put back on that account. This rarely happened to foreign captains'.

The copper smelting interests, in opposing the operation of the navigation laws, had to explain why freight charges fell immediately after the laws came to affect the ore trade. In 1842 the rate was

£5 6s. od. per ton on ores shipped from Chile to Britain; in 1843 £4 4s. od.; but in 1844, 'when the importation was exclusively confined to English vessels, the freights were £2 19s. 9d'; and the charges in 1845 were similarly low. One witness explained the levels of 1844–45 as being due to 'the uncertain state of things in the River Plate, which caused vessels to flock round to Chili and Peru'; and another adduced 'the fact that numerous vessels had brought cargoes which had gone to Chili in ballast . . . being attracted thither by rumours of high freights and had thus over-stocked the markets'.

Foreign vessels were not allowed after 1842 to take cargoes to Britain. Largely because of this there were 'left upon the west coast of South America a number of ships belonging to the United States, to Hamburgh, to Sweden &c. which could get no back freights; and those ships were induced to take cargoes at any rate of freight to any part of the world'. Thus 'to America, Sweden, Hamburgh, &c. the freights were less than to this country'. It was not known whether the low freights charged by the foreign ships were remunerative or not, but 'they were in such circum-stances very glad to get them'. Budd 'had no doubt that the United States ships would prefer a cargo home to one to this country'.

Freights on ore from Chile to Britain were about £2 per ton higher than those from Chile to the U.S.A., according to Boardman, and Budd agreed that the difference 'was more than £2. per ton [and] . . . amounted to 10 per cent on the cost of the copper'; but when Boardman claimed that this adverse differential was larger than the import duties his figures for the latter may have been incorrect. Budd emphasized 'that the amount of freight was not in itself of importance so much as the question of how much they had to pay compared with other countries'.

It is worth quoting the example given by Boardman of the difficulty encountered by his firm in October or November 1846. 'They were anxious to send a cargo home to England, but they could not get one at a less freight than five guineas per ton; and they were, therefore, compelled to charter a Danish vessel to carry it to the United States, and the freight they charged was only at the rate of three guineas per ton, thus making a difference of two guineas in the freight, though the difference in the voyage was not more than from five to ten days. Previous to the imposition of the duty there had been no exportation whatever to the United States. . . . By the last advices received from Chili he understood that they could not get an English vessel to bring a cargo to Swansea for a freight of £4 10s. per ton; and at the same time there were some Danish vessels lying there for cargoes. This had often happened and he had known their cargoes delayed for want of British ships as long as three months.' He also added that exports of manufactured goods from Britain to South America, which had been growing rapidly, were being restricted by the quantity of South American produce which England might take in return.

While Boardman, on rather insecure grounds as we have seen, considered the navigation laws more harmful to the copper smelters than the import duties, Brownell and Budd took the opposite view. Brownell thought the duty 'was a permanent evil while the other was uncertain and fluctuating'—a reference, undoubtedly, to the effect of changes in the numbers of British ships seeking cargoes at the copper-ore ports. Budd 'had no facts to go on in estimating what the freights would be in case the navigation laws were repealed; but he should think the freights would still be slightly in favour of the United States'. In copper smelting, however, citizens of the United States 'still . . . could not compete with England if there were no duty and no navigation laws, because they could not compete with us in coal. The bituminous coal in Pennsylvania is 200 miles from the coast, whereas, the English coal is no more than a mile from the coast.'

Budd's ideas were echoed by Thomas Boundy of Swansea commenting on a meeting in support of the navigation laws which was held at Bridgend in 1849.[220] 'A meeting for the purpose intended', he said, 'should have been held at Swansea, where the depressing result of the working of the *present* restrictive laws has been fairly tested to the manifest injury of the copper trade of this town'. He was 'surprised to see gentlemen advocating the present laws, who are large proprietors of that fuel most essential for the reduction of copper ores' and was 'prepared to prove that if the foreign ships had continued in our trade . . . not less than 5000 tons' more coal would be used weekly in the Swansea area. He found too that support for the navigation laws co-existed strangely with plans in Swansea 'for the construction of floating accommodation for (as was naturally supposed) the ships of all nations'. Finally he pleaded: 'Let the carrying trade be thrown open to all nations, and we shall again see this one of the most flourishing towns in the kingdom. We have all the natural advantages for smelting, it must be evident, therefore, that by throwing away all fetters connected with free admission of ores, we must become the competitors of the entire world.'

The well-known interdependence of tariffs and monopoly is

illustrated, on the one hand, by R. J. Nevill's reference to the import duties as an excuse for the low prices offered for foreign ores by the associated smelting firms in 1841[221] and, on the other hand, by the Chancellor of the Exchequer's statement in 1848 that a reduction of duties would undermine 'a combination among the smelters' which kept 'the price of copper to the British manufacturer . . . much higher generally than to the exporter to foreign countries'.[222] The fact that the smelting firms of south Wales associated to keep up the prices of manufactured copper and to drive down the prices of imported ores provided strong incentives to users of and dealers in copper, to the ore producers and even to entrepreneurs from outside the trade to establish smelting works in other countries. There is no basis, however, for saying with Mr. D. Owen Evans that 'the monopoly of the smelting trade was *the cause* of the decline of the industry in South Wales'.[223]

From the 1820s two or more copper firms often co-operated, temporarily, to drive up the price of the finished metal[224] or to force down the price of ores;[225] and from the middle 1840s the main smelting firms acted together to these ends on a more permanent basis.[226] They usually agreed on the terms of smelting contracts with the merchant houses importing Chilean and other ores.[227] There is evidence that the market for copper ores was a buyers' one in the statement to the Select Committee of 1847 that 'The value of a ton of copper ore was about £18 5s. and out of that sum there were charged for freights, land carriage &c. to the extent of about £11., and to this there was now to be added the duty of £1. 11s. 6d. per ton so that all that remained to the Chilean miner . . . was £5. 12s. 6d.'[228]

In 1856, though faced with a strong demand, the associated smelters of the Swansea area were refusing orders for copper, 'stating deliveries must be at their convenience' and yet retaining prices (fixed by themselves) at a lower level than demand conditions indicated. Varous explanations were adduced for such strange action. 'It is thought smelters are keeping prices down from an envious feeling [about rolling mills in Australia] so as, if possible, to make a failure with these new works'. Again it was suggested that the absence of 'a commander-in-chief or his deputy' from 'the usual monthly meeting' explained the continuance of prices at surprisingly low levels. In May 1858, on the other hand, prices were kept up despite falling demand; and though some orders then came in from those who, noting the firmness of the smelters, feared a rise in prices, such buyers held off as soon as the smelting firms 'exhibited more willingness to accept orders'. In November

1858 demand was stronger, but the group of smelters were again 'indifferent about orders', and prices were kept down because 'An advance in the price of English would only be attended with prejudicial results, as the holders of foreign would then be able to get out of their present stock . . . foreign holders not being able to sell at current rates'. The smelters—described as 'devotees of the holy cause of monopoly'—ignored the advice of *The Cambrian* to 'beware and treat their present customers with their due, or otherwise they may have to repent the mode adopted in their usual course of business; but few would commiserate with these staunch opposers of free trade and open competition'.[229]

Though it is very difficult to know what weight to give to the various causes of the decline of copper smelting in south Wales it seems likely that it was hastened by the tariff and navigation policies and by monopolistic practices. Some knowledge of such influences and of more important causes, in the discoveries of ores, coals, and new methods abroad, led a writer, in 1869, to say that 'the days of the copper trade are numbered' so that in that respect at least 'Swansea has seen its grand climacteric'.[230]

NOTES

1. E. H. Jones. 'The romance of Welsh inventors', *Wales and Monmouthshire*, II, May 1938.

2. For a discussion of the extent of this military demand see A. H. John, 'War and the English economy, 1700–63', *Econ. Hist. Rev.*, 2nd ser., VII, 3 (1955), 330–1: and R. O. Roberts, 'Copper and economic growth in Britain, 1729–84', *National Library of Wales Journal*, X (1957), 65–8.

3. Ulrick Frosse's letter of 7 March 1584 quoted by G. Grant-Francis, *The Smelting of Copper in the Swansea District* (2nd ed., London and Manchester, 1881), p. 20: W. O. Alexander, 'A brief review of the development of the copper, zinc, and brass industries in Great Britain from A.D. 1500 to 1900', *Murex Review*, I, 15 (1955), 391–6.

4. Rhys Jenkins, 'The copper works at Redbrook and at Bristol', *Trans. Bristol and Glos. Arch. Soc.*, LXIII (1942), 146, 162; and the same writer's 'Copper smelting in England; revival at the end of the seventeenth century', *Trans. Newcomen Soc.*, XXIV (1943–5), 73–80.

5. J. R. Harris, 'The copper industry in Lancashire and North Wales, 1760–1815' (Ph.D. thesis, University of Manchester, 1952), p. 3.

6. Cf. Rhys Jenkins, 'Copper smelting in England', pp. 73–4.

7. Cf. T. S. Ashton, *Iron and Steel in the Industrial Revolution* (Manchester University Press, 2nd ed., 1951), pp. vii–xviii, 30.

8. T. S. Ashton, *op. cit.*, pp. 26–8.

9. Rhys Jenkins, 'The copper works at Redbrook', 148; University of Liverpool Library, Rhys Jenkins papers, Count Gyllenborg's memorandum, p. 4.

10. J. Rowe, *Cornwall in the Age of the Industrial Revolution* (Liverpool, 1953), p. 4. Cf. W. Pryce, *Mineralogia Cornubiensis* (1778), p. x: J. A. Phillips and J. Darlington, *Records of Mining and Metallurgy* (London, 1857), pp. 28–9.

11. D. Lardner, *The Cabinet Cyclopaedia*, XVI (London, 1834), 19: J. Rowe, *op. cit.*, p. 9.

12. These imports were often costly, and were made more so by export duties imposed by King Charles XI of Sweden—cf. Rhys Jenkins, 'Copper smelting in England', p. 73.

13. Eli F. Heckscher, *An Economic History of Sweden* (Harvard University Press, 1954), pp. 92–3.

14. *Ibid.*, p. 87.

15. Rhys Jenkins papers, Odelstierna's 'Travelling description of foreign mines', p. 3 (English translation).

16. E. F. Heckscher, *op. cit.*, p. 85; cf. *Stora Kopparberg* (Stockholm 1955), pp. 28–33.

17. Cf. Sven Rydberg, *Svenska Studieresor till England under Frihetstiden* (Uppsala, 1951).

18. Cf. Rhys Jenkins papers.

19. T. S. Ashton, *op. cit.*, pp. 111–14.

20. Rhys Jenkins papers, extract from a memorandum by Count Gyllenborg in Anders Swab's letter of 27 October 1712, fo. 4. 'In January 1717', says Professor Ashton, 'Count Gyllenborg, the Swedish envoy to Britain, was arrested' for his part in a scheme for landing a Swedish force in Scotland to assist a new Jacobite rebellion (*op. cit.*, p. 111).

21. Rhys Jenkins Papers, *ibid.*, pp. 2–5.

22. N.L.W., Nevill MS. 6, 19 December 1827.

23. Derived by halving Swedish output, as Swab and Count Gyllenborg suggested. This output is given by Heckscher, *op. cit.*, p. 87.

24. Thomas Rees, *Miscellaneous Papers on Subjects relating to Wales* (London, 1867), p. 10.

25. J. Symons, 'The industrial capacities of South Wales', *The Cambrian Journal*, I (1854), 317; J. A. Scoffern, *The Useful Metals and Their Alloys* (London, 1857), p. 539. Walther G. Hoffman, *British Industry, 1700–1950* (trans. Henderson and Chaloner, Oxford, 1955), pp. 239, 309, gives valuable references for and a graph of British copper production after 1770: this graph, however, is open to question in certain respects (cf. R. O. Roberts, art. cit.).

26. *House of Commons Report on the Copper . . . Trade, 1799* (*Reports not inserted in the Journals*, X, 677), quoted by A. H. John, *The Industrial Development of South Wales, 1750–1850* (Cardiff, 1950), p. 108: cf. *The Commons Journal*, 11 April 1783.

27. Cf. W. G. Hoffmann, *op. cit.*, p. 309; D. Trevor Williams, *The Economic Development of Swansea* (University of Wales Press, 1940), p. 77.

28. J. Symons, art. cit., p. 317; Thomas Rees, *op. cit.*, p. 10; E. A. Smith, Zinc (Monographs on Industrial Chemistry, 1918).

29. Cf. C. D. J. Trott, 'The historical geography of the Neath region up to the eve of the Industrial Revolution' (unpublished M.A. thesis, University of Wales, 1946).

30. Cf. E. Lipson, *The Economic History of England* (London, 1934), II, 175; H. Hamilton, *The English Copper and Brass Industries to 1800* (London, 1926), chapters ii–iii.

31. Cf. D. Trevor Williams, *op. cit.*, p. 89; H. O'Neill, *Presidential Address* to the Swansea and District Metallurgical Society (1954), pp. 9, 13–14; D. Elwyn Gibbs and R. O. Roberts, 'The copper industry of Neath and Swansea: records of a suit in the Court of Exchequer, 1723', *South Wales Record Society Publication*, No 4 (1958).

32. Rhys Jenkins papers, Thomas Cletscher, 'Foreign mine relations, 1696'

p. 13. At the Conham Works near Bristol, however, the ore smelted before 1700 had to be brought from Cornwall (Rhys Jenkins, 'The copper works at Redbrook and at Bristol', p. 163).

33. Rhys Jenkins, 'The copper works at Redbrook and at Bristol', p. 167.

34. Morris MS., 'History of the copper concern ... from the letter books' (1774), pp. 21, 87, 95; this seems to be the only reference to a smelting enterprise at Hayle in the 1720s. On the works at Hayle later in the eighteenth century, see W. Pryce, *op. cit.*, p. 277; N.L.W. MSS. 15101-117 (ore purchase notebooks); A. K. Hamilton Jenkin, *The Cornish Miner* (1927), pp. 115-16.

35. Rhys Jenkins, 'The copper works at Redbrook and at Bristol', 167.

36. W. Pryce, *op. cit.*, p. 278.

37. J. Rowe, *op. cit.*, p. 71.

38. W. Pryce, *op. cit.*, pp. 242, 274, 279-80.

39. Ulricke Frosse, the German manager of the Aberdulais works, was well aware of this in 1584. Cf. G. Grant Francis, *The Smelting of Copper in the Swansea District* (2nd ed., London and Manchester, 1881), p. 23: John Percy, F.R.S., *Metallurgy* (London, 1861), p. 299. Rhys Jenkins, 'Copper smelting in England', p. 80. refers to the advantage of smelting together sulphide and carbonate ores.

40. Rhys Jenkins papers, H. Kahlmeter's 'Account of English mines', 1727, p. 22. Kahlmeter considered that Redbrook, Glos., where smelting had been in progress since the 1680s, was the most convenient place for producing metals (Rhys Jenkins, art. cit., p. 150).

41. Cf. J. Percy, op. cit., p. 307.

42. *The Commons Journal*, 11 April 1783, 366-7; cf. J. R. Harris, *op. cit.*, p. 130.

43. The small and short-lived copper works at Hayle and other places in Cornwall undertook not only a first reduction of the ores but full smelting.

44. P. Russell and O. Price (eds.), *England Displayed ... By a Society of Gentlemen* (London, 1769), II, 289.

45. Morris MS., p. 99. On the beginnings at Holywell, cf. Thomas Pennant *History of the Parishes of Whiteford and Holywell* (London, 1796), pp. 202-3. A. H. Dodd, *The Industrial Revolution in North Wales* (2nd ed., Cardiff, 1951, p. 20; J. R. Harris, *op. cit.*, pp. 44-5.

46. Royal Institution of South Wales, Mackworth MS., Cotes to P. Courteen, 26 February 1738.

47. H. P. Wyndham, *A Gentleman's Tour Through ... Wales in ... 1774* (1st ed., 1775), pp. 43-4.

48. W. H. Chaloner, 'Charles Roe of Macclesfield (1715-81); An Eighteenth Century Industrialist', *Trans. Lancs. and Chesh. Antiq. Soc.*, LXIII (1952-3), 73 fn. Cf. Grant-Francis, *op. cit.*, p. 78; J. R. Harris, *op. cit.*, pp. 254-6.

49. Cf. Birmingham Assay Office MS., 'Mining, smelting, and selling combined with the Welch collieries' (1786); H. Hamilton, *op. cit.*, pp. 229, 357.

50. *The Commons Journal*, 11 April 1783, p. 366.

51. J. R. Harris, *op. cit.*, p. 93.

52. A. H. John, *op. cit.*, p. 188.

53. Pascoe Grenfell to Michael Hughes of Sutton, St Helens, cited by J. R. Harris, *op. cit.*, p. 285.

54. G. Grant-Francis, *op. cit.*, p. 78; cf. A. H. John, *op. cit.*, p. 28.

55. Respectively Rhys Jenkins papers and *op. cit.*, pp. 43-4.

56. Rhys Jenkins, 'The copper works at Redbrook and at Bristol', p. 167.

57. Rhys Jenkins papers, Kahlmeter, *op. cit.*, pp. 7, 22, 36 and Thomas Cletscher, *op. cit.*, p. 5.

58. Cf. Dafydd Morganwg, *Hanes Morganwg* (Aberdar,1874), p. 215; A. H. John, *op. cit.*, pp. 109–10.

59. Yorkshire Imperial Metals Ltd MS., 'Short statement . . . on the copper activities of I.C.I. Metals Limited at Swansea', 23 July 1938.

60. James Davies, *Galvanised Iron, its Manufacture and Uses* (London, 1899), pp. 6 ff. Cf. *The Cambrian*, 19 November 1847; D. Trevor Williams, *op. cit.*, pp. 88, 90; H. W. Dickinson, 'A study of galvanised and corrugated sheet metal', *Trans. Newcomen Soc.*, XXIV (1943–5).

61. W. H. Chaloner, art. cit., p. 73; J. R. Harris, *op. cit.*, pp. 53, 56, 93; J. Rowe, *op. cit.*, p. 64.

62. Quoted by J. R. Harris, *op. cit.*, p. 282; cf. *ibid.*, p. 98.

63. Cf. A. H. Dodd, *op. cit.*, p. 193.

64. Cf. T. Neville George, *The Geology . . . of the Swansea District* (Univ. of Wales Press, 1939), pp. 43–4.

65. T. Mardy Rees, *The Quakers in Wales* (Carmarthen, 1925), pp. 256–7; J. W. Wright, 'The refractories industry', *Western Mail Commercial and Industrial Review*, January 1955.

66. W. Fairley, *Practical Observations ln the South Wales Coalfield* (1869).

67. Cf. *Slaters Directory—South Wales* (1858), pp. 6, 126.

68. Rhys Jenkins papers, Thomas Cletscher, *op. cit.*, p. 9.

69. Grant Francis, *op. cit.*, pp. 84, 92, and the same writer's *Original Charters . . . of Neath* (1845), p. 105. Clay called 'Stourbridge clay' did not necessarily come from the Stourbridge area.

70. W. Pryce, *op. cit.*, p. 32.

71. Cf. *The Cambrian*, 5 April, 15 and 22 August 1806.

72. Thomas Pennant, *Tours in Wales* (ed. John Rhys, Caernarvon, 1883), p. 67; Thomas Cropper, *Buckley and District* (1923), pp. 65–6; F. V. Emery. 'The Penclawdd Canal', *Gower*, IV (1951), 46.

73. Cf. *The Cambrian*, 24 May 1850, where there is a description of the localization in Swansea from the correspondent of *The Morning Chronicle*. R. J. Nevill in 1831 wrote of 'the greater difficulty there is in getting vessels to load ore for Llanelly than for Swansea after the end of October' (N.L.W. Nevill MS. 7, pp. 52–3).

74. I am indebted to my colleagues, Dr. D. E. Davies and Mr. A. P. Greenough of the Department of Metallurgy, University College of Swansea, for valuable guidance here.

75. Cf. Donald Hicks, *South Wales Coals and Some of their Industrial Uses* (Swansea Technical College paper, Gorseinon, 1935), pp. 7–8.

76. The works of John Vivian and Sons, established in that year.

77. N.L.W. MS. 15112C (Vivian MS., 'Penclawdd notebook'), 30 December 1810.

78. *Ibid.*, 10 February 1810.

79. W. O. Alexander, art. cit., pp. 410, 413.

80. J. Percy, *op. cit.*, p. 98; *The Efficient Use of Fuel* (H.M.S.O., 1944), p. 9.

81. *Op. cit.*, p. 150.

82. *The Cambrian*, 5 May 1848; cf. E. D. Peters, *The Principles of Copper Smelting* (New York, 1907), p. 173.

83. Cf. Grant-Francis, *op. cit.*, p. 9; C. J. Trott, *op. cit.*, chapter i.

84. Cf. Yorkshire Imperial Metals Ltd. MS., indenture of agreement dated 26 July 1811 between J. H. Vivian and partners, Hafod Works, and William Howell of Swansea, 'refiner or smelter of copper'.

85. E. D. Peters, *op. cit.*, p. 437.

86. *Op. cit.*, pp. 314–86, and his evidence in the *Report from the Select Committee*

on *Scientific Instruction together with Evidence* (1868), p. 83; cf. *The Cambrian*, 16 August 1850, and W. O. Alexander, art. cit., pp. 410–14, which reproduces a flow-sheet of the Welsh method drawn by William Terrill in 1877.

87. Art. cit., 34.

88. J. R. Harris, *op. cit.*, pp. 42, 285; J. Percy, *op. cit.*, pp. 317–18.

89. Cf. J Percy, *op. cit.*, pp. 337–45; Grant-Francis, *op. cit.*, pp. 157–60; Martin Phillips, *The Copper Industry in the Port Talbot District* (Neath, 1935), pp. 40–3.

90. W. H. Chaloner, art. cit., pp. 60–3.

91. Morris MS., 'History of the copper concern', p. 14; H. Hamilton, *op. cit.*, p. 251.

92. *Op. cit.*, p. 289.

93. Arthur Young, *A Six Weeks Tour through the Southern Counties of England and Wales* (London, 3rd ed., 1772), pp. 168–9.

94. Hamilton, *op. cit.*, pp. 119–20, based on *A Farther State of the Case relating to the Brass Manufacturers* (1720).

95. J. Latimer, *Annals of Bristol in the Eighteenth Century* (1893), p. 96.

96. A. K. Hamilton Jenkin, *The Cornish Miner* (1927), p. 91; cf. J. Rowe, *op. cit.*, pp. 8, 18.

97. Arthur Aikin, *Journal of a Tour through North Wales* (London, 1797), p. 140.

98. C. R. Williams, 'Treffynnon yn 1800', *Lleufer*, VII, 3 (Hydref, 1951), p. 118.

99. The *Census of Population* for 1851 gives the following employment figures for south Wales (including Monmouthshire): coalminers, 31,489; iron manufacturers, 15,013; iron miners, 10,275; and tinmen, workers, and dealers in tin, 2612.

100. Royal Institution of South Wales, 'Brief for defendant Pascoe Grenfell Esquire' (in a copper smoke action, *c.* 1832), pp. 11, 16.

101. J. Symons, art. cit., p. 317.

102. The categories for metal manufacture do not, at least in 1901 and 1911, include manufacture from metal. In 1901 and 1911 the numbers of workers who made goods from the non-ferrous metals were few. In Glamorgan (including the county boroughs) in 1901 there were 16 workers manufacturing from copper, 7 from zinc, 23 from brass and bronze, and 41 white metal and electro-plate ware manufacturers and pewterers.

103. These figures seem to be inflated by the inclusion of female 'other workers and dealers'—an inflation which was slight in the case of copper and appreciable for lead.

104. Cf. D. Trevor Williams, *op. cit.*, pp. 77, 79–80.

105. *The Cambrian*, 12 June 1850, based on information from Sir Hussey Vivian. J. Lewis, *Swansea Guide*, (1851), p. 9.

106. R. Oxland in *The Useful Metals and their Alloys* (ed. J. Scoffern, 1857), p. 551.

107. D. Trevor Williams, *op. cit.*, p. 170.

108. *South Wales Evening Post*, 23 February 1922.

109. J. J. Cartwright (ed.), *The Travels through England of Dr. Richard Pococke* (1889), II, 199.

110. E. Rowland Jones, *Heroes of Industry* (London, 1886), p. 120; cf .*The Cambrian*, 24 May 1850.

111. *Royal Commission on the Employment of Children in Mines*, XVII, 639, quoted in A. H. John, *op. cit.*, p. 139.

112. C. S. Hall, *Book of the Wye and the Coast* (London, 1861), pp. 338–9.

113. J. Heywood, *Illustrated Guide to Swansea and the Mumbles* (1911), p. 7. Heywood gave the annual gross value of output of steel in the hinterland of Swansea as £2½ millions and that of tin (i.e. tinplate) as about £5 millions.

114. *The New Swansea Guide* (1823), p. 32. The employment figure for the Swansea valley given here seems to agree with the estimate for Britain given above.

115. Samuel Lewis, *A Topographical Dictionary of Wales* (London, 1833), II, Loughor; R.I.S.W., 'Brief for defendant Pascoe Grenfell', p. 19.

116. *Proceedings of the Subscribers to the Fund for obviating the inconvenience arising from the Smoke produced by Smelting Copper Ores, etc.* (London, 1863), p. 83.

117. R. Oxland, *op. cit.*, p. 551. As mentioned earlier, Oxland exaggerates the number of the copper workers.

118. R.I.S.W., 'Brief for defendant Pascoe Grenfell', p. 12.

119. Quoted by A. H. John, *op. cit.*, p. 98.

120. *Op. cit.*, p. 10.

121. N. L. W., Nevill MS. 6, 15 January 1823; Nevill MS. 5, 7 October and 5 December 1823.

122. *The Cambrian*, 30 June 1832.

123. N.L.W., Nevill MS. 7, 4 December 1842.

124. Cf. A. H. John, *op. cit.*, pp. 108–11.

125. J. Symons, art. cit., p. 318.

126. R.I.S.W., 'Brief for defendant Pascoe Grenfell', p. 28.

127. D. Hicks, *op. cit.*, p. 13.

128. Tehidy MS. (Camborne, Cornwall), William Jenkin to John Vivian, 22 March 1805. I am grateful to Mr. A. K. Hamilton Jenkin for an extract from this letter.

129. Cf. A. H. John, *op. cit.*, pp. 189–90; *The Cambrian*, 11 February 1804. 28 May 1814.

130. *The New Swansea Guide*, 1823.

131. A. H. John, *op. cit.*, p. 115.

132. J. Rowe, *op. cit.*, pp. 7, 9.

133. J. R. Harris, *op. cit.*, pp. 116, 125; *The Commons Journal*, 11 April 1783, p. 367.

134. Loc. cit., p. 19; cf. the similar statement made in 1838 about the coal trade of Llanelly, quoted in A. H. John, *op. cit.*, p. 115.

135. D. Trevor Williams, *op. cit.*, pp. 152–3.

136. D. Lardner, *op. cit.*, p. 149, quoting a Dr. Paris.

137. R.I.S.W., 'Brief for defendant Pascoe Grenfell', pp. 13, 19.

138. *Ibid.*, p. 13.

139. *The Cambrian*, 27 September 1848.

140. Quoted by D. Lardner, *op. cit.*, pp. 149–50.

141. *Ibid.*, p. 20.

142. On the development of the aluminium industry see S. Moos, 'The structure of the British aluminium industry', *The Economic Journal*, December 1948; Northern Aluminium Co., Ltd., *Extraction and Fabrication of Aluminium* (Banbury, 1949); 'Aluminium', supplement to *Barclays Bank Review*, February 1953; Winifred Lewis, *The Light Metals Industry* (London, 1949).

143. A. H. John (ed.), *The Walker Family, Ironfounders and Lead Manufacturers, 1741–1893* (London, 1951), p. 5.

144. W. R. Jones, *Minerals in Industry* (Harmondsworth, 1943), p. 70.

145. D. Trevor Williams, *op. cit.*, pp. 87–8.

146. The U.S.A., Australia, Mexico and Canada are now the largest producers of lead.

147. Cf. J. Rowe, *op. cit.*, pp. 308–9, 323.

148. H. Heaton, *Economic History of Europe* (New York, revised ed., 1948). pp. 503–4.

149. David Turnbull, *Cuba* (London, 1840), quoted N. Brown and C. C. Turnbull, *A Century of Copper* (London, 1899 and 1900), Part II, p. 13.

150. *The Cambrian*, 3 July 1846; T. C. Barker and J. R. Harris, *A Merseyside Town in the Industrial Revolution: St. Helens* (Liverpool, 1954), p. 240.

151. J. Rowe, *op. cit.*, p. 130.

152. Statement by Mr. Boardman before a Select Committee of the House of Commons on 'The Copper Trade Question', *The Cambrian*, 30 April 1847.

153. Pascoe Grenfell and Charles Pascoe Grenfell, with Owen Williams and Thomas Peers Williams of the Anglesey group, were partners in the two works at Upper and Middle Bank, Swansea (University College of Swansea Library, Grenfell MS., indenture of 25 March 1828); and Pascoe Grenfell with John Williams (Scorrier, Cornwall) and Fox (? Lewis Fox) operated the Rose Smelting Works near Swansea from 1823 to 1829 (*The Cambrian*, 17 January 1824, 2 April 1825; G. C. Boase, *Collectanea Cornubiensis*, I, 1890. col. 1249; N.L.W. Nevill MSS., V, 3 June 1824, VI, 18 November 1826, 18 May 1829).

154. J. Rowe, *op. cit.*, p. 145.

155. J. F. Rippy, *Latin America and the Industrial Age* (New York, 1947), p. 188.

156. J. F. Rippy, 'British investments in Latin America, end of 1876', *Pacific Historical Review*, XVII (1948), 11–12. Cf. J. F. Rippy in *Pacific Historical Review*, XXI (1952), 342, and in *The Hispanic American Historical Review*, XXX (1949), 280, 284.

157. N. Brown and C. C. Turnbull, *op. cit.*, pp. 10, 13.

158. *Ibid.*, p. 11.

159. N. L. W., Nevill MS. 7, R. J. Nevill to C. P. Grenfell, 2 August 1830.

160. N. Brown and C. C. Turnbull, *op. cit.*, p. 16; C. J. Lambert, *Sweet Waters: A Chilean Farm* (London, 1952), p. 10.

161. Mr. Boardman's evidence to the Select Committee, *The Cambrian*, 30 April 1847.

162. *The Mining Journal*, supplement, 9 November 1872.

163. *The Cambrian*, 5 December 1851, 28 July 1854; Bank of England, Swansea branch letter book III (London to Swansea), 1 October 1852; Yorkshire Imperial Metals Ltd. MS., 'List of deeds (1885)'

164. *The Cambrian*, 23 and 29 September 1847; Yorkshire Imperial Metals Ltd. MS., 'List of deed (1885)'.

165. *Swansea and Glamorgan Herald*, 7 January 1852.

166. *The Cambrian*, 22 January 1847.

167. N. Brown and C. C. Turnbull, *op. cit.*, p. 17.

168. *Ibid.* and *The Cambrian*, 5 March 1847.

169. N. Brown and C. C. Turnbull, *op. cit.*, pp. 5, 17, 18.

170. *Ibid.*, p. 20; E. D. Peters, *op. cit.*, pp. 453–4: H. O'Neill, 'The invention of Bessemer in relation to non-ferrous metals', *Metallurgia*, LIV, 326 (December 1956), 270. I am very grateful for discussions with Professor O'Neill.

171. N. Brown and C. C. Turnbull, *op. cit.*, p. 28.

172. W. R. Jones, *op. cit.*, p. 45.

173. Pan-American Union, *Copper* (Washington, 1942), p. 7.

174. For the contents of various ores imported to Swansea in 1900 see W. O. Alexander, *op. cit.*, pp. 417–18.

175. D. Trevor Williams, *op. cit.*, p. 77.

176. N. Brown and C. C. Turnbull, *op. cit.*, pp. 9, 12.

177. Quoted in *The Cambrian*, 22 January 1847.

178. *Encyclopaedia Britannica* (9th ed. 1875)—Chile.

179. Glamorgan Record Office, Vivian MS., D/DGV/19, pp. 15, 20; N. Brown and C. C. Turnbull, *op. cit.*, pp. 18, 21.

180. The Great Lakes smelting area was later superseded, by a belt extending from Montana through Nevada and Utah to Arizona, as the main source of North American copper (S. Evelyn Thomas, *A Modern Geography* (London, 1932). II, p. 345).

181. Mr. Boardman's evidence to the Select Committee, *The Cambrian*, 30 April 1847.

182. N. Brown and C. C. Turnbull, *op. cit.*, p. 17.

183. *Ibid.*, p. 19.

184. E. D. Peters, *op. cit.*, p. 173.

185. *The Cambrian*, 11 December 1846.

186. N. Brown and C. C. Turnbull, *op. cit.*, p. 5.

187. Quoted, *ibid.*, p. iii.

188. E. D. Peters, *op. cit.*, pp. 172-3.

189. W. O. Alexander, art. cit., p. 422.

190. Dr. H. C. H. Carpenter, Cantor lectures to the Royal Society of Arts on 'Progress in the metallurgy of copper' (December 1917), quoted D. Owen Evans, art. cit., p. 23.

191. *The Cambrian*, 10 October 1856.

192. W. Smart, *Economic Annals of the Nineteenth Century, 1821–1830* (London, 1917), p. 278; T. C. Barker and J. R. Harris, *op. cit.*, p. 240; J. Rowe, *op. cit.*, pp. 122, 140-2, 308-9.

193. *The Cambrian*, 5 May 1848.

194. *Ibid*; N.L.W., Nevill MS. 8, 20 January 1841.

195. See p. 125.

196. *The Cambrian*, 5 May 1848.

197. Evidence of Edward Budd to Select Committee, *The Cambrian*, 30 April 1847.

198. N.L.W., Nevill MS. 8, 20 January 1841.

199. *Ibid.*, 1 January 1841.

200. *Ibid.*, 1 January and 4 October 1841. Cf *ibid.*, 21 and 28 May 1842 and Nevill MS. 9, 8 April 1843.

201. *The Cambrian*, 30 April 1847, 21 April 1848.

202. *The Cambrian*, 5 May 1848. Mr. Boardman gave the duty on ore as 'about £1. 10s. per ton,' *ibid.*, 30 April 1847.

203. *Ibid.*; N. Brown and C. C. Turnbull, *op. cit.*, p. 80; J. H. Clapham, *An Economic History of Modern Britain*, II (Cambridge, 1952), p. 542.

204. *The Cambrian*, 5 May 1848.

205. *Ibid.*, 30 April 1847; Thomas Boundy in *The Cambrian* of 20 April 1849 states that British works were 'deprived . . . of about *nine-tenths* of the foreign ores'.

206. *Ibid.*, 5 March and 30 April 1847, 5 May 1848.

207. *The Swansea and Glamorganshire Herald*, 26 April 1848.

208. *The Cambrian*, 5 March 1847, 5 May 1848.

209. *Ibid.*, 5 May 1848; cf. Boardman's evidence, p. 149.

210. See p. 148.

211. E. Budd's evidence, *The Cambrian*, 30 April 1847.

212. N.L.W., Nevill MS. 8, 31 October, 1845.

213. *The Cambrian*, 27 March 1846.

214. *The Cambrian*, 30 April 1847.

215 *Ibid.*; on manufacture see also R. J. Nevill's statement p. 145.

216. *The Cambrian*, 5 March 1847. The letter was signed 'Free Trade. Manchester —St. David's Day'.

217. Evidence to the Select Committee on the Copper Trade, *The Cambrian*, 30 April 1847.

218. J. H. Clapham, *op. cit.*, I, p. 133.

219. This statement and the account in the next six paragraphs are based on a long article about 'The Copper Trade Question' in *The Cambrian*, 30 April 1847.

220. *The Cambrian*, 20 April 1849.

221. N.L.W., Nevill MS. 8, R. J. Nevill to C. P. Grenfell, 1 January 1841.

222. *The Cambrian*, 5 May 1848.

223. Art. cit., p. 21; italics supplied.

224. E.g. N.L.W., Nevill MS. 9, R. J. Nevill to E. Budd, 13 May 1843.

225. E.g. N.L.W., Nevill MS. 7, R. J. Nevill to R. Mitchell, Truro, 17 July 1830.

226. I.C.I. Metals Division MS., 'Memorandum book', p. 185, H. H. Vivian to J. M. Williams, 11 May 1878.

227. *Ibid.* and Glamorgan Record Office, D/DGV/Ia, A. P. Vivian's business notebook, I, pp. 121–5.

228. Mr. Brownell's evidence, *The Cambrian*, 30 April 1847.

229. This paragraph is based on *The Cambrian*, 10 October, 7, 21 and 28 November 1856; 21 and 28 May, and 5 November 1858.

230. Quoted W. O. Alexander, *op. cit.*, p. 422.

PART THREE
BANKING

CHAPTER SEVEN

Early Banking in Cardiff

by T. M. Hodges

THE BANK, variously known during its existence as the 'Cardiff Bank', 'Wood Evans & Co'. and 'Wood, Wood & Co.', owed its origin to the enterprise of John Wood, senior, a Freeman of Cardiff, and its Town Clerk of many years standing. Wood was a man of considerable local importance and many parts, for besides possessing much valuable property in real estate, he held the offices of Treasurer to the Glamorgan County, Treasurer to the Cardiff Turnpike Trust and Captain of the Cardiff Cavalry.

It came within the scope of Wood's duties, both as Attorney and as Treasurer, to receive and pay large sums of money in cash, and also to remit and have remitted to him drafts drawn on London bankers.[1] His advent into the banking world was, therefore, but a short step outside his previous functions. He had accumulated a wide law practice in the surrounding district as a result of which he had gained a reputation for probity and honest dealing amongst local trades-people and country gentry. He was the custodian of large public funds both on account of local trusts and on that of the County itself. He had had, too, considerable practice in the negotiation of bills of exchange for and on behalf of his law clients. Furthermore, Wood was a man of quite considerable wealth, both in personal and real estate. On the personal side, there is evidence that he had an ambitious, speculative nature, and a love of power, a side of his personality which brought him into frequent conflicts with Turnpike Trustees in various parts of Glamorgan in his capacity as County Treasurer. Altogether, therefore, Wood possessed certain attributes, both material and otherwise, which his legal practice did not completely satisfy, but for which he found ample scope in his banking venture.

The exact date when the bank first commenced business is not recorded, but a statement in the bankruptcy proceedings against John Wood, junior, reads:

for several years previously to the year 1812 John Wood, the

Elder, Attorney-at-law, father of the defendant, carried on the business of a banker at Cardiff in partnership with William Tindall, Charles Evans and James Jelf, under the several titles of the Cardiff Bank, and Wood, Evans & Co.

The earliest direct reference to the 'Cardiff Bank' in the MSS. of the Wood family is 10 March 1807, on which day an entry in John Wood's Day Book contains a summary of a bill drawn by the Bank on Messrs Elton & Co. Old Bank, Bristol, which reads:

No. 663   CARDIFF BANK   Cardiff, *Mar.* 10*th* 1807
   £14 15s.
35 days pay J. Wood, Esq.

                                    for WOOD, EVANS & Co.
                                           J. W.

To MESSRS ELTON & Co.,
     OLD BANK, BRISTOL

Thereafter, frequent references to the Bank occur in the Day Book, all of which record similar summaries of bills or cheques drawn on Bristol or London banks, of which the two below are samples:

                     BRISTOL   *14th April* 1807
       MESSRS ELTON & Co., OLD BANK, BRISTOL
Pay Mr S. Strickland or bearer Seven pounds 8s. 6d.
(*Cheque*)
   £7 8s. 6d.
                               a/c CARDIFF BANK,
                               WOOD, EVANS & Co.
No. 2108   CARDIFF BANK, GLAMORGANSHIRE
                            CARDIFF, 20*th April* 1807
      £40
On demand pay Henry Lee Esq. or order forty pounds, value received.
(*Bill*)
                              For WOOD, EVANS & Co.,
                                J. WOOD

MESSRS ROBARTS, CURTIS & Co.
     LONDON

Taking as evidence the serial number of the first bill of which there is existing record, and comparing it with that of the bill recorded a month or so later, it may be conjectured from their rate of issue that the Bank started functioning at some date early in 1807, there being no reference to the Bank in the year 1806.

Wood, the elder, had four children—three sons, John, Nicholl and Frederick, and a daughter, Mary Ann—all of whom became directly or indirectly implicated in the affairs of the Bank by virtue of the fact that certain Trust moneys of theirs were borrowed at one time by John Wood, junior, to assist the Bank finances at a time of stringency. This experience of Wood's Bank illustrates in striking fashion the sort of contingency which was an indigenous part of country banking in those days owing to a combination of weaknesses in its structure.

The more serious of these shortcomings were the unlimited nature of the liability, the dangerously small amount of capital, the inadequacy of reserves, and the small possibility of spreading risks which were more often than not tied up in a very specialized part of trade. The danger to be avoided at any cost was that of arousing the extreme sensitiveness of the public to a suspected 'run on the bank'. No wonder that the country bank was considered 'a constant source of weakness in a flimsy, ill-balanced banking structure'.

John Wood, junior, and his brother Nicholl, followed their father's original calling in law, and were practising as attorneys and solicitors in partnership in 1812. In November of that year, however, John Wood, junior, at the age of thirty-two, was taken into partnership in the banking business, and from that date onwards made banking his main occupation. This was all to the good of the Bank. So many of the country banks, while deriving strength from the trade connections of their owners, were exposed simultaneously to the dangers arising from a lack of specialized direction which could only be remedied by unremitting efforts in banking as a sole occupation.

In April 1813, William Tindall, Charles Evans and (Sir) James Jelf, the three original partners of the elder Wood, retired from the Bank, though the latter two remained customers throughout its existence, being major debtors at the time of bankruptcy. No stronger reason is given for their retirement than the absorbing ambition of the elder Wood to make the Bank a purely family affair. The occasion was, however, used to take into partnership one Thomas Morgan, a minion of the family with some capital, and the name of the Bank was changed to 'Wood, Wood & Co.', though the alternative title remained in constant use throughout its history.

The three partners, John Wood, senior; John Wood, junior; and Thomas Morgan contributed capital and shared profits and losses in the proportions of 2:2:1 respectively, profits being distributed every six months. Unfortunately, the records do not state the amount of capital contributed by each, except to say that at the death of John Wood, senior, on 10 October 1817, he was indebted to the Bank to the amount of £8699 12s. 2d. Privately, however, the elder Wood at the time of his death was a comparatively rich man, owning property both in Cardiff and in the neighbourhood, besides possessing shares in a number of canal and tramroad companies. On the death of John Wood, senior, the Bank ownership became a purely family concern, for Thomas Morgan received his share of capital and profits and retired in order to take over the administration of the deceased Wood's estate, a special account being opened in the Bank for this purpose.

The prestige of family banks in those days was influenced far more by the disclosed fortune of a deceased member than by the extent of the bank capital owing to the unlimited liability attaching to bank ownership. The knowledge that such fortune remained at the call of the surviving members as a sort of reserve to be made available in times of temporary financial embarrassment served to allay the incipient fears of the bank's customers.

From the date of his father's death onwards, John Wood, junior, continued as sole owner of the Bank, and in the next year gave up his law partnership with his brother Nicholl in order to devote the whole of his time and energies to banking. Notice of the dissolution is recorded thus: 'This partnership was dissolved in March 1818, when John Wood was (at his own request) struck off the Roll of Attorneys.'

It was the very essence of country banking to maintain intimate contact with the big private banks in London, who acted as agents. Country banks held current accounts with these agents upon whom they drew in order to discharge distant debts for their local customers. They augmented these London balances from time to time by ordering metropolitan debtors to meet their obligations by paying into the banks of the London agents. The latter cashed the country bank-notes which by arrangement could be cashed at the bank of origin or in London. Other functions fulfilled by these agents, acting in co-operation with the country banks, were the negotiation of bills of exchange, drafts, letters of credit, etc. Finally, they constituted a sort of final reserve for surplus funds, and were also extremely useful on occasion in providing accommodation when funds were tight. Contact between London and the provinces at best was perfunctory owing to the poorness of communications, and depended entirely upon the regularity of the mail coach services.

For this reason, amongst others, some country banks were prevented from having London accounts. The Cardiff Bank was very fortunate in that a daily coach service connected it with the metropolis. This coach started daily from Stag Lane and arrived in Cardiff each morning *en route* to Milford Haven to meet the Irish Mail at Hubberstone, Pembrokeshire, returning thence through the vale of Glamorgan and connecting such places as Swansea, Neath and Cowbridge *en route*. That the coach was put to the service of the Bank regularly is evidenced by references to money being sent by this means, e.g. 'A/c of Thos. Bassett, Bonvilstone, with Wood, Wood & Co. Dr. entry June 1820. Notes by coach, £100.'

The London agents of the 'Cardiff Bank' were Robarts, Curtis & Co., later known as Sir William Curtis & Co., and early references in John Wood's Day Book show that John Wood, senior, in his function as attorney and treasurer had had dealings with Robarts, Curtis & Co. before his banking days. In the year 1812, the 'Cardiff Bank' had a favourable balance with Robarts, Curtis & Co. to the amount of £1293 12s. 3d., and by the date of Thomas Morgan's entry into partnership in 1813, the credit balance had grown to £5435 14s. 2d. No doubt, an appreciable part of the increase was due to the new partner's capital contribution to the Bank. During the next few years, however, this favourable position was no longer enjoyed, for by the year 1817 there was an adverse balance with the London bankers to the amount of £8089 16s. 10d. At the time of the death of the elder Wood, on 10 October 1817, the assets of the Bank amounted to £43,295 15s. 10d., made up of debts from sundry persons. The liabilities of the Bank at that date amounted to £43,329 14s. 11d. While this position apparently showed only a small adverse balance, the true position was not so healthy in that, of the debts due to the Bank, the Woods themselves, father and son, owed £15,002 10s. Of this sum, the estate of the deceased Wood was liable for £8699 12s. 2d., while the remainder was chargeable against the private estate of John Wood, junior.

Subsequent to the death of the elder Wood, the Bank under his son's sole ownership and direction prospered sufficiently to wipe off all the debts with the exception of the sum due to Sir William Curtis & Co., which was chargeable against the estate of the deceased Wood. In order to achieve this favourable position, the younger Wood had secured a loan of £8000 in February 1818, from the trust fund of £20,500 created by Henry Hurst's marriage settlement to his daughter, the elder Wood's wife (deceased), and administered for the benefit of her children, of whom John Wood, junior, was the eldest. On 21 March 1818, the latter applied £5000 of this loan towards liquidating his Bank's indebtedness with its London agents, while the remaining £3000 he advanced to his brother Nicholl, securing a mortgage on the latter's property as collateral.

Like many other contemporary Welsh banks, the 'Cardiff Bank' was a note-issuing bank. Notes were issued of the following denominations: £1, £1 1s., £5 and £10, payable on demand either at Cardiff or London. The notes carried a picture of a castle executed on the left side of the note, which bore the inscription underneath, 'Mutlow s.c. London'. There is a memorandum showing a list of holders of £1 and £1 1s. bank-notes to the total value of £41 6s., which were called in at the time of the Bank's failure. These were all held by local people, most of whom were persons of small means, such as labourers, small farmers, tradespeople, and small gentry. The amount of note issue is not stated, but in the Bank's account with its London agents for 1819—taking this as a representative year—a debit item 'Notes' appears regularly every week for an average amount of £450, with a total for the year of £22,274 5s.

It would be highly satisfactory to be able to give exact statistics of notes issued, bills negotiated, loans made, interest charged, and the number and kind of investments. Unfortunately, this is not possible, partly because the method of keeping accounts in those days left much to be desired in the proper classification of items. An omnibus account into which a heterogeneous mixture of debits and credits was entered seemed to be the core of the accounting system, whose chronological merits only serve to accentuate its lack of classified information. Some idea of the scope of the banking business may be gleaned, however, from the total quarterly debits and credits of the 'Cardiff Bank' in the books of Sir William Curtis & Co., the London agents. These show quarterly totals on the debit side for amounts ranging from £25,000 to £42,000. Corresponding credits fell short of these in all quarters between the years 1819 and 1823, except for that ending June 1820, when a net credit balance of £598 8s. 10d. was shown in favour of the 'Cardiff Bank'. The gradually worsening position of the Bank is shown by the increasing size in the debit balances from 1820 onwards, reaching the amount of £17,384 3s. 4d. at the time of the Bank's failure.

Cardiff banking connections with the industrial hinterland were meagre at this time. This may be attributable to the fact that Cardiff had not yet developed greatly as an outlet for inland industrial products, and drew its prosperity from the surrounding agricultural area. More important still, however, was the fact that there existed in Merthyr Tydfil two banks, one known as the 'Merthyr Tydfil Bank', owned by Thomas Peirce, David Williams & Co., and the other known as the 'Cyfarthfa Ironworks Bank', owned by the iron-masters Crawshay, Hall and Bailey, whose London bankers were Messrs Were, Bruce, Simson & Co. Nearby, in Aberdare, where iron-making was also well established, though on a smaller scale, was the 'Abernant Ironworks Bank', owned by James Tappenden and Francis Tappenden. It is not surprising, therefore, that nearly all the customers of the 'Cardiff Bank' resided either in Cardiff itself, or in the agricultural vale of Glamorgan. These customers were for the most part small traders from Cardiff and district, or farmers and gentry. The Bank's main functions in this community seemed to be those of receiving local deposits, issuing notes, settling distant debts for its customers, and lending money to finance deals in property and real estate, accepting collateral on these loans in the form of deeds.

No exact figure is given of the number of individual accounts at any one time in the books of the Bank, but at the time of its failure there were 210 separate debit and credit balances, of which 109 were debit items of debts due to the Bank, amounting in all to nearly £15,000. The listed credit items forming the remaining one hundred odd accounts amounted to over £46,000, of which the debt due to the London agents formed by far the largest single entry, being over half the total. The above total does not include the individual accounts kept by the London agents on behalf of the 'Cardiff Bank', the number of which would bring the total up to well over 300.

Many of the chief local gentry and industrialists availed them-selves of the Bank's services from time to time for the settlement of debts due in London or Bristol. One entry in the name of the Mar-quis of Bute, dated 22 June 1823, was for £5201, representing a transfer of funds for the purpose of a debt settlement in London. Entries crediting prominent local industrialists such as Crawshay, Guest & Co., the Dowlais Co., and Harford, of the Melingriffith Tinworks, Whitchurch, appeared frequently. Those in the name of Crawshay were for sums varying from £400 to £600 in single items, being no doubt sums paid in London for ironwork shipped from Cardiff. The credits appearing in the name of a prominent local coalowner, Robert Thomas, probably originated in payments for shipments of coal to London, which were just then commencing. Curiously enough, very few entries carried the names of other banks, though entries for relatively small sums appeared in the names Coutts & Co., Glyn & Co., Barclays & Co., and Sir John Lubbock & Co.

John Wood, junior, seemed to confine his own investments to

three types, namely, real estate, canals and railroads, and exchequer bills, of which the first absorbed by far the greatest amount of his capital outlay. At the time of his bankruptcy, his investments in canal and similar undertakings were relatively small. They included:

	£	s.	d.
Five shares in the Monmouthshire Canal	1203	16	2
Four debentures in the Monmouthshire Canal	394	11	8
Two shares in the Meath Navigation	244	19	6
Five shares in the Aberdeen Canal ⎱	200	0	0
One share in the Hay Railway ⎰			
One debenture in Remmer's Bridge Trust	100	0	0

Curiously enough he held no shares in the Glamorganshire Canal which ran through his own town, and which contributed so materially to its early prosperity and growth. This may be attributed to the fact that the local industrialists, like Crawshay, who had initiated the enterprise at the end of the eighteenth century, had concentrated the ownership of this very lucrative venture into their own hands.

The 'Cardiff Bank' suffered like many other country banks from excessive concentration of resources on too narrow a range of investments. Had these banking pioneers had the opportunity or the perspicacity to spread their assets while maintaining a due regard for liquidity, they would have been better able to minimize their risks and so weather the economic storms of the era following the Napoleonic wars. So often, however, they had tied the fortunes of their banks to those of a few trades or firms whose misfortune spelt disaster to the banks. In the case of the 'Cardiff Bank', its owner had concentrated on real estate investment which, however lucrative, was not the best form in which to maintain bank assets, especially when the slightest rumour of stringency was likely to cause a local 'run' on the bank. It was such a lack of liquidity which compelled Wood to draw more and more on his London agents for accommodation, who naturally soon acquired a large proportion of his collateral.

Conditions got steadily worse throughout 1822. The assets of the Bank, largely tied up in fixed capital, became immobilized in the hands of the London agents, as security for debts already outstanding with them. The news that all was not well with the Bank leaked out in 1822 from several quarters. For instance, on 25 July of that year Thomas Bassett, Solicitor, of Bonvilston, wrote to Mr George Jenner, Gentleman, of Wenvoe:

Mr Wood owes money to the Aubrey Arms Club and has evaded payment by repeatedly ignoring demands. I will pay the debt myself and send the Bond to the Bank to be deducted out of what I owe there and for which I am now paying exhorbitant interest.

In the same year, too, the finances of the Cardiff Cavalry, of which John Wood was an Officer and Treasurer, were the subject of inquiry. Around about this time, too, John Wood and his brother Nicholl brought a successful action for slander against a local tradesman, the publicity of which did not improve matters despite the result. It is not surprising, therefore, that rumours that the Bank was in difficulties caused a 'run', and on the morning of 17 September 1822, the townspeople of Cardiff were thrown into consternation by the appearance of the following notice attached to the Bank premises in Duke Street:

> Messrs Wood, Wood & Co., Bankers, Cardiff, having stopped payment, a Meeting will be held at the Town Hall, in Cardiff, on Saturday next, at 12 o'clock, when and where the creditors are requested to attend.
>
> Cardiff, 17th Sept. 1822.

A little less than a year later John Wood was declared a bankrupt, and his estate was thenceforth sold by auction to discharge his Bank's indebtedness.

The contributory causes of the Bank's failure are not suggested in the bankruptcy proceedings, but an examination of the Bank's activities, or what amounts to the same thing, those of its owner, supports what has already been said about the unwiseness of tying up the bulk of his assets in fixed investments like real estate, which made it impossible for him to meet the demands of his customers for cash in return for the Bank's notes. Accommodation from London became no longer available when his agents refused to honour his notes. By the time of his bankruptcy he had deposited deeds with them to the value of £26,386 3s. 4d. to cover debts to that amount. Furthermore, the assignees appointed by the Commission of Bankruptcy proved additional debts due to the amount of £19,759 10s. 10d. As the title deeds of a great portion of Wood's estate had already been appropriated to secure the London debts, the sum of £19,759 10s. 10d. was unsecured by collateral, and a dividend of 6s. in the £1 was declared. The £6000 odd necessary to meet this dividend came from the residue of Wood's estate not already secured by Curtis & Co., and included debts received, money in the Bank, together with proceeds of the sale of furniture and farm stock.

The failure of the 'Cardiff Bank', which for sixteen years had been the sole depository, issuer and lender in the area, naturally caused a first-class sensation in the neighbourhood. Wood, in a letter written at the time of his failure, says 'the Gentleman who has been in treaty with me for my Banking concern is to let me know his answer to-morrow and if he does not accept the proposals I have another in view'. This suggests that others hoped to succeed where he failed. No record exists, however, of a successor until the West of England and South Wales Bank opened years later. The echo of the failure of 'Wood, Wood & Co.' did not die away for another twenty-two years, for in the year 1845 an announcement by printed bill advised all creditors of the payment of a final dividend.

NOTE

1. John Wood's Day Book (1806–7), Cardiff Library. John Wood, senior, was entered on the Roll of Attorneys in 1785.

CHAPTER EIGHT

Bank of England Branch Discounting (1826-59)

by R. O. Roberts

I N May 1826 the Government placed beyond doubt the right of the Bank of England to set up provincial branches, and it pressed for their immediate establishment. The Bank quickly complied and created 'Branch Banks' which shared with Threadneedle Street the aim of 'monopolizing to themselves the circulation of the country'.[1] This object was largely to be furthered by the Branches through paying out their own notes for bills discounted with them. The following account of such discounting is largely based on the records of the Branch Bank at Swansea,[2] where the nature of the operations, though not their magnitude, seems to have been fairly typical.

It has been suggested that the Branches were established not in the places most in need of financial rehabilitation but in those offering the best opportunities of making profits and combating the newly legalized joint-stock banks.[3] The Branch Bank at Swansea was opened in October 1826, and the story of its establishment shows the Bank of England as seeking to serve both society and its shareholders by choosing to operate in a place that promised a good profit.[4] In the region of this new Branch Bank—to be precise, in the 'district' of the banks of Wilkins & Co. in Brecon and Merthyr—'very few' Bank of England notes circulated before 1826.[5]

A discount account at a Branch was allowed only after Threadneedle Street had investigated thoroughly the credit-worthiness of the proposed discounter—and the Branch Bank Letter Books are, therefore, a useful source of entrepreneurial history. L. W. Dillwyn, who had done much to bring the Branch to Swansea, was refused an account, despite his 'high Credit', because he was not 'actually engaged in Trade'; and where a discount account was granted to a trader it was given an upper limit. During its early years the Branch Bank allowed a number of discount accounts, with limits up to £20,000, for iron and copper firms.

A discount account could be granted to an agent acting on behalf of a firm, upon the guarantee of the latter, as in the case of John Borlase Jenkins acting at Swansea for Pascoe Grenfell & Co., the copper smelters. The agents of the Branch Banks, however, were continually enjoined to be cautious in their review of lists of discounters and, following the insolvency of Messrs. Hindes & Derham at Leeds, they were to watch especially those who had additional discount accounts at other banks.

Discount accounts 'for circulation' at specially favourable rates were granted from 1830 onwards to such banks as gave up issuing their own and other country bank notes and agreed not to re-issue bills.[6] These facilities were extended to a number of banks in the Manchester and Liverpool area which, as is well known, did not issue their own notes.[7] Such 'Circulation Accounts' were sometimes confusingly known as 'Loan Accounts' and the accommodation granted through them was secured by the deposit of title deeds of property and, if it were considered necessary, by a legal mortgage. Discounted bills or bonds also 'might be taken . . . as Collateral Security, and the amount as received . . . become immediately at their disposal, other bills of equal value . . . being deposited with you in their stead'. One bank could provide a guarantee for another, as Cocks, Biddulph and Biddulph of Charing Cross did for their 'friends' Biddulph Brothers and Co. of Carmarthen. A banker satisfying the conditions could have a discount account with a fixed amount at a relatively low rate (e.g., 3 per cent in 1835) if he did not fall below the fixed maximum by more than 12 to 15 per cent—a range 'found quite sufficient' to allow for fluctuations of business. Or the amount of discounts could remain 'open' and the banker 'would pay the current market rate as fixed by the Bank, and on an average of years does not much exceed 3 per cent'. At least one bank, Biddulph Brothers & Co., agreed not to discount elsewhere while the amount under discount at the Swansea Branch was below their maximum—which was £46,000.[8]

Bills, whether presented by traders or bankers, were closely scrutinized by the Branch before discounting,[9] but it was found difficult to obtain 'sound information in Swansea' about discounters, and the exact nature of the bills sometimes eluded the staff of the Branch, 'even with the extended means of information which you have so judiciously obtained'.

Bills, drawn by the customer of a Branch were favoured less than those, drawn by someone else, which had come into his possession in the normal course of trade.[10] It was stated in 1828 that 'it certainly never was contemplated to discount bills drawn' by customers, whereas negotiable bills coming into the hands of 'Country Gentlemen and others receiving rents' would be discounted in order 'to check in a limited degree their circulation as money'. If a customer regularly pressed upon the Branch his own drafts 'and never offers business bills, *not drawn by himself*, it may without hesitation be assumed that he is leaning on the bank for capital'; and such an account should be judiciously reduced.

It was a 'fundamental Rule' of the Bank that each bill should have 'two distinct securities independently of our Discounter'. The standing of the drawee and the other acceptor(s) was of course carefully investigated; and bills drawn by one branch of a firm upon another were rarely accepted. A number of such bills were refused in 1827 and 1828 since they clearly represented attempts to obtain additional capital.

The bills of a corporation were not discounted if there was uncertainty about the authority of the person accepting them. Bills accepted outside Britain were not welcomed in the early years of the Branch, and if possible bills should be payable at banks. The endorsements on 'indirect bills' had to be well examined, and renewed bills were discouraged.

'Accommodation bills' were frowned upon by the Branch Banks Committee in 1826, and it was explained in 1829 that discounts granted by the Branch Bank were 'presumed to be *occasional* accommodations'. To be eligible for discount at the Branch, bills should be the result of 'bona fide transactions' and should 'really represent the Trade of the district'. It was explained that 'Discounts are effected by the Bank not to enable manufacturers to *hold* but to dispose of their goods—to give facilities to actual traders and not to encourage the increase of manufacturers which the present state of the market evidently proves to be unnecessary'. These sentiments and, indeed, the terminology echoed the earlier theories (though not the practice) of Liverpool merchants.[11]

Banks such as Wilkins's of Brecon habitually advanced on good iron trade bills 'even six months after date', but the bills discounted at the Branch Banks were normally of the three-month variety, which the Bank had allowed since 1822.[12] In 1830, however, it was conceded that advances might '*with due discretion*' be made to the much-favoured firm of Vivian & Sons upon bills of four or six months' usance.

The Swansea Branch Bank agent wrote in 1842 that in his locality 'the Colliers do a considerable Business but the great one of the place is smelting copper, imported and paid for by Bills on London'. Much of the discount business which the Branch Bank transacted was undertaken for the copper smelting firms, but the Branch handled only a small proportion of their bills. No evidence has been found that paper representing purchases of ore by the copper firms was discounted at Swansea. As for the finished metal, it was 'shipped to London, Liverpool, Bristol, etc., and then sold chiefly on credit' and largely, though not wholly, for six-month bills. It was believed that the smelting firms discounted such bills 'in the cheapest market, occasionally to a large extent': Vivian & Sons, for example, divided their discount transactions between London and Liverpool; and their desire, in 1836, to confine their discounts to the Swansea Branch did not bear much fruit. Indeed, like other copper smelters, Vivian & Sons used the Branch Bank mainly for making wage, duty, freight and other current payments on behalf of their works near Swansea.

Various other types of bills were discounted at the Branch Bank. Those of the coal trade were for sales of coal to copper works, and, sometimes with ironstone, to ironworks. There were bills for iron supplied to tinplate manufacturers, but usually the iron trade's bills, arising from the sale of metal, were six-month bills and thus ineligible for discount. (Only a few of the iron firms, such as Crawshay & Co. and Harford & Co., seem to have obtained discount accounts at the Branch.) Arrangements were made as the Branch Bank in 1855 for discounting bills arising from deliveries of ores to the Landore silver works. Bills, payable at such houses as Cocks's and Child's, and drawn by merchants dealing in coal, 'Drugs, Wine, Groceries and Oats', were also discounted as long as the acceptances were good. Despite the relatively high rate of stamp duties on them, medium and small bills of this kind were common in South Wales—for 'such . . . is the system of doing business in these districts'.[13] Bills drawn by railway-construction contractors upon railway companies were not to be discounted at the Branch Banks.

The discounting of bills for bankers had as its purpose 'the entire withdrawal of their own circulation', for without this 'the circulation of the Banker . . . must drive out that of the Bank while it rests upon it.' Here the comment from Threadneedle Street in 1831 on the application of a Cardiff bank, Towgood & Co., for a discount account at the Swansea Branch is illuminating: 'If the request to discount with you was made merely to uphold their own circulation it cannot of course be admitted, it being a clearly ascertained fact that monies so obtained are not used for country circulation but are transmitted immediately to London to meet the Bills due in London drawn in payment of the said circulation—your issue for that purpose becomes therefore *substantially* a London issue, and extends so far the liabilities of the Bank to sudden demands for gold.' The aim of the Bank was not 'monopoly in order to profit, but . . . a more manageable circulating medium throughout the country.' In 1827 and 1828 the Swansea Branch Bank opened temporary discount accounts for local banks to enable them to obtain sovereigns for the £1 notes which were then being withdrawn.[14] Under what was known as 'Rule 32', such accounts were granted to Walters, Voss & Walters of Swansea, Williams & Rowland of Neath, Wilkins & Co. of Brecon, and Waters, Jones & Co. of Carmarthen. Discounts to Waters, Jones & Co. reached 'upwards of £35,000' in the shadow of their Loan Account due to lack of vigilance on the part of the agent. It was made quite clear from the start, however, that 'general' discount accounts would be arranged only for such banks as agreed not to issue their own notes.[15] In February 1829 (a year before the concessions for non-issuing came into force in the case of the Birmingham Banking Co.),[16] Walters, Voss & Co. were granted 'a Discount and Drawing Account for general purposes' with £10,000 as the limit of the discounts allowed at any one time. In 1831 Waters, Jones & Co. were to be informed that, in order to have a general discount account, 'not only . . . they should discontinue issuing and circulating their own paper, but that also of other Bankers'. Walters, Voss & Co. and another Swansea bank, Eaton, Knight & Stroud, had their accounts threatened with closure in 1835, after Threadneedle Street had been 'reliably' informed that they had issued notes other than those of the Bank of England. (The informants were the bankers Messrs. Biddulph of Carmarthen and Henry Verity of Bridgend.) In 1836, however, Eaton & Co. still held their account, and that of Walters, Voss & Co. was continuing in 1841. As mentioned earlier, a discount account having a specified range was opened in 1834 for the bank of Biddulph Brothers & Co. of Carmarthen, and in the following year a 'fixed' account of this type was obtained by Edmund J. Jones of Hereford and by Henry Verity of Bridgend. (Verity's account was at first to remain 'open' for a trial period of twelve months.) By 1841, however, immediately after the union of Walters, Voss & Co. with the Glamorganshire Banking Co., the Swansea Branch held only one 'fixed' account—that of Biddulph Brothers & Co., which was wound up at the close of 1844.[17]

A list of the 'open' discount accounts at the Swansea Branch Bank is shown in the following quotation: 'An Account of the Country Banks which have been supplied with or are now receiving Bank Notes and Coin, and which Act only with Bank of England Paper, but which do not take a fixed amount for circulation, from 1832 to 1847 both inclusive:

Year	No. of banks	Names
1832	1	Eaton, Knight and Stroud
1833	2	Eaton, Knight and Stroud
		R. J. Nevill
1834	2	Eaton, Knight and Stroud
		R. J. Nevill
1835	3	Eaton, Knight and Stroud
		R. J. Nevill
		Jones, Williams & Co.
1836	4	Eaton, Knight and Co.
		Jones, Williams & Co.
		Rowland & Stroud
		Glamorganshire Banking Co.
1837	2	Jones, Williams & Co.
		Glamorganshire Banking Co.
[1838–47	1	Glamorganshire Banking Co.]'

Upon the advice of its London agent, Samuel Jones Loyd, the new Glamorganshire Bank in 1836 decided not to issue its own notes, and the Branch Bank opened an account for it.[18] The Glamorganshire Banking Co., however, were dissatisfied with the terms (a discount account up to £10,000 at the market rate) allowed to them in exchange for withdrawing the very popular Williams and Rowland notes, and for displacing National Provincial notes by 'pushing' those of the Bank of England. Their protest, in which they were supported by the Branch agent, failed to move the Governors.[19]

By the Bank Charter Act of 1844 (7 and 8 Vict., C.32, Sections XXIII and XXIV) agreements previously made between the Bank of England and other banks, whereby the latter refrained from issuing their own notes, were to terminate on 31 December 1844; and thereafter the Bank of England could allow to such banks 'a Composition' of 1 per cent per annum on the Bank of England notes circulated by them. Biddulph Brothers & Co. was one of the banks named in the schedule attached to the Act; and it operated under the system specified.[20] The Glamorganshire Banking Co. did not appear in the official schedule though, from the beginning, it had not exercised its right of note issue.

The movements of discounts at the Swansea Branch and at all the Branch Banks is shown in the following graph and in the table on page 186. The data for the early years support Clapham's statement that the Branches were 'quickly and uncommonly successful' in obtaining discount business.[21] The course of total discounts was fairly similar at Swansea to what it was at all Branches until the 1850s—though there was a sharper fall in Swansea than in all Branch discounts during the slump of 1836–8, and also though the subsequent rapid recovery of total discounts at all the Branches in

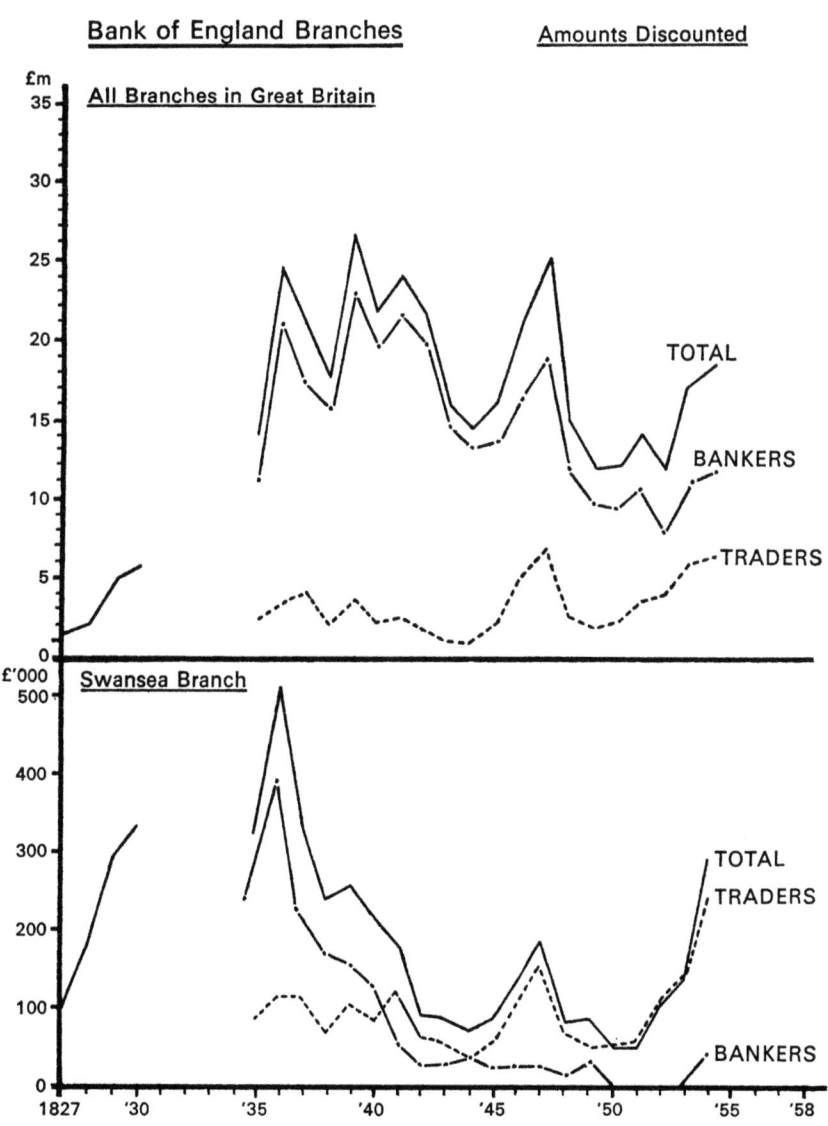

Bank of England Branches   Amounts Discounted

All Branches in Great Britain

Swansea Branch

TOTAL

BANKERS

TRADERS

TOTAL
TRADERS

BANKERS

1838–42 was not reflected in the Swansea figures. Discounts at Swansea as at all Branches climbed from a trough in 1844 to another peak in 1847.

Unfortunately the amounts of Branch Bank discounts are given only for whole years, and this prevents close study of their relationship to trade cycles. What does emerge is that total Branch discounts —on which the rates were relatively stable—increased in years of financial stringency and fell when credit could be obtained more freely. (The significance of Branch Bank discounts is underlined by the fact that, except perhaps for 1836–7, they were larger than those of Threadneedle Street from 1831–2 until the Act of 1844: thenceforth until 1914 they remained nearly as large and occasionally larger.)[22]

Discounts to traders at Swansea were very similar in their movements to those at all Branches throughout the period. Discounts to bankers, however, moved dissimilarly, and their failure to recover at Swansea after 1836 is the most notable feature of the Swansea statistics. This failure was due very largely to the sending of bills to London by the dissatisfied Glamorganshire Bank, and it was a very serious matter for the Swansea Branch since most of its discounts until 1840—as of those of its much larger counterparts in Birmingham, Liverpool and Manchester over a longer period—were for the banks. Sir John Clapham refers to these towns as 'the three principal centres of the tied-bank system'.[23]

Even during the period when the secular trend of Swansea Branch discounts was steadily upwards some uneasiness was felt at the Bank. The Principal of the Branch Banks Office, J. R. Elsey, observed as early as 1833 that the discount accounts at Swansea for 'the Brecon Bank and some few manufacturers in the District' were 'operated on but to a very trifling extent'. And he stated 'with regard to the Bankers generally and Mr. Nevill in particular they will not come to you for discounts while they can do without your aid'. As for discounting directly for manufacturers and traders, 'the Coal and Copper Works are the chief Sources of Trade, but most of the parties engaged therein are attached to the local Bankers'.

Statistics for the creation of inland bills of the medium and long varieties display a secular growth during the period covered by this paper;[24] and, therefore, the failure of discounts at the Branches to expand after 1836 seems not to have been due to any lack of bills.

The discount business at the Branches was, of course, kept down, probably from the very beginning, by the strict rules described above governing the grant of discount accounts and the nature of the bills handled. The Swansea Branch letters contain good examples of the way in which these restrictions prevented the growth of discount business. The general restriction to bills of three months prevented the Branch Bank from obtaining more than a small part of the rapidly growing business of the South Wales iron works. Again, in 1842 and 1848, assistance was refused to the Cobre Mining Association, which was 'probably the largest' importer of copper ore to Britain. Under revised tariff arrangements in 1842 they became liable to pay upwards of £35,000 annually in duties, and difficulty was encountered because 'the major part' had to be paid when the cargoes arrived, whereas the latter required 'some little time to sell'. (Though duties were lowered in 1842, imported ores could no longer escape taxation by being smelted in bond and the produce exported.) To explain the refusal of the Bank to advance on the bills offered by the Association, the Governor reiterated that 'the drafts of the Agents on their principals could not be eligible for discount'. Unfortunately, no London to Swansea letters for the period 15 August–21 September 1842, seem to have survived; but a letter in the other direction shows that the Monmouthshire and Glamorganshire Banking Co., which already transacted business for the Cobre Association at Swansea (charging 5 per cent with ¼ per cent commission for discounts), lost the additional business arising out of the import duties to the Glamorgan Banking Co. who undertook it at their current rate and without any commission.

The restrictions imposed by the Bank are also illustrated by the sudden contraction of discounts at the Branch Banks for bankers and for traders in the spring of 1847—a contraction which did not enhance the reputation of the Branches.[25] The refusals of discounts during that period of financial panic were said by the Governor to be due to the Bank's inability to allow the agents at the Branches 'the same discretion as we can exercise in London'.[26]

The rates of discount charged at the Branch Banks had a considerable effect on the amount of their business. The financial importance of the Branch Bank rates was more generally recognized in the early period of open market operations when, in 1831, the Court of Directors of the Bank of England resolved that 'in the event of the Governor and Deputy Governor not being able to proceed with a sale of Exchequer Bills while a continued loss of treasure is incurred they are authorized to resort to an advance in the rate of interest at the Branch Banks . . . first communicating with his Majesty's Ministers'[27] In the early 1830s they offered accommodation on relatively favourable terms: their rates for non-issuing bankers with 'fixed' accounts were 1 per cent below the Bank rate and, unlike the country banks, they did not also charge a commission.[28] Nevertheless, Mr. King concluded that these advantages were so offset by the 'red tape' which enveloped their discounting operations that they did not take away much business from other banks; and his view receives a little support from the statistics of a Liverpool bank provided by Dr. Pressnell.[29]

In the late 1830s the maximum and minimum rates of discount at the Branch Banks were the same as those of Threadneedle Street but this equality was ended in September 1844 by the much discussed lowering of the Bank Rate.[30] Discount rates at the Branches henceforth exceeded the published Bank Rate by amounts varying (at least from $\frac{1}{4}$ to $1\frac{1}{2}$) according to the prevailing charges of banks in the vicinity of the Branch Bank. Thus the Swansea minimum in 1845 was 4 per cent as against $2\frac{1}{2}$ per cent in London, and at the Birmingham Branch 'the rate is the London rate with the addition of $\frac{1}{2}$ per cent for bank bills, and 1 per cent discount for general commercial bills'.[31] Five Liverpool banks presented a united front in 1848 and even secured that the discount rate at their local Branch would be $\frac{3}{4}$ per cent below the Bank Rate.[32] The relationship in practice between Branch discount rates and Bank Rate is obscured, however, by the fact that the Bank sometimes charged considerably more than the published Rate.'[33] Nevertheless, the Swansea Branch, like probably all the others, became greatly concerned at its high discount charge. John Biddulph, the newly-appointed agent, was asked in 1845 to enquire 'as to the probability of an increase of discounts in the event of the rate . . . being more assimilated to that of London . . .' and he found that the price elasticity of demand was considerable. He observed: 'Mr. Joseph Price of the Neath Abbey Iron Works, who has a discount acct. with us but never makes use of it because he can get his bills cheaper done in London, stated to me . . . that he would bring us all the bills he now sends to London if he could have them discounted at the same rate as he pays there, vizt. 3 per cent for Bills having not more than 3 mos. to run, $3\frac{1}{2}$ per cent do. of 6 mos. date and under. Messrs. Benson & Co. and Messrs. Vivian & Sons have led me to believe the same—the former never make use of the disc acct which has been granted to them and the latter only for the use of their Works.' Lower rates also 'might eventually induce the Glamorganshire Banking Compy to discount with the Branch instead of sending to London as they must now do'. Biddulph concluded that 'all we require to procure a share of safe paper, is an approximation to the London rate of discount', and suggested 'that *two* rates might be applied advantageously to this Branch—the lowest I conceive would include the Bills generally offered by our principal customers'. Such an arrangement was in fact adopted, following the definition of first class and of second class bills in June 1847 and March 1850. In 1851 the Directors resolved: 'That until otherwise instructed the Agents be authorized to discount . . . at ½ per cent above the Bank's minimum rate in London, or ¼ per cent above the minimum rate at the Branch Banks.'

There is no doubt that the smallness of the discount business at the Swansea Branch from the late 1830s onwards was partly due to penetration of the area by joint-stock banks. As early as 1835 the private banks of Morris & Sons, and Waters, Jones & Co. of Carmarthen were 'annoyed by Branches of Joint Stock Banks interfering with the ground which they have occupied for years'; and the joint-stock banks were only beginning to influence south Wales at that time. In the following year, the Bank of England was 'disinclined to enter into new arrangements with Joint Stock Banks' before the publication of a report on them by the Parliamentary Committee then sitting, but such arrangements were then made for the Gloucestershire and the Glamorganshire Banking Companies.[34] In 1841 the Monmouthshire and Glamorganshire Banking Co. obtained a discount account at the Bristol Branch Bank with a drawing account at the Swansea Branch; and in 1847 the Glamorganshire Banking Co., which had been the largest circulator of Swansea Branch notes, obtained a new discount account at the Swansea Branch Bank. The latter was continually on guard against joint-stock banks that issued notes. In 1841 T. L. Whitehouse commented on the projected non-issuing bank of Thomas and David Walters at Swansea that 'we have clearly the command of the Circulation thro' the Glamorganshire Banking Company and the Walters cannot keep out any addition to our actual amounts tho' their taking the ground may prevent the Natl. Provincial, North and South Wales or any other issuing body from attempting to come here.' In addition, a new rule had been adopted by the Bank in the mid-1830s whereby bills bearing the endorsements of such joint-stock banks would not be discounted in Threadneedle Street or the Branches,[25] but no example has been seen of its operation in south Wales. It was stated, however, in 1859, when the Swansea Branch Bank was closed, that the West of England and South Wales Bank and the Glamorganshire District Bank 'commanded the whole Trade of the Town and vicinity of Swansea', and that they did so by 'the discount of Paper not admissible at the Bank of England Branch'.

During the second quarter of the nineteenth century the Bank of England was not very important as a direct provider of business finance, though the discount services which its Branches provided directly for industrial and trading firms 'might very well have become . . . important'.[36] The net effect of the Branch Bank discounts on the supply of short-term finance is difficult to assess, however, since it is necessary to include the rather obscure consequences on the supply of credit by country banks of their 'circulation account' arrangements at the Branches.

At the time of the establishment of the Branch Banks a number of people in the City and elsewhere held the view that the Bank of England was planning to attract to itself the best discount business.[37] They expected that the Branch Banks would accommodate only 'first rate traders and manufacturers', giving them 'additional advantages' over 'the middling class of trades-people'. Further, it was held that the latter would be injured because the country banks that financed them—and financed them on the same terms as applied to the larger merchants—would find it impossible, after losing their profitable connections with the large traders, to continue in business.[38] Nothing like this happened—the Branch Banks do not seem to have discriminated between discounters according to the size of their business; and the country banks continued to provide advances for all classes of traders. The amount of accommodation provided by the country banks, however, was affected in various ways by their connections with the Branch Banks.

It seems that the Bank of England Branches did not abstract much discount business from the country banks, but they had certain, more indirect, effects. Their coming enabled at least one country bank to reduce its reserve of bullion and Bank of England notes by about a half;[39] and this would allow it to grant accommodation more freely. Parry Wilkins explained that 'the Branch Bank is very accommodating; for a payment in London, they will let us have any sum we want in Bank cash or notes'.[40] Coppieters, however, has emphasized that the Branch Banks, owing to transport difficulties, were faced with 'a danger of depletion of local reserves before the arrival of the horse carriage with gold from London'.[41]

Again, non-issuing banks having 'fixed' circulation accounts tended, said J. W. Gilbert, to discount more in order to reach the minima stipulated.[42] This, however, would probably not represent a large expansion, since the minima were fixed on the basis of experience, and since they were only minima.

On the other hand, in country towns the non-issuing banks having circulation accounts were reported as becoming 'more select as to the persons they lend their money to'—because their gross returns from discounting were eaten into by the discount payment they had to make to Branch Banks. This effect was not so marked in the industrial areas where the banks were favoured by larger deposits.[43] Again, country banks depending on circulation accounts had reason to complain, on certain occasions in the 1830s and 1840s, of the withdrawal, with little or no warning, of Branch Bank discount facilities.[44] This would tend to make them more guarded in supplying credit. (Coppieters errs in his statement that 'the agents . . . were not instructed to restrict their issue in periods of inflationary pressure'.[45]) Finally, in south Wales and possibly in other areas, the Branch Banks did not, as they did in Lancashire, force down the rates of discount and cause new discount business to appear.[46]

The latter tendencies making for a contraction of the accommodation granted by country banks were stronger than those making for its expansion, if we can accept the evidence of a customer of the Swansea Branch that 'much of the Banking accommodation which formerly existed' had been lost as a result of the establishment of Branch Banks. His statement, however, may be coloured by his belief that he was being badly treated by the Swansea Branch.

In areas such as south Wales where the Branches did not attract much discount business by relatively low rates, such connections as existed between the local bankers and traders and the London money market were not severed; and they may well have been strengthened by the facilities granted to the country banks for the transmission of bills to their London correspondents via the Branch Banks. The Swansea agent was told in 1835 that if a non-issuing banker proposing an open account 'deemed it more to his interest to act on the London Money Market, he might transmit thro' you his bills to his London correspondent'. (Even in the case of Lancashire, where the lowering of the Branch Bank discount rates had the first effect of attracting business away from London, King believes there was probably the secondary effect that London would obtain some of the additional discount business that accompanied the lowering of rates.)[47] The connection with London was also strengthened in that rates of discount at the Branch Banks become related to the published Bank Rate in London.[48]

Despite the establishment of the Branch Banks, and the disfavour with which they regarded country banks that re-issued bills, small bills continued to circulate; the average amounts of the short-term (twenty-one-day and seven-day) bills circulating from the Swansea Branch and from all the Branches were respectively £2,258 and £80,901 in 1832, and £4,839 and £253,384 in 1856.[49] The circulation of small bills of 'unmercantile character' in Wales, however, could not easily be terminated by Branch Bank action, since it was due, according to the Swansea agent in 1840, to the continuing lack of wealth of the country.

Regarding the major purpose of the discounting business as, indeed, of all the operations of the Branch Banks, the agent at the Swansea Branch could state in 1842 that 'all country issues in this part of Wales are quite out of vogue, the public do not like paying to get them exchanged and they have ceased being current here: in Monmouthshire also they must have felt the check'. Undoubtedly, the discount business of the Branch Bank contributed to this result; but it also extended its own note issue through the encashments by holders of drawing accounts and, to a limited extent, through making advances and loans. The average circulation of Branch Bank notes, however, was not very large: that of the Swansea Branch at its peak in 1845 was less than that of Wilkins's two banks in 1825–8.[50] The decline in country note circulations, in fact, was primarily due to factors other than the issue of Branch Bank notes—notably the withdrawal from 1829 of all notes for less than £5 (by an act of 1826),[51] and the growing competition of cheques.[52]

Indeed, in the discussion of 1826, bank notes had been over-emphasized to the exclusion of other means of payment;[53] and the subsequent rapid growth in the use of cheques, and of gold sovereigns and half-sovereigns in replacement of the smaller notes,[54] greatly reduced the relative importance of bank notes. This, and the legislative provisions of 1844 for ousting country notes may have caused the Bank of England to lose interest, as Professor Sayers says, 'in using branch discount facilities as a bribe to persuade the country bankers to refrain from issuing their own notes'[55]—though immediately after 1844 Threadneedle Street and at least one Branch were greatly concerned to increase the discount business.

The Branch Bank at Swansea was closed in February 1859. Its failure to yield much profit to the Bank—which was regarded as a serious matter—is reflected in the Letter Books from 1842 onwards. and its chief public service to south Wales in the 1850s—'the facility of exchanging Notes for Coin and Coin for Notes' to a very small extent—'could be effected with equal facility from the Bristol Branch, and at a very small additional expense'.

AMOUNTS DISCOUNTED AT BANK OF ENGLAND BRANCHES

All branches (£)

Year	For bankers	For traders	Total
1827			1,583,766
1828			2,223,503
1829			4,921,926
1830			5,485,756

1835	11,079,287	2,720,915	13,800,202
1836	21,107,903	3,638,206	24,746,109
1837	17,405,705	3,953,098	21,358,803
1838	15,657,522	1,977,097	17,634,619
1839	22,950,300	3,645,600	26,595,900
1840	19,942,001	2,285,509	22,227,510
1841	21,717,656	2,564,447	24,282,103
1842	20,199,322	1,874,747	22,074,069
1843	14,725,299	1,221,996	15,947,295
1844	13,549,808	998,662	14,548,470
1845	13,905,084	2,219,684	16,124,768
1846	16,598,364	4,775,781	21,374,145
1847	19,165,676	6,001,474	25,167,150
1848	12,190,875	2,766,357	14,957,232
1849	9,961,740	2,108,141	12,069,881
1850	9,834,093	2,423,839	12,257,932
1851	10,708,904	3,571,497	14,280,401
1852	8,174,028	4,146,656	12,320,684
1853	11,366,482	6,071,980	17,438,462
1854	12,030,277	6,491,655	18,521,932

Swansea branch (£)

1827			98,820
1828			176,835
1829			291,658
1830			330,875
1835	235,418	88,305	323,723
1836	394,531	113,459	507,990
1837	219,100	111,822	330,922
1838	167,936	71,237	239,173
1839	153,500	103,900	257,400
1840	129,755	83,824	213,579
1841	59,685	120,135	179,820
1842	30,037	62,127	92,164
1843	28,627	54,932	83,559
1844	32,773	36,002	68,775
1845	24,513	57,282	81,795
1846	26,601	102,237	128,838
1847	25,515	155,601	181,116
1848	12,841	70,854	83,695
1849	32,958	54,267	87,225
1850	—	51,875	51,875
1851	—	50,001	50,001
1852	—	105,563	105,563
1853	—	139,250	139,250
1854	42,299	243,707	286,006

NOTES

1. Quoted in J. H. Clapham, *The Bank of England* (Cambridge, 1944), II, 114.
2. The Governor and Company of the Bank of England are thanked for granting access to some of the Bank's Court and Letter Books, on which this paper is based. Sources other than the Bank's records are shown in footnotes.
3. *The Times*, 26 September 1826, p. 3, col. 3; *The Cambrian*, 5 August 1826; L. H. Grindon, *Manchester Banks and Bankers* (Manchester, 2nd edition, 1878), p. 223; J. H. Clapham, *loc. cit.* and *Economic History of Modern Britain* (Cambridge, 1950), I, 276.
4. Cf. R.'O. Roberts, 'Financial Crisis and the Swansea Branch Bank of England, 1826', *The National Library of Wales Journal*, XI (1959).
5. The evidence of J. Parry Wilkins to the *Committee on the Charter . . . of the Bank of England* (B.P.P. 1831–2, VI), Q.1628.
6. Cf. Clapham, *The Bank of England*, II, 140; W. T. C. King, *History of the London Discount Market* (London, 1936), pp. 55–6; E. Coppieters, *English Bank Note Circulation, 1694–1954* (The Hague, 1955), p. 31; L. S. Pressnell, *Country Banking in the Industrial Revolution* (Oxford, 1956), p. 179.
7. Cf. King, *op. cit.*, p. 58; S. G. Checkland, 'The Lancashire Bill System and its Liverpool Protagonists', *Economica*, May 1954, 141; *The Three Banks Review*, September 1952, 48–49.
8. Cf. W. T. C. King, *op. cit.*, p. 56.
9. *Ibid.*, p. 52; S. G. Checkland, *art. cit.*, pp. 138–8.
10. King, *ibid.*, p. 51.
11. Cf. S. G. Checkland, *art. cit.*, pp. 134–9.
12. Evidence of J. Parry Wilkins, *loc. cit.*, Q. 1718, 1804; W. T. C. King, *op. cit.*, p. 35.
13. Cf. *Select Committee on the Operation of the Bank Act of 1844* (B.P.P., 1857, X), Part II, Appendices, p. 324; A. D. Gayer, W. W. Rostow and A. J. Schwartz, *The Growth and Fluctuation of The British Economy, 1790–1850* (Oxford, 1953), ii. 907; S. Checkland, *art. cit.*, p. 130.
14. Cf. Clapham, *The Bank of England*, II, 107.
15. Cf. W. Norman's evidence, quoted by W. T. C. King, *op. cit.*, p. 55.
16. Clapham, *The Bank of England*, II, 140; R. S. Sayers, *Lloyds Bank in the History of English Banking* (Oxford, 1957), pp. 142–3.
17. *Second Report from the Select Committee on Banks of Issue* (B.P.P., 1841), Appendix 2, p. 259.
18. R. S. Sayers, *op. cit.*, p. 143.
19. *Ibid.*, p. 144.
20. *Ibid.*, and T. E. Gregory, *Select Statutes Relating to British Banking, 1832–1928* (London, 1929), I, 146.
21. *The Bank of England*, II, 115, 140–1.
22. Clapham, *The Bank of England*, II, 142, 433–4.
23. *Ibid.*, II, 141.
24. *Report from the Select Committee on the Operation of the Bank Act of 1844* (B.P.P., 1857, X), Appendix 39; Gayer, Rostow and Schwartz, *op. cit.*, II, 908.
25. *Report from the Secret Committee on . . . Commercial Distress* (B.P.P. 1847–8, VIII), evidence of the Liverpool banker, Adam Hodgson, Q.513,520, the Birmingham merchant, P. H. Muntz, Q.1259–63, and W. Cotton, a director of the Bank of England, Q.4269–72, 4285. See the graph.
26. W. T. C. King, *op. cit.*, p. 145 fn.
27. Cf. *ibid.*, pp. 84–5; Clapham, *The Bank of England*, II, 295.
28. King, *op. cit.*, pp. 53, 56–7.

29. *Ibid.*, p. 53; Pressnell, *op. cit.*, p. 516.

30. *Report from the Secret Committee on . . . Commercial Distress* (B.P.P. 1847–8, VIII), Vol. III, Appendix 15.

31. *Ibid.*, and Vol. II, evidence of P. H. Muntz, Q.1265.

32. R. S. Sayers, *op. cit.*, pp. 147–8.

33. E. Victor Morgan, *The Theory and Practice of Central Banking* (Cambridge, 1943), p. 144.

34. R. S. Sayers, *op. cit.*, pp. 144–51.

35. W. T. C. King, *op. cit.*, pp. 60–61.

36. Cf. R. S. Sayers, *op. cit.*, p. 152.

37. *Leeds Patriot* quoted by *The Times*, 26 September, 1826, p. 3, col. 3.

38. *The Cambrian*, 5 August 1826, which, while quoting the argument, added that it was based 'upon a supposition that may be altogether false'.

39. Evidence of J. P. Wilkins, *loc. cit.*, Q.1758.

40. *Ibid.*, Q.1753.

41. *Op. cit.*, p. 98.

42. *Secret Committee on the Operation of . . . Joint Stock Banks in England and Ireland* (B.P.P. 1837, XIV). Q. 2059.

43. Evidence of J. P. Wilkins, *loc. cit.*, Q.1792–7.

44. W. T. C. King, *op. cit.*, p. 59.

45. *Op. cit.*, p. 98.

46. King, *op. cit.*, p. 58.

47. Cf. *ibid.*, pp. 54, 58–9.

48. Cf. Sayers, *op. cit.*, pp. 147–8.

49. *Report from the Select Committee on the Operation of the Bank Act of 1844* (B.P.P., 1857, X), Appendix 2.

50. Evidence of J. P. Wilkins, *loc. cit.*, Q.1599, 1600; *Report from the Select Committee on the Operation of the Bank Act of 1844* (B.P.P., 1857, X), Appendix 2.

51. Evidence of Wilkins, *loc. cit.*, Q.1618–20, 1653, 1708, 1749–50, 1791; Clapham, *The Bank of England*, II, 106.

52. Cf. Sayers, *op. cit.*, pp. 150–2.

53. Cf. Clapham, *The Bank of England*, II, 106.

54. Cf. Sayers, *op. cit.*, p. 151.

55. *Ibid.*, p. 152.

CHAPTER NINE

The History of the Newport and Caerleon Savings Bank (1830-88)

by T. M. Hodges

O N 25 October 1830, five gentlemen of high local standing met in the Hanbury Arms, Caerleon, in the county of Monmouthshire. The purpose of their meeting was to discuss proposals for the establishment of a local Savings Bank. As a result of their deliberations, they came to the conclusion:

That the establishment of a Savings Bank in accordance with Act 9. Geo. IV. Cap. 92, in the town of Caerleon will be of great benefit to the industrious persons in the neighbourhood.[1]

Caerleon, situated about three miles north of the town of Newport, was at that date little more than a village, having a population of only 1071. The neighbouring parishes between them could muster no more than a further 4037 people. Its environs were predominantly agricultural: with the exception of a few landed proprietors and well-to-do industrialists, the bulk of the population, and that of the surrounding villages, consisted of working-class folk of very small means.

Up and down the country, there had been for a number of years, similarly well-intentioned men of the better class, who had met on like occasions and with the same motives. By the year 1830, their united efforts had produced 480 Savings Banks, and 427,830 working-class depositors had accumulated more than £14,616,900 in small savings.[2] Four such banks had already been established in south Wales, at Bridgend, Cardiff, Pembroke and Haverfordwest. None of these places could then reckon its populations above a few thousands; but if they were small and not very wealthy, they were just the environment in which Savings Banks flourished best.

The names of the gentlemen mentioned above were: Major Digby Mackworth, of Glen Usk, a local landowner; Richard Fothergill, owner of the local ironworks; the Reverend William Thomas, Vicar of Caerleon; and John Jenkins, also of Caerleon, one of the local gentry. Since the venture was new to them these gentlemen resolved to seek the advice of others in south Wales who had already had previous experience in drawing up an acceptable constitution. Consequently, it was decided:

> That the rules already in force in the Bridgend Savings Bank, under the direction of the Hon. Sir John Nichols, shall be adopted as the basis for those at Caerleon.

In accordance with the above, the affairs of the institution were to be conducted by Trustees and Managers, the former not to exceed six in number, and the latter not to exceed twelve. These officials were to have the power to fill any vacancy which might occur in their number, and to appoint a treasurer. Also in accordance with the voluntary nature of the Savings Bank movement throughout the country, neither the treasurer, nor the trustees, nor any other person having control in the management was allowed to derive any 'benefit from deposits made in this Bank, nor receive any remuneration whatever for his or their services'.

The gravity of the trust imposed on these voluntary workers, in whose hands were placed the savings of the depositors, was fully realized by requiring the 'Treasurer and any other person or persons acting in the capacity of Secretary, or Actuary, to give security to the Clerk of the Peace for the just and faithful execution of such office or trust as two Trustees and three Managers may approve'. Accordingly, Richard Fothergill, the Treasurer, and John Salter, the Actuary, were required to deposit bonds to the value of £200 and £50, respectively, with the Clerk of the Peace for Monmouthshire. Some such security was universally demanded from active officials, though no guaranteed minimum amount was fixed by Act of Parliament until 1848, when £100 was declared the minimum guarantee.[3] The security bore some relation to the amount of funds collected as deposits. Later on, when total deposits in Caerleon, amounted to many thousands of pounds, the security demanded from the then acting Treasurer was £600, and that from the Actuary, £200. For many years before 1870, the total securities of the chief officials had been increased to £1000.

The following is the list of original Trustees and Managers:

Trustees	Residence	
Lord Granville Somerset, M.P.	Badminton	Hon. Trustee
Sir Charles Morgan, Bart., M.P.	Tredegar	—
Sir Thomas Salusbury, Bart.	Llanwern	Trustee
Capel Hanbury Leigh, Esq.	Pontypool	—
William A. Williams	Llangibby Castle	—

All these Trustees and Managers were leading figures in the locality, or had strong local attachments. In this regard, Caerleon was especially fortunate in being able to secure the goodwill of men of such high standing as Lord Granville Somerset, M.P., of Badminton, and Sir Charles Morgan, M.P., of Tredegar Park, whose kinsman gained fame at Balaclava. Throughout the country were to be found similar men, far removed from the lower orders by birth and position, who gave not only their blessing, but often their active assistance to the Savings Bank movement.

This inspiration and guidance is not surprising, seeing that there were amongst the middle and upper classes, men with a strong sense of the rightness of helping the working classes to a better realization of the value of thrift. The habit of saving was an admirable trait, revered only a little less than godliness. Especially was this to be inculcated and encouraged in the lower orders by those in higher social position as a practical method of demonstrating that, while the sin of poverty was a personal affair, the Almighty had a habit of helping those who helped themselves. If as a result of long years of saving, an annuity could be bought sufficient to maintain the saver from falling a burden on the poor rate during old age, what more laudable line of conduct could the poor pursue? How better could they atone for their lowly condition than by making themselves at least as little dependent upon the help of others as thrifty living could make them?

In some cases the Trustees were men who were willing to give financial backing to a Savings Bank, but did not wish to do the actual work of attending weekly at the place of business. The Managers were, in such cases, the voluntary workers, who gave their services in assisting to receive deposit books, make payments, and sanction withdrawals, etc. No hard and fast distinction could be drawn, however, for Trustees, even of aristocratic birth, could be found, who undertook, and conscientiously carried out, the most unimportant tasks in the bank whenever their turn of duty came round. In the case of the Caerleon Savings Bank, whilst it is true that the two most wealthy, and prominent of the original Trustees, namely Lord Granville Somerset, M.P., and Sir Charles Morgan, M.P., were merely Trustees in an honorary capacity, several of the other Trustees, like Major Digby Mackworth, and Richard Fothergill, both wealthy industrialists and property owners, took a continuously active part in the day to day operations of the Savings Bank, the former in the capacity of Chairman for many years, and the latter as Treasurer until 1837. The Managers, in the main, were neither as wealthy, nor as influential, but were, nevertheless, prominent local figures, drawn from the more prosperous tradesfolk and professional classes. The original list of Managers had a strong ministerial flavour: no less than eight of the original eighteen being drawn from one or other of the religious denominations. The strength of the clerical contingent is not surprising seeing that the movement itself owed its origin to one of the cloth, and clerics were prominent in nearly all the Savings Banks in the country. After all, what better practical application of Christian virtue could they find than in an institution providing for the thrift which formed the burden of so much of their pulpit oratory?

There is strong evidence, in the respective positions of Trustees and Managers, that there was some class distinction between the two types of officials. This distinction was evidenced also, in other parts of the country, especially in the early days of the movement. It was probably encouraged in order to win the sympathy and powerful support of prominent people as Trustees, whose very names would not only be beyond reproach locally, but would also carry weight with the National Debt Office. Later on in the history of the movement, less weight was placed on such class differences, and though in many places the post of Manager was a sort of apprenticeship for later Trusteeship, the distinction was not universal throughout the country, and everywhere grew less so with the passage of time, and the growth of the movement in popularity.

According to the rules and regulations of the Caerleon Savings Bank the maximum number of Trustees was six, and that of Managers was twelve, but in the original list of Trustees, ten names appear in the Day Book, and no less than eighteen names of Managers. No doubt some form of roster was drawn up for a given period, and the requisite number laid down for each type of official was selected from amongst the possibles willing to give their gratuitous services to the bank.

An examination of the Day Book shows that at least two people, sometimes more, never less, put in an attendance at every day of business. Usually it was the Managers who attended, but occasionally one finds the name of a Trustee. It was not until the passing of the Savings Bank Act of 1863 that it became compulsory for at least two to be in attendance on business days.[4]

It was necessary to have a large number of Managers, not so much to secure as long a list as possible of influential names, as because of the need for spreading over as wide a circle as possible the duties of attendance at the receipt of custom, and so reducing the amount of voluntary service required from each Manager. An examination of the attendances of Managers, as recorded in the Day Book of the Savings Bank under consideration, shows that the ministers of religion did a very large share of the work, even allowing for the fact that they formed nearly 50 per cent of the Managers. Perhaps this was as much because they had more time at their disposal to do so, as to the fact that they may have regarded the conscientious fulfilment of their duties as a moral obligation.

One of the first acts of the newly constituted Savings Bank was to deposit the signatures of the Trustees with the Commissioners for the reduction of the national debt, with whom all savings, over and above withdrawals, were invested in what were known as the 'Funds'. This procedure required two of the Trustees to make out an order to invest this surplus, and send it through a London agent to the National Debt Office, which would in turn instruct the Bank of England to credit the sum to the 'Fund for the Banks of Saving'. A form of debenture was at first issued to the Trustees in return for the investment, but as this was found to be inconvenient, since it had to be surrendered at the Bank of England whenever money was withdrawn, a simple form of receipt was substituted later on.[5] By the time the Caerleon Bank had been established the second method had become the rule. For instance, a Minute in the Day Book, dated

19 February 1831, reads: 'That £100 be sent to the Bank of England, and a receipt required from the Commissioners for the Reduction of the National Debt for the interest of the first £100.'

Usually, when a bank was established, circulars were prepared, and sent out to prospective depositors, pointing out the dangers of hoarding money at home, and exhorting them to save for old age or a rainy day, and so make themselves independent of the help of others. There is no record of any such printed circulars having been sent around the Newport area; but an announcement drawing attention to the opening of the Savings Bank appeared in the *Monmouthshire Merlin*, the county newspaper on 12 February 1831. There were, however, ready at hand, far more effective instruments of propaganda in the local ministers of religion, of whom eight were Managers. By means of formal announcements from pulpits on Sundays, or by exhortations in sermons and buttonholing at home, a campaign of proselytizing prospective savers was launched on all the neighbouring villages.

The Savings Bank started in fact in a very humble way, and with little or no equipment. A room in the Caerleon National School was hired once a week, on Saturdays, and remained open to receive deposits and make withdrawals, from 12 o'clock noon until 2 p.m. Business was first commenced on 19 February 1831. The only equipment consisted of a ledger for recording depositors' names, addressses and occupations, and the amounts deposited or withdrawn; a day book to record the minutes of meetings; another to record the annual statement, or balance sheet; and finally a supply of deposit books. An interesting item of expenditure given in the first General Statement was

January 1st, 1831 purchase of iron chest   £3. 11s.

It does not require much imagination to assign a function for this very necessary piece of bank equipment. On the same day, the Day Book records the appointment of Mr John Salter, as the first actuary of the Savings Bank, at a salary of £5 5s. per annum. This nominal sum as remuneration was the only departure from the purely voluntary nature of the organization.

The first General Statement issued by the Caerleon Savings Bank was for the period ending 20 November 1831. This date was that fixed by the Commissioners for the return of General Statements each year. According to this return, the total number of original depositors was thirty-three. Of these, one was a Trustee, whose deposit of £20 represented a loan to the Savings Bank for the purpose of providing the necessary ready cash to purchase initial equipment, and to provide petty cash for small disbursements or withdrawals until such time as a large enough surplus was accumulated to meet expenses. By this gesture from a Trustee, the Caerleon Savings Bank was saved the rather chancy alternative forced on some Savings Banks in Scotland, where it was the custom to pass the hat round at the inception to secure sufficient money to buy the bank's accounts books, etc., and to pay for the hire of a room.[6]

By the end of the first year of the Savings Bank the total sum invested by the thirty-three depositors amounted to the modest sum of £190 6s. 1d. Of this sum, £55 6s. 3d. was kept as money in hand by the Treasurer to meet withdrawals. The expenses of running the bank for the first year amounted to £34 4s. 8d., and the balance of £100 odd was invested with the Commissioners for the reduction of the national debt.

The amount of interest allowed by the Commissioners to the Saving Bank was £4 11s. 3d. per cent, and the interest paid to depositors was fixed at £3 6s. 8d. per cent. This left a balance of £1 4s. 7d. per cent for working expenses. Since the prevalent rate of interest in Consols was 3 per cent, the Savings Banks were in an extremely favoured position. Parliamentary opposition to the generous terms offered to Savings Banks was continuous, and in 1844 they succeeded in getting the interest payable by the Commissioners reduced to £3 5s. per cent, with a maximum payable to depositors of £3 0s. 10d. per cent.[7] Few Savings Banks were able to pay this latter amount to depositors and leave enough for working expenses. The Newport and Caerleon Savings Bank—as it had by then become known—paid £2 18s. 4d. per cent and continued to do so until 1880 when the maximum paid to depositors was reduced to £2 10s. per cent.

Of the thirty-three original depositors, thirty held balances not exceeding £20 each, and two depositors held balances between £20 and £50.[8]

It is a great pity that ledgers showing a complete record of individual deposit accounts for the Newport and Caerleon Bank have not been preserved. The only light thrown on the names and occupations of the individual depositors is that shown in a ledger giving amounts paid in and withdrawn for the two years 1847 and 1848. An examination of this record reveals that depositors consisted of:

Servants	Minors
Labourers	Seamen
Wives, widows, spinsters	Dressmakers and milliners
Clerks (mostly railway clerks)	Small farmers and farm-servants

Craftsmen: masons, smiths, coopers, cobblers, pattern-makers,
    carpenters, mechanics

Clothing Clubs	Friendly Societies
Charitable Societies	Building Societies
National School Clubs	Penny Banks

By far the largest single class of depositor consisted of minors either
depositing in their own names, or, when under seven years of age,
in the names of their guardians. The next largest was the servant
class. This is not surprising, seeing that domestics, though earning
little more than £5 or £10 per year, usually lived free of board, and
were wont to place the whole of their yearly wages for safe-keeping
for their old age in the bank. Such people were also most open to
persuasion by well-intentioned masters. The latter sometimes opened
accounts for their servants to give them a start in a career of thrift,
and also opened accounts for their children, with the same object in
view. Criticism was frequently levelled against this practice on the
grounds that many such minors were children of well-to-do people
for whose benefit the Savings Banks were never intended. However,
the strict limits set to the maximum amounts which could be deposited restricted much abuse of the Bank's true function by this
class of depositor.

Amongst the co-operative devices for encouraging petty savings
to meet particular contingences were the Clubs of various kinds, of
which the Clothing Club was a humble, but popular example.
Such efforts in petty saving have survivals to this day amongst the
lower income groups. Of the several Clothing Clubs banking with
the Newport and Caerleon Savings Bank was one in particular
which is worthy of a brief mention by virtue of its relatively large
deposit. This Club, known locally as Mrs Gethin's Clothing Club,
ran for more than a dozen years, and had at one period as much
as £331 16s. to its credit. Considering that this sum was made up of
individual amounts rarely exceeding £1, Mrs Gethin's venture
must have had wide popularity, and no doubt formed a very lucrative sideline to the enterprising Mrs Gethin's clothing establishment.
In addition, there were several other Clothing Clubs with credits
ranging from £35 to £60. These clubs were more often than not
run by the shopkeepers themselves, many of whom were not above
taking advantage of the ignorance of the poor to indulge in sharp
practices, to their own pecuniary gain.

Between the minimum deposit of 1s. and the maximum of £200,
by far the largest number of accounts ranged below £100. Taking
two representative years, 1852, which was the first year for a de-

tailed classification of deposits to be given, and the year 1887, it may be seen from the figures given below, that of the 797 depositors (excluding Penny Banks, Friendly and Charitable Societies), one-half held deposits below £10 in 1852. In the year 1887, of the 1142 depositors (again excluding Societies and Penny Banks) more than 50 per cent were below £10. This distribution of depositors was usual throughout the history of the Bank.

TABLE COMPILED FROM ANNUAL GENERAL STATEMENTS, 1852 AND 1887

No. of depositors (in 1852)	No. of depositors (in 1887)	Distribution of accounts	Amounts (in 1852) £	s.	d.	Amounts (in 1887) £	s.	d.
63	220	Not exceeding £1	29	17	7	67	1	5
196	210	£1-£5	489	5	3	525	9	4
131	146	£5-£10	929	8	2	1,055	2	11
94	79	£10-£15	1,134	16	11	950	6	4
40	57	£15-£20	667	9	5	984	10	7
102	99	£20-£30	2,443	13	6	2,463	6	10
77	83	£30-£40	2,518	10	2	2,816	9	0
24	41	£40-£50	1,067	11	11	1,808	6	6
38	64	£50-£75	2,310	2	4	4,065	2	0
12	39	£75-£100	1,050	10	11	3,453	0	2
6	32	£100-£125	689	2	11	3,596	16	6
5	33	£125-£150	684	17	7	4,578	15	1
9	39	£150-£200	1,461	8	1	6,732	7	7
797	1142		15,476	14	9	33,096	14	3
9	18	Charitable Societies	674	12	8	794	15	8
17	23	Friendly Societies	3,842	4	4	2,991	12	0
—	4	Penny Banks	—			145	15	10
823	1187		19,993	11	9	37,028	17	9

Definite limits were set by the Commissioners to the amount which could be deposited by savers. While no deposit less than 1s. could be taken, the maximum which could be deposited by any one depositor in a year was fixed at £30. This figure was the limit fixed by the Savings Bank Act of 1828 when the maximum was reduced from £50.[9] No depositor was allowed to make any further deposits when the sum of £150 had been reached, and when total deposits and interest had amounted to £200, no further interest was payable on any deposit thereafter.

The purpose of setting limits to annual and total deposits was to prevent wealthier people from using the Savings Banks in order to reap the benefit of the higher rate of interest payable, while on the other hand to offer a handsome inducement to the poor. These maxima were relaxed for certain classes of depositors, such as working-class societies, towards which the Savings Banks acted in the capacity of banker. Trustees or Treasurers of any Charitable Society were allowed to deposit any donation or bequest for the maintenance of education or benefit of the poor to the amount of £100 per annum, but were not allowed to hold a balance of more than £300 *in toto*, exclusive of interest. Friendly Societies, established prior to the Act of 28 July 1828, were allowed to deposit the whole or part of their funds. Any Friendly Society formed after that date was limited to a total blance of £300 in principal and interest.

The progress of the Savings Bank from its inception up to the year 1837 was continuous, but the rate of advance was slow. From 1831 to 1837 the bank had been known as the Caerleon Savings Bank, and had drawn its depositors from the villages of the neighbourhood. On 15 April 1837, however, a decision of importance in the history of the Savings Bank was made. It is recorded in the Day Book in the following words:

> Resolved that it is found expedient to remove the office of this Savings Bank from the National School in Caerleon to more convenient premises in the Borough of Newport.

A further resolution on 20 April 1837:

> Resolved that the change of address be inserted three times in the County Paper. Henceforth the Bank should be known as the Newport and Caerleon Savings Bank.

The move was a wise one, for Caerleon was a much smaller place than Newport, and the prospects of further expansion were strictly limited by the sparse and relatively static population. Newport, on the other hand, was not only a more populous area from which prospective depositors might be drawn, but it was developing rapidly as a port and commercial and industrial centre. By the year 1841 its population amounted to 13,766 and was rapidly increasing.

On 1 July 1837, business was commenced at the Newport premises, and with the departure of the Savings Bank from Caerleon, Richard Fothergill, the Treasurer since its inception, and one of the founders, resigned, having faithfully fulfilled his moral obligation to see the bank well and truly established on a firm foundation. His resignation marked the end of the purely disinterested official. Such men were to be found, here and there, despite the indifference to the economic frustration of the working classes with which men of their class have often been charged. Henceforward the Treasurers though still performing their duties gratuitiously, were drawn almost exclusively from local bankers. Fothergill was succeeded by a 'William Williams, Banker, of Newport', who filled the post until 1852, when he, in turn, was succeeded by the Manager of the West of England and South Wales Bank, Newport. The amount of security demanded from the latter, as Treasurer, was raised for the first time from £200 to £600, on account of the growth in deposits in the meantime.

By the end of the first ten years of its existence, the Savings Bank could show an appreciable increase of business. The number of accounts had grown from 33 to 327. The amount deposited within a single year had increased from £178 5s. to £2648 18s. 3d.; the total amount standing to the accounts of depositors from £190 6s. 1d. to £7484 13s. 11d.; and the balance of investments from £100 6s. 3d. to £7298 18s. 3d.

From the year 1837, when the bank's activity for the first time embraced Newport, the number of new accounts opened each year was about forty, and the total amount of the deposit accounts increased annually up to 1841 by approximately £1000. The average percentage of withdrawals to annual new deposits was 42·9 per cent, or about 18·5 per cent of total accounts. A characteristic of withdrawals was their increase in proportion to the amount of new savings. For example, from 1837 to 1841, they ranged from 47 to 69 per cent. This was not necessarily a cause for alarm. One of the chief inducements to prospective depositors was that they could withdraw their money with comparative ease, and when they wanted. Many cautious depositors would often try this out just in order to satisfy themselves that their money was actually there. Having assured themselves that this was so, they would then reinvest the money later on.

Despite the fact that the early 1840s saw the spread of a type of Friendly Society with elaborate ritual, which set out to appeal to the workers as a more attractive alternative to Savings Banks, the latter did not suffer thereby, since they became the repository of both the Friendly Society and Charitable Society funds. By the late 1840s there were seventeen Friendly Societies and nine Charitable Societies which were regular depositors with the Newport and Caerleon Savings Bank. The total deposits of the former, in 1852, amounted to over £3842, with an average of £226 per Society, while the total deposits for the latter amounted in that year to over £674, averaging £75 each.

The 1840s also saw the appearance of the Penny Banks. Their great advantage over the Savings Banks, as a repository for small savings, was that the humble penny could more easily be saved than the initial shilling necessary to start a deposit in a Savings Bank. The appeal of the Penny Bank to children, and even to the adult of lowly circumstances, was therefore very strong, especially since the secretary or treasurer of the latter might well be a neighbour or the local minister who would be willing to take such small offerings at any time, whereas the nearest local Savings Bank might be some distance away, and only open once a week for a few hours. Here again the Savings Banks gained an ally rather than suffered a rival, for they became the Penny Banks' banker.

The principle of the Penny Bank did not gain popularity in the Newport area until much later than elsewhere. In fact the first local Penny Bank did not appear in the books of the local Savings Bank until 1867.

Thenceforward, however, there were never less than four Penny Banks amongst its list of depositors. They were not as wealthy as the Charitable or Friendly Societies, and held deposits averaging from £35 to £40.

During the 1840s a series of defalcations by officials of a number of Savings Banks occurred in many parts of the country, following the relaxation in Trustees' responsibilities, brought about by the Savings Bank Act of 1844. As a result of the scandal caused by the Cuffe Street Savings Bank, Dublin, in 1848, the Rochdale Savings Bank, in 1849, and others, a score or so banks closed their doors, while withdrawals overtopped savings in many more, and widespread damage was done to the reputation of the movement.[10] In 1848, for the first time in its history, the Newport and Caerleon Savings Bank paid out more money within the year than it collected. Its 1848 withdrawals amounted to over £6358 as against new deposits of £5433, despite the fact that the actual number of accounts was up on the previous year. These large withdrawals halted the hitherto steady increase in total accounts by several hundreds of pounds, while the balance of invested funds fell correspondingly.

The setback was purely temporary, for by the year 1851, the total savings had reached over £20,165. Annual new savings by the 827 depositors amounted to £5218 15s. 4d., which was double the amount of 1841. There was, however, a far higher rate of withdrawals during this decade than ever before. On an average they amounted to 79 per cent of new savings invested, while during the year 1848 as much as 17 per cent more money was withdrawn than was deposited. There never was any cause for alarm, however, for

Q   201

withdrawals never formed more than about 22 per cent of the total balances held by depositors.

By the middle 1850s the number of depositors had reached 1376, and the amount of funds invested exceeded £30,000. Consequently, the Trustees sought to acquire new premises. They approached the Commissioners on 9 February 1856 with the view to being allowed to mortgage the future funds invested as security for the new building. As a result of the inquiry, the reply they received from Mr Tidd Pratt, the Barrister for the Commissioners, was as follows:

> As Trustees of a Savings Bank you can not mortgage the future funds of the Bank to pay the expenses of erecting such a building. There is no objection to your undertaking the responsibility as private individuals, nor will there be any objection to any future surplus being applied to repay such expenses.

In April 1858, negotiations proceeded for the lease of a piece of land at the foot of Stow Hill, belonging to Sir Charles Morgan, M.P., one of the original honorary Trustees of the old Caerleon Savings Bank, and on 3 July of the same year a loan was advanced by 'a certain gentleman' to purchase the site and erect a building for £200.

Savings Banks came in for a great deal of criticism from the press during the 1850s, antagonists seeing in them a design on the part of promoters to keep the poor off the rates, and so save their own pockets. Such controversies, though ranking as important news in the national press, percolated only very slowly into the minds of the locals, who were quite content to repose their confidence in their local bank, whose officials they knew and trusted. The sure test to them was whether they could withdraw their savings easily whenever they wanted.

The continued high proportion of new savings in any given year to withdrawals bore out this fact. Provided depositors did so within the limits set out in the rules and regulations printed in their deposit books no hindrance was placed on withdrawals, so that cautious depositors could easily satisfy themselves as to the existence of their savings. It is true that the person who withdrew his savings was not allowed to reinvest them again within the same year: a necessary precaution to prevent panic withdrawals by depositors.

The importance of making withdrawals as easy as possible was fully appreciated, and, as soon as a new Savings Bank had accumulated a sizeable balance, the time limits for withdrawals were relaxed. For instance, the regulation relating to withdrawals at the inception of the old Caerleon Bank ran as follows:

Any depositor may withdraw the whole or any part of his deposit on any of the appointed days at the time appointed for business, provided a week's notice be given in the case where the sum required does not exceed fifty shillings, but for any sum above fifty shillings, a month's notice of such intention must be given.

By the 1850s, however, this rule was considerably relaxed, and any sum up to £2 could be withdrawn without notice, while sums from £2 to £10 could be withdrawn after three days' notice.

During the 1850s, the activities of the Newport and Caerleon Savings Bank doubled, e.g.:

	1851			*1861*		
No. of depositors	827			1651		
Total amount deposited	£20,165	18s.	2d.	£38,621	19s.	2d.
Balance of investments	£19,765	2s.	9d.	£38,381	5s.	1d.
Annual new savings	£5,218	15s.	4d.	£9,991	5s.	0d.

The figure of £10,970 10s. 3d. for new savings in 1859 was the highest reached for any single year in the Bank's history, before or after.

The year 1861 saw the passing of Gladstone's Post Office Savings Bank Act, and the early demise of the old Savings Banks was prophesied as a result of this new means of saving offered to the working classes. The advantages which the Post Office Savings Bank had over the old banks were many. Perhaps the most important, apart from the element of greater security, was that of added convenience: Post Offices were to be found in every village and hamlet in the land, and were open every day, and for long hours. These were advantages which were confidently expected to outweigh the advantage of slightly higher interest rates enjoyed by the old Savings Banks. The immediate effect was the closing of thirty small Savings Banks in the first two years of the Act, but, although by 1870 there were about 143 less Trustee Banks in existence than a decade before, the wholesale collapse of the movement which was prophesied did not take place, and most of the largest banks in the country remained untouched by the appearance of a more powerful rival.[11]

The effect of the 1861 Act was certainly felt by the Newport and Caerleon Bank, for a halt was called in its expansion for the first time. The year 1861 had been the peak year in its history both for the number of depositors and total balances. From then on a decline set in which lasted until 1870. The number of depositors decreased to 1153, and the total deposits and investments fell to £30,017 and £29,412 respectively. Transfers of deposits to the Post Office over the period amounted to nearly £2000, averaging approximately £360 a year from 1862 to 1865. The year 1866 was one of great distress throughout the country, due to industrial failures, the repercussions of which were felt locally. More than £12,489 of savings were withdrawn from the local Savings Bank, a sum which was nearly twice that saved in that year.

After the first detrimental effects of the rival Post Office Savings Bank had been felt in the 1860s, the Bank once more began to accommodate itself to the new situation. In fact, it seemed to take on a new lease of life during the 1870s with depositors and total deposits increasing year by year until 1877, when total accounts reached their maximum for the whole of the Savings Bank's history, at £38,905 15s. 1d. This annual progress to date had been maintained despite the depressed state of trade in the district during the year 1875, when strikes and lock-outs lasted for five months. Local distress from trade depression continued throughout 1876, and again in 1878, without seriously reducing deposits, despite the large withdrawals in the latter year.

Though the bank made little substantial progress during the 1880s there were no serious setbacks; despite the fall in the number of depositors in 1887 from 1316 to 1187, total deposits had actually increased somewhat to £36,969 3s. 3d. In 1880 the rate of interest payable to depositors had been decreased from £2 18s. 4d. per cent to the level paid by the Post Office, namely £2 10s. 0d. per cent. This removed the only real advantage which the old Savings Banks had had over their Post Office counterpart, apart from the traditional personal attachment which had succeeded through the years in weaving a strong sentimental bond between Savings Bank officials and depositors.

In 1887 the Savings Bank movement received a body-blow from the Cardiff Savings Bank scandal of that year, from which it never really recovered.[12] Its effect on the Newport and Caerleon Bank, situated only twelve miles away, was as decisive as it was to many others in the country.

The publicity caused by the Cardiff revelations, and the public discussion which followed on the duties and liabilities of Trustees, together with the reduction of interest payable by the Commissioners to the Banks to 2½ per cent resulted in a host of Savings Banks throughout the country, though perfectly solvent, abdicating in favour of the Post Office. In four years 101 banks representing nearly £5 million of funds closed their doors. Amongst these was the Newport and Caerleon Savings Bank, which ceased operating in 1888.

NOTES

1. Day Book of the Caerleon Savings Bank, MSS. f. M. 160 (332. 1), Newport Library.
2. H. Oliver Horne, *History of Savings Banks* (Oxford U.P., 1947), p. 386 and Appendix II.
3. Horne, *op. cit.*, p. 123.
4. Horne, *op. cit.*, p. 213.
5. Horne, *op. cit.*, p. 79.
6. Horne, *op. cit.*, p. 51.
7. Horne, *op. cit.*, p. 106.
8. Annual General Statement, 1831.
9. Horne, *op. cit.*, p. 100.
10. Horne, *op. cit.*, p. 124.
11. Horne, *op. cit.*, p. 209 and Appendix II.
12. Horne, *op. cit.*, p. 241.

PART FOUR
LABOUR

CHAPTER TEN

'Scotch Cattle' and Early Trade Unionism in Wales

by E. J. Jones

Nothing in the pages of history is more romantic than the history of the gradual self-organization of labour. At one time organized with their employers in craft guilds, the workers were deprived of the benefits of association by the capitalization of industry and the consequent diversity of interests which arose between the employers and their employees. The workers, thus cast adrift by the system which made them but mere hirelings, remained for centuries in a state of social chaos. Unscrupulous employers, who, often with the connivance of the Government, evaded the laws enacted in the interests of the workers, compelled the labouring classes, in the closing decades of the eighteenth century, to essay some attempts at organization.

The element of success which attended their efforts so alarmed the employing classes that they induced the unreformed Parliament, which saw in the rapidly spreading combinations something more than economic organizations, to still further jeopardize the position of the artisan classes by passing, in 1799, the notorious Combination Laws, thereby making workers' associations illegal. A combination of circumstances made still more hazardous the economic position of the workers; for the enclosures, the Napoleonic wars, and the Corn Laws confronted them with problems of an ever-increasing supply of labour, falling wages, a rising price level, and a burden of taxation that was to go on increasing for many years. Combinations entered into for the purpose of defending or improving their economic status being illegal and punishable by imprisonment, the workers degenerated into slaves of the new wage-paying system.

In July 1806, five rope-makers in the employ of Messrs. Grove and Co., of Swansea, were committed to Cardiff gaol for three months for a conspiracy to raise wages.[1]

The invidious character of the class legislation of the unreformed

Parliament, though it denounced as illegal the organizations of the most impotent members of the community, tolerated the formation of identical associations by the employing classes. In 1802 the ironmasters of south Wales had a powerful organization which met quarterly to regulate the price of iron and the wages of the workmen. At first the members were required to pay an annual subscription of one guinea; but a later arrangement imposed on new members a fee of 10s. 6d., the alleged cost of the bowl of punch imbibed by the ironmasters at each of their meetings.[2]

The workers persevered, however, with their unions; and though the laws enacted against them compelled them to meet surreptitiously, they created a series of undercurrents so strong as ultimately to throw the country into a state of appalling confusion. Squalid hovels and the necessity of sending their children to work in the mines and the factories helped to make the workers violent and subversive.

The system which permitted the employers to organize yet imprisoned the workers for doing likewise drove the workers to take the law into their own hands and to demonstrate by a campaign of terror the fatuity and futility of repressive measures. Secret societies were everywhere formed, and 'Scotch Cattle' prevented miners taking strangers underground without the express sanction of the 'lodges'. Anyone sufficiently intrepid to ignore the decrees of the lodges received a warning which, if disregarded, was followed by a nocturnal visit from some neighbouring band of 'Scotch Cattle'. The transgressor's house and furniture was often destroyed, bodily injury inflicted, and sometimes even murder was resorted to by these gangs of ruffians. To prevent identification the 'Scotch Cattle' not only blackened their faces and assumed disguises, but arranged that a transgressor in one district should be visited by a herd from another district. The terrorists were usually led by a 'bull', the strongest and most pugnacious scoundrel in the herd, and heralded their approach by lowings and growlings. On arrival at the house of their unwilling host, they destroyed its contents with a thoroughness that was appalling. A victim who showed any signs of resistance or attempted to reason with them was immediately chastized. Thus in November 1834, murder was committed at Blackwood[3] in the name of the 'Scotch Cattle'.

The recurrence of scenes of wanton violence continued unchecked for many years. Numerous arrests were from time to time made, but seldom did convictions follow, the injured being fearful to give evidence lest the revenge of the 'Scotch Cattle' should again fill their lives with terror and dismay. The impunity with which they defied the law encouraged the ruffians to intimidate not only recalcitrant employers, but also members of the general community sufficiently indiscreet to denounce their barbarous activities. In July 1834, for example, the shop of Thomas Rees, of the Rock, in the parish of Bedwellty, was destroyed for his denunciation of the men who combined against their employers.

Repressive legislation having failed to crush the spirit of the rebellious workers, the Government, in 1824, decided to repeal the Combination Laws. Toleration was all that resulted from the 1824 Act, for though it was no longer a criminal offence for a worker to belong to a union, the union had no legal status in the law-courts. The strike was still a dangerous weapon to use, for every worker who arranged or assisted in the arrangement of a demonstration of this kind was still liable to transportation for conspiracy. In 1825 the Act of 1824 was revised, some of its concessions being withdrawn and others accorded in their stead. Still liable to punishment for conspiring to combine and in other ways hindering and obstructing the due course of industry, the workers perforce continued their secret activities. Strikes degenerated into riots which necessitated the intervention of the military and the shedding of blood.

Merthyr Tydfil, the centre of a district which gave employment to over 100,000 persons, became the storm centre of the workers. In September 1831, considerable ferment prevailed among the workers in the ironworks; for the firemen, miners, and colliers of Monmouthshire and Glamorganshire, cognizant of what had transpired in the north of England, formed themselves into clubs or lodges, the avowed objects of which were said to be mutual assistance when unemployed and vigorous resistance to the arbitrary demands of the employers for wage reductions. It was generally believed, however, that, in addition to such laudable objects as were publicly proclaimed, the workers' lodges had as an ulterior object the desire to so harass the employers as ultimately to place the virtual control of industry in their hands. As the employers had regulated wages without regard to the cost of living, so the workers proposed to control industry without regard to profits. Illegal oaths were said to be the bonds of union between the workers, a connecting link strongly deprecated by those who saw in the workers' lodges a fruitful cause of confusion, distrust, and dissatisfaction between employers and employed.

Coercion and violence were the weapons used by the workers to persuade the hesitant to join the lodges. In the works and in the streets the refractory workers were persecuted by the unionists to the detriment of the employers and the employees. The handicap imposed on the employers by the schism among their workers determined them to contrive a plan of campaign which it was hoped would smash the union movement; members of the unions were to be discharged and their places filled from the large army of surplus labour. A bitter conflict ensued in which the 'Scotch Cattle' again became prominent.

Some forty or fifty men employed by the Neath Abbey Iron Works having joined a 'Union Club', the works agent served them with notices to quit. Unpleasant consequences were obviated by the immediate intervention of the principal proprietor, who, informed of the circumstances, invited his workmen to meet him to discuss dispassionately the advantages or disadvantages attaching to membership of the union clubs. Approximately 150 workers accepted the invitation. Mr. Price, having read the rules of the society to which the men had subscribed, proceeded to enumerate the several merits and demerits of the unions and to express his readiness to encourage and further any movement that had for its object the welfare of the workers. Several of the employees also addressed the meeting, some contending, in support of the unions, that combinations of workers by organizing a strike fund would make labour less perishable and therefore, as far as bargaining strength was concerned, more on a par with capital. The meeting had lasted about an hour when it was determined to take a vote of the men present; those in favour of the union to move to the right and those against to the left; and it was said that everyone moved to the left. Mutual congratulations followed the interment of this union club at Neath. The same plan of settlement was adopted in October by the colliers employed at Mr. Coffin's collieries at Cwm Rhondda.

A more difficult task confronted the proprietors of works at Dowlais and Merthyr. After many petty moves had been made by both sides, the employers posted a notice to the effect that after 24 September 1831, none but non-union men would be employed. The men thereupon ceased work, approximately 2000 persons being affected at Dowlais alone. The proprietors anticipated a long struggle. It was said that at Dowlais the employers had accumulated a stock of coke large enough to keep the furnaces in blast for nine months and several of the furnaces at the Plymouth and Dowlais works were blown out.

Though the depression in the iron trade caused that portion of the Aberdare Works formally managed by Messrs. Scale to close down, the workers continued to battle for their unions. Hunger is, however, in all struggles between labour and capital, a potent and relentless factor. By October many of the workers were in a parlous plight. Inadequately supported by the unions, which paid the workers from 4s. 6d. to 5s. per week, the workers were forced to solicit relief. On 7 October, many of the Dowlais and Plymouth workers applied to the magistrates for an order on the Select Vestry, it having refused them relief on the grounds that they were voluntarily unemployed. The application was refused.

In November, large numbers of impoverished workers, deserted by the 'Union Preacher' Twiss, renounced their unions and returned to work. The Plymouth workmen had decided to offer their labour to their employers on 14 November, but were deterred by the intervention of large numbers of workmen from Cyfarthfa and Nantyglo. Thus while many returned to work, the more headstrong among the workers continued to suffer for their unions. In January 1832, hundreds of the workers at Merthyr were still out, and in consequence the magistrates were continuously employed removing families to their parishes of origin, chiefly Carmarthenshire, Pembrokeshire, and Cardiganshire. It was estimated that the cost of removals from the Parish of Merthyr since the union club agitation commenced exceeded £500.

It has been said that illegal oaths formed the bond of union between the members of the newly formed lodges. No objection was taken to the body of rules openly published, save perhaps rules 13 and 14, which constituted the workers' Committee and Inspectors, the sole and irrevocable judges of the wage rates to be paid by the men's employers. The secret oaths, however, were roundly denounced. The following is an example of them:

'Prepare, prepare, for dust thou art, and unto dust shalt thou return.

'So, therefore, fall down on your knees, and lay your right hand on this Holy Book, and your left hand on your heart, and say after me this solemn obligation—

'Question: What is your name?—A. B.

'Is it of your free will that you come here to join this Friendly Society of Coal Mining?—I do.

'1st. I most solemnly and sincerely swear, with my hand on the Holy Book and on my bended knees, that I never will tell who gives me this obligation, or these witnesses present, as long as I live.

'So help me God.

'2nd. I will enter this Society and will pay according to the rules, or as the Committee thinks proper, or as far as lies in my power.

'So help me God.

'3rd. I never will instruct any person into the art of coal mining, tunnelling, or boring, or engineering, or any other department of my work, except an obliged brother, or brothers, or an apprentice.

'So help me God.

'4th. I will never work any work where an obligated brother has unjustly been enforced off, or standing up for his price, or in defence of his trade.

'So help me God.

'5th. I will never take any more work than I can do myself in one pay, except necessity require me to do so; and if I do, I will employ none but an obligated brother, and will pay him according to the master's price, or according to his work.

'So help me God.

'6th. I will never leave my work, to be supported by this Society, without first acquainting the Committee, and will pay my share down justly and truly, and will act accordingly.

'So help me God.

'7th. I will never injure an obligated brother, or anything belonging to him, before I acquaint him of his foreseen danger.

'So help me God.

'8th. I will never in a boasting manner make known how much money I can get, or in how short a time.

'So help me God.

'9th. I will never make known any signs, tokens, passwords, or guess or write them on stone, sand, wood, tin, lead, or anything visible or invisible to the eye.

'So help me God.

'10th. I never will make these obligations known to either master, manager, or under-looker, over-looker, book-keeper, or any person, except to a legal obligated brother.

'So help me God.

'Numbers, 30th Chapter, 2nd verse; Deut., 23rd chapter, 21st, 22nd, and 23rd verses.'[4]

In Denbighshire and Flintshire, where the average wage was 8s. to 9s. per week, the colliers were much distressed by the fluctuations that recurred in their industry. In January 1831, a threatened renewal of the conflict between the masters and themselves led the colliers in the Ruabon district to organize a 'Combination Fund' on the plan of and in conjunction with similar organizations in Lancashire.

The agitation for Parliamentary Reform inspired the workers, oppressed by recurring trade depressions, heavy taxation, the laws against trade unions, and the fluctuations of mismanaged currency, to abandon economic controversies and to divert their energies to securing such a reform of the House of Commons as would lead to an amelioration of the conditions under which they lived and worked. Politics were embraced simply because the workers were persuaded that their economic emancipation could only be achieved through a direct representation of their interests in the House of Commons. With characteristic fervour they participated in the agitation for reform and contributed in no small measure to its ultimate success. But the provisions of the Reform Act disillusioned the aggrieved workers, who once again reverted to their trade unions and the secret associations of the 'Scotch Cattle'. The country was again convulsed by the atrocities perpetrated by gangs of ruffians.

In February and March 1832, the districts round and about the Nantyglo, Blaina, and Coalbrook Vale ironworks were the scenes of violence and the destruction of property. Approximately one month before the Anti-Truck Act became effective, Messrs. Russell and Brown, the proprietors of the Blaina Works, proposed to their employees a wage reduction of from 5 per cent to 6 per cent, and a simultaneous reduction of from 10 per cent to 15 per cent in the price of provisions at the company shop. These offers, supplemented by a proposal to make advances in cash two or three times a week or oftener if desired, were accepted by the men, some of whom returned to work. The majority, however, intimidated by the workers in other areas, refrained from entering the levels. At a place called the Cornish Pit an assembled throng of workers were ordered by their leaders to turn their coats and blacken their faces preparatory to an attack on the cottages of two marked men. On arrival at the cottages, 'headed by a man blowing a horn', they destroyed the furniture and savaged the men 'in a most brutal manner'. Mr. Brown, his two sons, nephew, and agent, who sallied forth armed to meet the nocturnal visitors, failed to recognize any of them so complete was their disguise.

On the following day the Rev. William Powell and F. H. Williams, Esq., proceeded to Blaina to swear in special constables, while Messrs. Russell and Brown offered a reward of £50 to anyone furnishing such information as would lead to the apprehension of any of the offenders. The Secretary of State for the Home Department, informed of the disturbance, offered an additional reward of £100, 'with the promise of a free pardon to an accomplice'. Retribution soon overtook the malefactors; for a confederate of the 17th, who had returned to work the following morning, was so severely chastized by his former accomplices that he informed against five of them, who apprehended, were subsequently committed to take their trial at the impending assizes.

Though the victims of terrorism evinced an increasing readiness to testify against the wrongdoers, the 'Scotch Cattle' persisted in their nocturnal exploits. So widespread did their activities become that it was not considered safe to leave a house after dark. 'No person can travel from Risca to Tredegar without shuddering at the work of violent and wanton devastation that presents itself to the eye,' wrote a contemporary.[5] In November 1834, the Independent Order of Oddfellows at Tredegar passed resolutions designed to prevent their society 'being contaminated by fellowship with any of these scoundrels';[6] but so treacherous were the times and so widespread the ramifications of the clandestine 'Scotch Cattle', that a worker who had appended his signature to the resolutions received the dread warning of the 'Scotch Cattle'.

While the young and unruly members of the working classes were inspiring the community with terror, the more rational among the workers were persevering with their unions and enduring the tribulations so commonly the lot of pioneers. Thus the workers employed by C. H. Leigh, at Pontypool, who had subscribed to a trade union, were instantly dismissed, while the unionist employees of Messrs. Crawshay, Merthyr, were informed that unless they forthwith seceded from their unions the furnaces would be blown out.[7] This attitude of the employers became general, for they were determined to make yet another attempt to crush incipient trade unionism. In pursuance of this determination the ironmasters requested the workers to sign a declaration renouncing all 'connection, direct or indirect, with every club or union not sanctioned by the constitutional laws of the realm'.[8] A fierce resistance to this demand was made by the workers. The furnaces at Blaenavon and Hirwaiun were blown out and the iron industry practically brought to a standstill. The proprietors of the Varteg Iron Works, apprehensive lest a mob attack should be made on the firemen who had signed the declaration, requisitioned a considerable body of military. Fortunately their services were not required, for the struggle was of brief duration and not marked by scenes reminiscent of Merthyr in 1831. The workmen at Blaenavon signed the declaration in July, a lead immediately followed by the workers at other places.

The 'Scotch Cattle', however, continued their activities throughout 1835, though their immunity from arrest was becoming increasingly jeopardized. Judges and magistrates inflicted upon those who were apprehended the most severe sentences in the hope that such punishments might serve as warnings to others. In April 1835, Edward Morgan was hanged at Monmouth for the murder of Joan Thomas, at Blackwood; John James and William Jenkins for their connection with the outrage at the Rock were also condemned to death, but were subsequently reprieved and transported for life.[9]

With the advent of the Chartists the discontented, dissatisfied, distressed and restless workers transferred their affections from 'Scotch Cattle' and union clubs to the lodges of the Chartists, persuaded that, by supporting the agitation for a parliamentary reform more radical than that of 1832, they might materially benefit themselves. Once again politics seemed to them to be a lever to improve their economic status.

NOTES

1. *The Cambrian*, 18 July 1806.
2. C. Wilkins, *History of the Iron, Steel and Tinplate Trades* (Merthyr, 1903), p. 67.
3. *The Cambrian*, 10 April 1835.
4. *On the Oaths Taken in the Union Club.* By a Looker-on (Newport, 1831).
5. *Monmouthshire Merlin*, 26 July 1834.
6. *Ibid.*, 15 November 1834.
7. *Ibid.*, 26 July 1834.
8. *Monmouthshire Merlin*, 2 August 1834.
9. *The Cambrian*, 10 April 1835.

CHAPTER ELEVEN

The South Wales Sliding Scale, 1876-79: An Experiment in Industrial Relations

by J. H. Morris and L. J. Williams

THE history of an early example of the adoption in a major coalfield of a sliding scale which linked changes in wage-rates with variations in the selling price of coal has a more than local interest. It was no isolated innovation. In the later nineteenth century the device spread, for shorter or longer periods, to most English coalfields, to Lanarkshire, and to the anthracite mines of America. It illustrated the general desire of both owners and men for a durable agreement about wage-rates and some easy, almost mechanical, method of adapting them to changes in selling prices in an industry where wages formed a large element in costs and where price fluctuations revealed a considerable range and frequency. If a scale achieved these ends it enabled the mines to work more regularly because not only were changes in wage-rates achieved without industrial stoppage but also because coalfields could better maintain their competitive position when costs were quickly adjusted to market conditions. The scale also formed part of the general movement towards a more conciliatory stage in industrial relations when both sides were willing to form a joint committee to discuss industrial differences. It was, too, an arrangement appropriate to the phase when men's unions were fitfully growing to strength without having acquired it and when, accordingly, they were still prepared to accept the selling price of coal as the prime factor governing their wage-rates—particularly if the safeguard of a minimum were conceded. This early experience of the scale in south Wales, however, also demonstrated that it was no facile panacea—neither a full conciliation board nor frictionless adjustment to the instability of the industry was in fact achieved.

I

For the first five months of 1875 the bulk of the south Wales coal industry was idle because of a wage dispute, the third major stoppage of the industry in the short space of five years. There was, however, an essential difference between the strike of 1875 and the stoppages of 1871 and 1873. The earlier disputes had taken place against a background of rapidly rising coal prices which had enabled the miners to emerge from them substantially victorious; by the beginning of 1875 prices had already been falling for nearly a year and this continuous decline in trade, together with the steady fall in union membership which accompanied it, created a situation much more favourable to the employers.

During the decline from the unprecedented boom conditions of the early 1870s the men had already accepted two wage reductions—each of ten per cent—since May 1874; it was the demand for a further reduction of ten per cent which the employers wished to enforce from 1 January 1875 that led to the 1875 struggle. As the strike dragged on it became increasingly clear that the colliers, who steadily drifted away from a union which was unable to offer them any significant support, must eventually succumb; and the owners, for whom the prolonged strike was costly and who could see no sign of a trade revival, tended to stiffen their terms. The final settlement, which was concluded on 28 May, was, nevertheless, more moderate than many of the owners would have wished. It provided for a reduction of 12½ per cent in wages—which was more than had been demanded in January but less than many owners considered appropriate in May. This reduction was, however, subject to an important qualification: it was to apply for three months during which time a joint committee of twelve (six from each side) was to negotiate the details of a sliding scale under which future changes in wage-rates were to be regulated by variations in the selling price of coal .

This brief background helps to throw some light on the attitudes with which the two sides entered upon the first sliding scale agreement. Generally speaking the owners at this time accepted the new principle with reluctance and misgivings. The reasons for this are obvious and substantial enough. During the coal 'famine' of 1872–3 the abnormally high earnings which had accompanied the soaring prices had, in the owners' view, made the men more unruly and unmanageable. The owners, therefore, were reluctant in 1875 to grant any concessions to the men, not only because they considered that a substantial reduction in wages was unavoidable, but also because they viewed the struggle as 'largely an attempt to impose discipline'.[1] From this standpoint it was important that the employers should not merely win the struggle but that they should be unequivocally seen to win it. Most of the owners, moreover, welcomed the evident decline in union strength and were opposed to any solution that contained an element of arbitration which, it was considered, would give 'fresh life to the Unions that are now dying out'.[2] For both these reasons the sliding scale principle was not widely welcomed by the owners. On the other hand the owners genuinely desired to find some way of avoiding the ruinous conflicts which had beset the industry in recent years. It was undoubtedly the strength of this desire which enabled the minority of influential coal-owners, who took a strong stand in favour of the sliding scale principle, to carry the day.

Once the owners had decided on this policy they met with ready co-operation from the men's leaders. To be sure, the view that 'the men were compelled to accept a Sliding Scale'[3] has plausibility since its introduction followed a long strike in which they had been clearly defeated.[4] Nevertheless this view cannot be sustained. One of the miners' leaders, Henry Mitchard of Blackwood, had, even before the strike began, urged the Employers' Association to adopt a sliding scale.[5] Moreover the evidence of both the records of the negotiations and the contemporary press reports suggests that the miners' leaders—far from resenting the principle as an imposition —welcomed it as the winning of a significant concession. There were good reasons for this attitude. By May it was obvious that the colliers' long resistance was crumbling. Thus the sliding scale presented itself as a promising 'face-saver' for the men's leaders because it brought gains which offset the loss of the immediate reduction of wages. It had secured the granting by the owners of some recognition to the workmen's representatives. Moreover it liberated future variations in wage-rates from the arbitrary control of the employers. Much of the stubbornness of the men's resistance to the proposed reduction in January 1875 had derived from its seemingly arbitrary nature. They had already accepted two reductions in the previous seven months; they argued that the owners should now be obliged to demonstrate, not simply to assert, the necessity for this additional cut, and that the final verdict should be left to some impartial outsider. The sliding scale did not go as far as this, but since it made future wage changes subject to a clearly ascertainable regulator— the average f.o.b. price of coal—the men could fairly claim that their demands had been partially met.

A further reason for the welcome the men's leaders gave to the sliding scale rested on less solid grounds. The provision that any disputed points which arose in the bargaining over the terms of the scale could be referred by the joint committee to an umpire for final decision led them to state, in their circular to the colliers, that 'from this it will be seen that the masters have conceded the principle of arbitration in all future disputes'. As later events showed, this greatly exaggerated the concession which the owners had made.[6]

On 28 May 1875, the agreement which ended the bitter, five-month struggle was signed. The employers thereupon invited the men's representatives to dinner—'a sumptuous repast' with an 'abundant supply of champagne'—and the belief grew that the day's agreement was likely to have some permanence.[7] The belief was, in part, prophetic because, apart from one short interval, the wage-rates of the south Wales colliers employed in the pits of the Associated[8] owners remained regulated by a sliding scale until the end of 1902. In part, it was delusively optimistic because the first wage scale survived for less than four years, dying, as it had been born, in a stoppage of work over a wage reduction. Nevertheless in this first scale, brief though its life was, there was much of interest: the issues raised during the bargaining over its creation; the degree of control that the joint committee considered that it could appropriately exercise over the course of industrial relations; the difficulties of the application of the scale in a period of falling selling prices of coal; and the extent to which both sides, learning from the experience of these four years, modified their initial attitudes to the scale.

II

The friendly feelings which were engendered when the strike was settled were soon disturbed. Indeed before the joint committee formed to devise a scale had even met a personal squabble arose which threatened to wreck the whole scheme. In a heated speech during the 1875 strike, Alexander Macdonald, M.P., had denounced the great families of Wales who, he said, had enriched themselves at the expense of the workers. He had expressed the hope that, when the social history of Wales came to be written, 'names like those of Crawshay and Fothergill, and Vivian, and Davies, and others would go down to posterity with infamy as poltroons who attacked women and children'.[9] When Macdonald was selected as one of the workmen's representatives, Henry Hussey Vivian, although he sat in the House of Commons with Macdonald as a member of the same party, and although he had himself urged the importance of forgetting the bitter feelings engendered by the strike, declined to sit with him. The owners, reluctant to follow the easy path of accepting Vivian's resignation, wanted Macdonald to apologize before the joint committee met, whereas the men reasserted their faith in Macdonald.[10] Ultimately both Vivian and Macdonald resigned and the sliding scale discussions were thus undertaken by a committee of ten members, but the incident had revealed how quickly the feelings of both sides could still be aroused.

In the bargaining that ensued, both sides felt that they had claims which deserved special consideration. The owners wanted a price-wage relationship which would give them a sufficient margin to cover the interest they could have received by investing their capital elsewhere and, in addition, a further return to cover the extra risk of mining and to provide for capital redemption. Moreover, the owners claimed that recently their costs of production had risen, largely through the operation of the Mines Regulation Act of 1872 which extended the compulsory safety precautions and which, through limiting the hours for boy workers, had in effect limited hours for all.

The workmen claimed that the wage-rate should be fixed sufficiently high to compensate them for the recent increase in food prices and house rents. They suggested that, to maintain wages, the owners should keep up prices by a deliberate restriction of output. The men were, in effect, asking that instead of wages being regulated by prices, prices should be regulated by wages; that there should be a minimum level of wages which could be guaranteed if coal prices were prevented from falling below a corresponding minimum level.

The proposal for a policy of price maintenance was rejected outright by the owners as both impracticable and unsound in principle. It implied a greater control of the market than the owners of south Wales possessed. Welsh coal, heavily dependent as it was on export markets, was subject to the competition from coal produced in other mining districts, both British and foreign. This issue apart, however, compromise was likely as both sides were vividly aware of the loss and misery that a resumption of industrial strife would occasion. The sense of the importance of the discussion may be inferred from the proposal that Gladstone, Premier of England until the defeat of his party in the 1874 election, should be invited to act as umpire—although in the end the committee had to rest content with the less ambitious choice of the Rt. Hon. Arthur Lowe, late Home Secretary.[11]

Before the end of the year a scale had been agreed, based, with modifications, on the price-wage relationship which had existed in 1869. Both sides, as a rough compromise, accepted this as a 'standard' year which was representative of economic conditions before the abnormal boom of the early seventies. But some recognition was also afforded to the special claims of each side. Thus the minimum wage-rate was to be 5 per cent higher than the rate paid at the respective collieries in 1869 to compensate the increased cost of living since that date. The selling price accepted as equivalent to this minimum wage-rate was 12s. a ton for the steam-coal collieries and 11s. a ton for the bituminous collieries, these prices—higher than those which had prevailed in 1869—being taken as covering all the claims of the owners in respect of the extra cost of producing coal under the Mines Regulation Act of 1872.[12]

Account was taken of the diversity of the industry by dividing the collieries of the Association into three groups, consisting of the steam-coal collieries, the bituminous collieries of Monmouth-shire and the Caerphilly district of Glamorgan, and the bituminous collieries of the rest of Glamorgan, a group which included most of the collieries in the Neath and Swansea districts. To balance the minimum wage-rate inserted into the scale there was also provision for a maximum. Wage-rates were to rise by 7½ per cent for every complete shilling increase in price until the prices reached 21s. and 20s. for steam and bituminous coals respectively. Thereafter, however high prices might go, wage-rates were to remain un-changed. To set the scale in motion the average prices at which coal had been sold in November and December 1875, were to determine the wage-rates paid for the first six months of 1876; subsequently rates were to rise or fall according to the audits of prices covering six-month intervals. Either side could end the operation of the scale by giving six months' notice.

III

The results of the first audit, declared in February 1876, showed that coal had been selling at prices of between about 10s. 8d. and 11s. 3d. for the three groups, prices which were sufficiently low to justify a general reduction of wage-rates to the minimum. The colliers who had gained most from the fluctuating trade conditions of the early seventies now lost most. While the steam-coal men were faced with a 7 per cent reduction in the wage-rates they had been recently receiving, the reduction for the bituminous-coal colliers in most of Glamorgan amounted to 21½ per cent and to even more in some of the Monmouthshire collieries.[13] A host of minor difficulties arose when attempts were made to apply this award. Some of the colliers complained that these reductions brought their wage-rates below the agreed minimum of 5 per cent added to the 1869 rates, while others complained that they were excessive for types of labour other than hewing—for example, the ripping of roof, the making of headings, and the work of the hauliers—which had not shared fully in the general advance of wages in the recent boom. There were men, from some Monmouthshire collieries especially, who claimed that their wages had been below the general rate in 1869 and that these had since been 'levelled up', so that the strict application of the award to them would reimpose injustice. Difficulties arose, too, over collieries which had been idle in 1869 or had been sunk since that date, while at other collieries it was claimed by the owners or the men, according to who would benefit by a change, that their colliery was included in an inappropriate group. These complaints were brought before the joint committee, a body which, having devised the sliding scale, was now reconstituted into one to administer it. The principles which were to govern the committee's policy did not immediately emerge as at first it took no decisions but merely limited itself to hearing evidence from both sides, supplemented, if necessary, by the production of colliery pay sheets. If further investigation was required the committee deputed two of its members, one chosen from the owners' representatives and one from the men's, to visit the colliery to meet the officials and the men and to enquire more fully about local conditions. The committee did, however, publish in the press its resolution that it would not consider disputes which had already led to a stoppage of work or to the handing in of notices to terminate contracts, as it was only by refraining from such precipitate action that the men could conform with the spirit of remedying grievances by discussion and mutual understanding which the committee represented.

Nevertheless it soon became clear that, contrary to the expectations of the men, the committee was not to develop into a general board of conciliation. After considerable discussion the view of the owners' side—that the committee existed simply to enforce the sliding scale award and to allow no departure from it in any particular—prevailed. The grievances already submitted to it were decided on this principle, while in some complaints it declined to interfere. It took no action in a dispute at Crawshay's Gethin and Castle pits, for example, where the colliers were dissatisfied both with the allowance for 'clod' (rubbish) contained in the seam and with the rates paid for ripping roof, as the committee said that it was not its province to adjust any dispute between owners and men once the rate had been fixed. It did nothing to appease the hauliers even though the workmen's representatives on the committee 'strongly urged' it to make 'some trifling concession'—even if only $\frac{1}{2}$d. a day—'so as to keep so important a class as the hauliers at peace'. The committee, to avoid the possibility that the knowledge that it had at least discussed the hauliers' complaints might delude other workmen into pressing for concessions, decided to publish in the press that it had conceded no advance to the hauliers because it did not feel justified 'in varying the terms of the award in any particular'.[14]

A further example of this narrow conception of the function of the joint committee was the expression of the owners' view in February 1877, that it was not expedient for it to hear disputes as they arose at the various collieries 'because it would be constituting the Joint Committee into a perpetual Board of Arbitration, and that was not intended when they were appointed'.[15] This policy of dealing solely with disputes which arose out of alleged violations of the sliding scale agreement of 1875 and not with all disputes usually meant the rejection of appeals for intervention brought forward by the men. When the Glamorgan Coal Company, for example, on the grounds that the seam had become less faulty, was reducing the wage-rates paid at Llwynypia (a pit opened since 1869) to equate them to those paid in neighbouring collieries the committee declined to intervene when the men complained.[16] The policy was, however, not so one-sided as would appear at first sight because similar complaints from the owners rarely reached the committee owing to the policy of the Association of discouraging its members from bringing them forward. The Committee, thus, poured only a limited amount of oil on the troubled waters of the industry and many disputes were left to be settled, or to rankle, at colliery level.

The committee was an experiment, but one less ambitious than it might have been and than the men expected it to be. There were precedents for joint bodies with a wider scope. The joint committee established on the west Yorkshire coalfield in 1873, modelled on the committee already in operation in Northumberland and Durham, could deal with all questions relating to wages, the mode of working, and any other subject which might arise between owners and men at any colliery. More general questions could also be referred to this committee and, if these could be settled in no other way, an umpire with the power of final decision could be appointed.[17] The committee in south Wales was certainly not hampered from developing along these lines by any weakness of personnel. On the owners' side men like David Davis of Ferndale, William Menelaus of Dowlais, William Thomas Lewis, agent to the Marquis of Bute, and Archibald Hood of the Glamorgan Coal Company were all authoritative figures. On the men's side there were Thomas Halliday, of national importance as a union leader, Henry Mitchard, a leading figure in Monmouthshire, John Prosser and David Morgan of Aberdare, and William Abraham ('Mabon'), already winning fame through his silver-tongued oratory. But in south Wales the employers were determined that the joint committee should have strictly limited powers and the men were compelled, despite their reluctance, to accept this view.

IV

Even though the employers at first had wished to keep the sliding scale agreement inviolate the pressure of events soon impelled them to seek modifications of it. In conceding a minimum wage-rate the owners had realized that at times they must be prepared to work at a loss, but it was believed that the workmen's concession of maximum rates would enable any such loss to be recouped. No one had anticipated, however, that the depression after 1876 would be as deep or enduring as it proved to be. From the end of 1875 until the beginning of 1880 the selling price of coal moved steadily downwards, the average price of steam coal, for example, falling during this period from about 10s. 8d. to about 8s. 3d. a ton. The demand for coal by the iron trade was dwindling with the fall in the production of pig iron in south Wales from nearly 715,000 tons in 1874 to about 670,000 tons in 1879. The iron industry of the region was hard hit by the collapse of its mainstay, the export trade in rails to America. In 1877, for example, the works of the Aberdare valley, the glow of their furnaces quenched, were described as 'gaunt and silent spectres'[18] while elsewhere, as at Cyfarthfa, other ironworks were idle with little prospect of restarting. The stagnation in demand was general. The slowly growing export trade in Welsh coal formed a solitary exception, but even here the acuteness of competition precluded any hope of an immediate revival of prices; not only were the iron companies tempted to send more of their coal to the market but also the extensive collieries initiated during the boom years of the early seventies were now becoming productive.

Debarred by its agreement from making a direct attack on minimum wage-rates, yet acutely conscious that its membership accounted for only half of the production of the coalfield, the Owners' Association sought desperately for other means of reducing costs. In 1876 it revived a plan to establish a set of contract rules which would, for example, compel a greater regularity of attendance at work and an acceptance of greater flexibility in working methods, but this attempt foundered, as it had in 1874, on the opposition of the men.[19] The owners also attempted to secure some relief by lengthening the working week. They informed the men of their intention to return to the hours, for adults, which had been general before the Act of 1872—namely, 69 hours a week instead of the current 52.[20] The men's representatives claimed that the sliding scale had settled hours as well as wages through the allowance for the costs of the 1872 Act conceded to the owners in fixing the equivalent selling price under the scale. Some of the largest owners disregarded this protest; indeed, in August 1877, it could be asserted that 'the system of lengthened hours had . . . really become general in the Aberdare valley'.[21] Nevertheless an increase in hours could not be a satisfactory remedy in an industry suffering from over-capacity, with many collieries already unable to secure enough orders to work their pits full time.

A more serious situation arose when some of the members of the Association started to negotiate reductions of wages with their own workmen outside the scale, a process which had already made some headway among non-member firms. The issue was brought to a head by the announcement, in May 1877, that the colliers employed by the Plymouth and Aberdare Company had accepted a reduction of 10 per cent below the minimum wage-rates provided by the scale.[22] This direct attack on the scale was condemned by most of the Associated owners who were still anxious to honour their agreement with the men. The reaction of the colliers was even more antagonistic. Already uneasy owing to the attempts by some owners to increase the number of hours, but ultimately willing to yield on this provided the advantage of the minimum wage-rates under the scale was retained, they could never countenance actual wage reductions at individual collieries if the scale was to keep any meaning at all. In the event, the reduction proposed by the Plymouth Company was not effected as its colliers, under pressure from their fellow-workmen, withdrew their acceptance of it.[23]

The issues raised by this incident, however, could not be ignored. The loyalty of the members to the Association, not free as competitors were to reduce wages, was under a strain which could have been relieved only by a marked change in the trend of prices—and of this there was no sign. Thus, in December 1877, the Associated owners felt compelled to inform the men's representatives on the joint committee that the current state of trade made the continuance of the agreed minimum wages-rates impracticable and that, if no concession were granted, notice would have to be given to end the scale. The men, well aware that they had been sheltered from a general onslaught on wages only by the existence of the scale, agreed to accept a reduction of 5 per cent below the minimum.

The formal integrity of the scale was maintained by the promise of the owners that, as soon as the recovery of trade brought prices above the minimum standard, this 'loan' would be returned by the grant of a 5 per cent increase additional to the scale.[24]

Any relief that the owners had gained was negatived in the following year by a further deepening of the depression which reimposed all the old strains. At the end of 1878 the owners put forward new demands for the recognition generally of a sixty-hour working week and for the removal of the minimum from the scale. To the colliers these demands seemed unreasonable. The reduction in wage-rates they had already accepted was by no means the full measure of their distress since, with irregular working causing almost universal under-employment, earnings had dropped much more drastically. At a delegate meeting, held at Merthyr on 13 December 1878, the owners' request was rejected;[25] the owners thereupon gave the necessary six months' notice to end the scale.

The intention was not to abandon the idea of a scale, but merely to secure the freedom to effect a reduction in wage-rates. The principle of a scale was not now objectionable to the owners—far from it—and they had indicated that they would be 'most happy to discuss a new arrangement'[26] which would be more in keeping with trade conditions. During the negotiations in the first half of 1879 the owners' demands solidified into a request for a 10 per cent reduction in wage-rates, this being considered essential to meet the competition from the North of England where hours had already been increased and wages reduced. Moreover the owners of the non-associated collieries in south Wales were imposing reductions in the wage-rates of their colliers and members were beginning to leave the Association to gain freedom to behave similarly. Some of the men's leaders were aware of the futility of resistance. Halliday, for example, advised the colliers to 'agree with thine adversary quickly, while thou art in the way with him',[27] but this scriptural advice was unheeded and no agreement had been reached by the time the owners' notice expired. During the first week in July there was a complete stoppage at the 170 pits belonging to the 59 members of the Association, but thereafter the colliers gradually trickled back on the owners' terms. The first scale had ended, as it started, in conflict.

V

The successful negotiations for a revised scale early in 1880 afforded convincing proof that, despite the stresses of its existence, the first sliding scale had revealed advantages which commended it to both sides. Any agreement which could not be revoked at short notice and which evinced some power to endure was welcome to the owners because buyers were more likely to place their orders in south Wales if they felt that the honouring of long contracts would not be interrupted by industrial strife. The men also gained from the regularity of earnings which accompanied this regularity of trade. Still more were they aware that for much of its course the 1875 scale had protected them from attacks on their wage level during a period of unusually depressed trade. They were patently weak and disunited; the scale not only removed wage-rates from the arbitrary control of the employers but also promised automatic improvements in them when trade should revive.

Experience soon made both sides realize, however, that the scale had unfavourable implications which had largely been overlooked in 1875. Many owners strongly resented the growing interest, inevitable when wages were tied to prices, which the men took in their commercial policies. They also resented the greater difficulty they experienced in introducing new working methods since the men could often claim that these changes, by affecting the basis of the scale, constituted a departure from it. These resentments ultimately made the owners, if not eager to abandon the scale, less willing to strive for its retention. The grounds for the men's discontent were more fundamental. They were—and were to remain—disappointed in their hope that the scale would be supplemented by a general 'Board of Arbitration'. They were frustrated in their hope that they could secure the co-operation of employers in the restriction of output and, in the absence of this, suspected that by allowing prices to govern wages they were encouraging their employers to indulge in competitive selling which served merely to depress their own standard of life. The men, too, suspected that the collapse of unionism could not be wholly ascribed to the depression of trade, since the impulse towards unionism was sapped by the apparent automatism of the scale.

Nevertheless the scale could be credited with having averted a repetition of the bitter industrial conflict of the early seventies which had involved losses and sacrifices which long remained fresh in the memories of the leaders of both sides. For some years, then, the belief in the general principles of the scale predominated and efforts were concentrated simply on amending the details of its construction. It was clearly realized by 1879 that a scale which seemed eminently satisfactory under one set of trade conditions could, as these conditions altered, contain implications which were intolerable. When this happened the scale could be maintained only if there was a readiness on both sides to negotiate a new basis for it in a conciliatory spirit. For many years this readiness existed and the flexible attitude both owners and men were willing to adopt helps to explain the unusually long survival of the scale in south Wales.

To the far-sighted the seeds of the downfall of the scale could have been apparent in 1880 because, by the new agreement of that year, the employers succeeded in abolishing the provision fixing any minimum for wage-rates. This loss the men lamented as the abandonment 'of that principle which gives us the right to determine the lowest wage-rate we shall take for our labour'.[28] Slowly the men became mistrustful of the assumption, implicit in the scale, of the over-riding identity of interests of capital and labour and they put as their foremost aim the securing of a wage which, as a prior charge on the industry regardless of the selling price of coal, would provide them with a reasonable minimum standard of living. They could then feel that, even if the stability of trade and the industrial peace the scale promoted were blessings, they were blessings which could be bought too dearly.

NOTES

1. *Owners' Association Minutes*, 28 May 1875.
2. *Ibid.*, 14 August 1874.
3. G. D. H. Cole, *A Short History of the British Working Class Movement, 1789–1947* (London, 1948), p. 183. A similar view is implied in R. Page Arnot, *The Miners* (London, 1949), p. 60.
4. This view also seems plausible because the ultimate effect of the automatic adjustment of wage-rates under the scale was to retard the growth of trade unionism in south Wales. This, however, became apparent only later; it was by no means obvious—or, indeed, inevitable—in 1875.
5. *Colliery Guardian*, 12 June 1874.
6. *Ibid.*, 28 May 1875.
7. *Ibid.*, 4 June 1875.
8. The sliding scale agreement applied only to the colliers employed by members of the Coalowners' Association, although, normally, it had a considerable influence on the wage policy of the owners who were not members.
9. *Colliery Guardian*, 24 September 1875.
10. *Western Mail*, issues 1 September–15 October 1875. The men's choice of Macdonald is explicable by his position as an acknowledged miners' leader. Possibly, too, his mistrust of sliding scales had not yet hardened into vocal opposition. Macdonald welcomed the principle of joint consultation embodied in the Welsh experiment. It was the spread of this 'principle of arbitration' which occasioned his comment in mid-1875: 'Look at the glorious state of things in England and Wales.' See S. and B. Webb, *The History of Trade Unionism* (London, 1920 edn.), p. 338.
11. *Minute Book of Joint Committee*, 28 October, 10 December 1875.

12. *Colliery Guardian,* 31 December 1875. It was clearly to the interest of the owners to fix the selling price that was to be equivalent to any given minimum wage-rate as high as possible. Had the 1869 selling price of (roughly) 9s. been taken as equivalent to the minimum wage-rate in the steam-coal collieries the men would have received an increase when the price rose to 10s. As it was under the scale they did not get an increase until the selling price of steam coal rose to 13s. a ton.

13. *Colliery Guardian,* 18 February 1876.

14. *Minute Book of Joint Committee,* 27 May 1876.

15. *Ibid.,* 14 February 1877.

16. *Ibid.,* 14 February 1877.

17. F. Machin, *The Yorkshire Miners,* I (Barnsley, 1958), 177–8.

18. *Mining Journal,* 27 January 1877.

19. *Minute Book of Joint Committee,* 24 October 1876.

20. The owners were legally entitled to take this action as the Act of 1872 restricted the hours only of boys under 16.

21. *Minute Book of Joint Committee,* 28 August 1877.

22. *Western Mail,* 26 May 1877.

23. *Ibid.,* 30 July 1877.

24. *Minute Book of Joint Committee,* 28 December 1877.

25. *Western Mail,* 14 December 1878.

26. *Minute Book of Joint Committee,* 14 December 1878.

27. *Colliery Guardian,* 6 June 1879.

28. *Minute Book of Joint Committee,* 24 May 1880.

PART FIVE

HOUSING

CHAPTER TWELVE

House Building in the South Wales Coalfield, 1851-1913

by J. Hamish Richards and J. Parry Lewis

SUMMARY

THIS paper attempts to plot the course of residential building in the South Wales Coalfield[1] during the period 1851–1913. The primary material is similar to that used by the late Mr. Bernard Weber in his path-breaking article, 'A New Index of Residential Construction, 1838–1950'.[2]

One of the duties imposed on local authorities by the Health Act of 1848 was the drawing up, and enforcement, of Building Bye-Laws, based on model bye-laws issued by the Central Board of Health. Before any building could be erected, the local boards, guided by the surveyors, had to approve the plan. Many local authorities have records showing details of the plans approved, and these form the main source of our information.

A local board was set up only after an area had attained a certain degree of urbanization. In 1851, the only towns in our region which had local boards whose records are still preserved were Cardiff and Swansea. Aberdare and Newport have records from 1855, and Merthyr Tydfil from 1856. No more local board records have been found for the years before 1865, and it is 1878 before there are as many as ten different series. The available information, therefore, covers only the larger towns in the earlier years, but eventually comprises the whole of the coalfield and its dependent ports. Undoubtedly, from 1865, onwards most of the building was in towns covered by the information available to us; but there was other building, unhampered by these bye-laws, or of which we have no record, in other areas.

Plans submitted to the local boards were recorded by the Surveyor in a Register of Plans. The exact content and usefulness of these registers varies from place to place, but generally the register gives the plan number, the type of building proposed, the site, the date on which the plan was submitted, the date on which it was approved or rejected, and the name of the person for whom the building is being done. Some of the registers give the dates of commencement of building, of inspection of drains and damp courses, and of completion; but unfortunately this information was rarely recorded with sufficient consistency for it to be of much use. Amongst the areas with really complete records are Merthyr Tydfil, the Rhondda, and Llantrisant and Llantwit Fardre. Generally the plans were entered in the order of submission; but sometimes they were entered under street names, which made the study of particular streets very easy, but complicated the task of ascertaining how many plans were approved in a particular period for the whole town. In other cases the register was not preserved.

Fortunately, however, democracy generates the duplication of records. Not only did the surveyor mark his register 'approved' or 'rejected', but his committee made some note of the matter in the minutes. Sometimes it was the Works and Sanitary Committee. At other times the Road and Bridges Committee, while one authority, with a strangely modern touch, had a Housing and Plans Committee. The minutes of these committees were usually well kept. Often, however, the committee was, in fact, a committee of the whole council, and in such cases the records of plans approved is to be found in the minutes of the Council itself. The information to be obtained from these depends to a great extent on the standard set by the first Clerk. Some contain a copy of the Surveyor's Monthly Report; others give a list of plans approved each month; yet others, intent on economy, record baldly that 'the Surveyor's Report was read' or that 'all the plans mentioned in the Surveyor's Report were approved'. This form of economy was widely practised in north Monmouthshire.

But if economy was in the air, so was public health, and many of the M.O.H. reports for the local areas were written by doctors whose liking for statistics rivalled that of Florence Nightingale herself. Some of these give the number of houses built in each year; others the number planned. Some give the number inhabited at the end of each year. Usually these reports gave figures for the calendar year and the monthly material available from the more primary sources just mentioned has therefore been collected on this basis. For Cardiff, however, the information is for years ending 31 August. This particular series is given in Table I but is not included in any of the composite indices.

In a few areas we have series showing both the number of house plans approved and the number of houses actually built. Examination of these suggests that, on an average, houses took about nine months to pass from the planning to the completion stage, and that about a tenth of the houses planned were never built. In the two cases where we have failed to find complete records of plans approved, we have been able to obtain data about houses built. This information has been used to estimate series of plans approved for Mountain Ash (1903–14) and Aberdare (1909, 1910, 1913 and 1914). In Mountain Ash, the amount of building going on in these areas during the years covered by these estimates was considerable. Where the houses concerned were council houses, the number of plans has been taken as identical with the number of houses built in the following year.

Because the series of house plans approved for the different local boards begin in different years it is not possible to reach any useful conclusions by simply adding the series together. We can, however, obtain a useful series for four towns (Swansea, Newport, Aberdare and Merthyr Tydfil) beginning in 1856. This series, expressed in *per capita* terms, is shown in Diagram I. Although it relates to building in only four towns, it is probably a reasonably good indicator of house-building in the South Wales Coalfield, including, as it does, two ports (one of which was so concerned with metal industries and both with coal), a predominantly coal area, and a large iron area.

Diagrams I and II also show indices for six towns (the four just mentioned and Llanelly and Mountain Ash) commencing in 1867; for fifteen towns commencing in 1881; for twenty towns commencing in 1887; and for twenty-eight towns commencing in 1893. The composition of these indices is shown in Appendix I. In each the number of house plans approved has been divided by an estimate of the population.

Unfortunately it is far from easy to obtain annual estimates of population of local board areas. In some cases local M.O.H. reports contain population estimates which appear to be fairly reasonable. But usually the estimate has gone more and more awry as the last Census has passed further into history; houses were far easier to count than people.

Considerable time was spent on this aspect of the problem and many methods were tried before a decision was finally taken. In each case we began by obtaining the population of a local board area in two consecutive Census years. The figures have been easily available for 1871 onwards, but 'plans approved' series exist for seven areas before that date. For most of these the local board area has been easily identified with areas for which the earlier Censuses give population figures; but in the case of Mountain Ash

House Plans Approved per 10,000 population

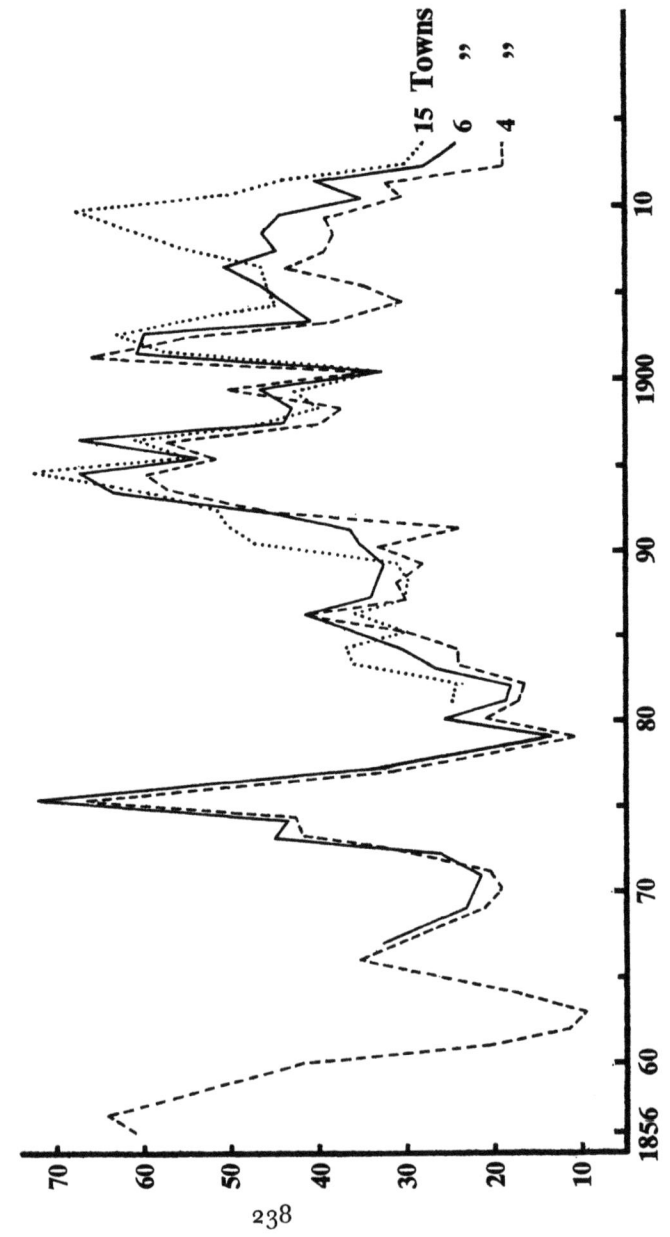

DIAGRAM I.

DIAGRAM II.

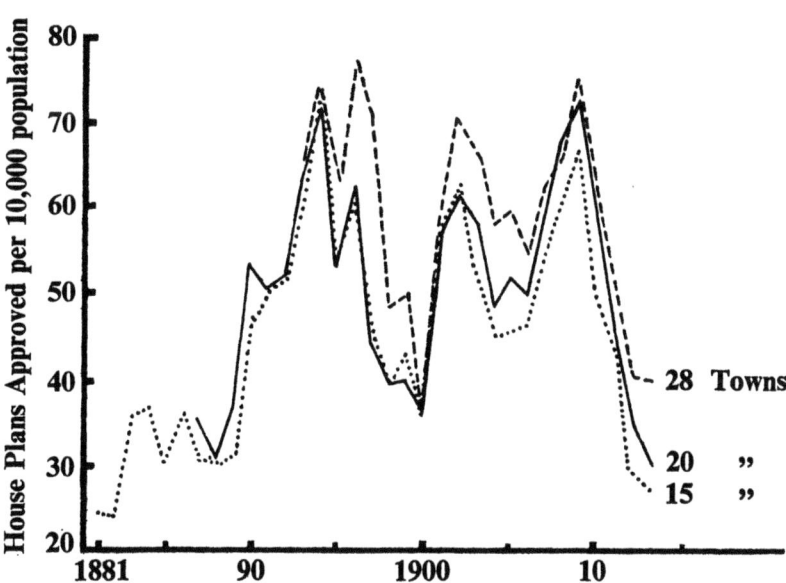

(whose plans approved series begins in 1867) it was quite impossible to perform such an identification, and the 1871 population had to be projected backwards for a few years on an arbitrary basis.

The main difficulty was that of estimating the population in the inter-census years. One method we considered was that of relating the annual change in population to the amount of house-building going on. Thus, if the inter-censal increase in population was 1000, and the total number of plans approved during this period was 200, then in a year in which 30 plans were approved, we would assume that the population increase was 150. A reasonable modification of this would be to let the increase in population occur in the year before the plans were approved, since the building of houses might very well have lagged behind population increase. Unfortunately there were several difficulties. In some cases there was a decrease in population accompanied by an increase in the number of houses (probably due to emigration from one part of the area, leaving empty houses, and a lesser immigration to another part of the same area, where there was a housing shortage, but perhaps, an expanding industry). A second difficulty arises the moment we consider the earlier years of any series. For example, the Penarth series of plans approved starts in 1877. The method we have just outlined can be used from 1881 onwards, but since we know nothing about the number of plans approved between 1871 and 1876 our method is inapplicable in the first few years. Boundary changes cause further trouble. Any one of these difficulties by itself could be surmounted with a reasonable degree of confidence; but when the three complications occur within one single area, the prospect is dark. One way around these objections would be to make a study of the economic development of the separate areas, relating population change not only to house planning but also to the opening and closing of mines and iron works. But the immense amount of labour involved, and the persisting uncertainty about the final product, made us decide against attempting this Herculean feat.

Various modifications of the above method were considered, and the estimates were made for some of the more manageable towns, but eventually it was decided that one big devil is preferable to a lot of little ones. We fell back on linear interpolation. The only difficulty here arises out of boundary changes, and we surmounted it as follows. Suppose that in 1891 an area has a population of 10,000 and that a boundary change occurs in 1897. This new area has a population in 1901 of 12,000 and the 1901 Census reports that in 1891 its population was 10,400. We assume that the population of the new area increased uniformly from 10,400 in 1891 to 12,000 in 1901. This gives an estimated population of 11,360 for the new area in 1897; 11,520 for 1898, etc. For the population of the old area in 1891–6 we assume that the 1891 population increased annually by the average increase of the preceding decade. For the particular area concerned, this procedure is unlikely to give a highly accurate result; but except in the nineties there were never many boundary changes in the same decade, and the error becomes of less importance in the aggregate. Where there is reason to believe that linear interpolation gives us a population figure that is too low, the *per capita* index will be too high, and *vice versa*. Careful examination of the raw data and of all reasonable departures of the population from our estimates has suggested that none of the important peaks or troughs in our series occupies a wrong position.

We may now consider these fluctuations. The immense peak in the late fifties in the Four Towns series reflects, in particular, the building boom in Swansea and Aberdare. In the former town, whose population grew from 25,000 in 1851 to 34,000 in 1861, over 700 houses were planned in 1858, the total for the years 1857–1860 being over 1400. In Aberdare, where the population rose from 15,000 in 1851 to 32,000 in 1861, there were over 453 houses planned in 1855, 392 planned in 1856, 234 in 1857, 97 in 1858 and 164 in 1859. In Newport, a town of about 23,000 people, 130 houses were planned in 1858. In Merthyr Tydfil 198 houses were planned in 1856, 293 in 1857 and 163 in 1858 at a time when the population was about 49,000. The trough of the early sixties, the subsequent minor peak, and the trough of the early seventies are all common to Cardiff and to each of the Four Towns; but the peak of the mid-seventies arose chiefly out of very high activity in Swansea and high activity in Aberdare and Newport. The late seventies saw depression in Cardiff and each of the Four Towns.

The period from the late seventies until the early nineties saw a great increase in building activity which, thanks largely to the development of new collieries, safely absorbed the trade cycle whose peak was in the mid-eighties. The last decade of the century began with feverish activity in Barry, and the continued growth of new colliery towns. In Swansea there was quite a sizeable peak when 479 houses were planned in 1893—when the population was about 91,000. Aberdare, after a decade of almost zero activity, reached a peak in 1894 with 200 houses, for a population of 40,000. About the same time Cardiff reached a peak with 1500 houses in 1895. Newport, with 760 houses planned in 1896, when its population was about 61,000 reached its highest-ever *per capita* figure; and Merthyr Tydfil leapt to its greatest heights between 1899 and 1902, when 3000 houses were planned in four years for a population of 70,000.

At this time, when Merthyr Tydfil attained its zenith, building in almost all other towns was low. The two short cycles which characterized the pre-war years were most marked in the new colliery towns.

Finally we may compare our results with those of Weber. In 1863, when Cardiff, Swansea, Aberdare, Newport and Merthyr Tydfil were all in a trough year, Weber's index (which included at this time Birkenhead, Birmingham, Bradford, Hull, Liverpool, London, Newport (Mon.) and Wolverhampton) showed a minor peak. The peak around 1867 corresponds roughly to a trough in Weber's series (which then had a slightly wider coverage), and the trough in 1870 to a minor peak. But in 1875 comes a prominent peak common to Weber's series and to our own series. The down-swing in the second half of the seventies reached bottom sooner in south Wales (as far as we can judge from our 4-Town, 6-Town, and 15-Town series) than in the towns covered by Weber; and the eighties witnessed a fluctuating but definite increase, leading to a boom in the nineties which anticipated the national boom by five or six years, and lasted that much longer. But the trough of 1900 was all the more severe. Indeed, in south Wales we cannot describe this as anything but a major trough, while in Weber's index it is nothing more than a ripple caused by the Boer War. The steady decline of 1902–1914 in the national index has no real counterpart in south Wales, as a whole, although in some towns such as Cardiff, for example, it was very apparent.

The examination of the various components of the south Wales and national indices has not yet been undertaken with the careful attention necessary to formulate any definite conclusions, but it seems very likely that between 1880 and 1914 the course of construction in south Wales was dominated by fluctuations in the export sector which in turn was positively correlated with the building cycle in the United States. The analysis suggested that, whereas the index of building in Great Britain as a whole moved inversely to that of building in the United States, the course of building in south Wales was not in line with that of the aggregate. The south Wales building cycle was export-determined.[3]

TABLE I

HOUSE PLANS APPROVED

	Cardiff		Swansea		Newport		Aberdare		Merthyr Tydfil	
	Plans approved	Plans per 10,000	Plans appr.	Plans per 10,000	Plans appr.	Plans per 10,000	Plans appr.	Plans per 10,000	Plans appr.	Plans per 10,000
1851	380	234	272	109						
2	328	185	252	98						
3	190	99	199	74						
4	123	59	100	36						
5	192	86	82	29	93	42	453	207		
6	356	150	51	17	114	51	392	166	198	41
7	284	112	187	62	103	45	234	92	293	61
8	240	90	704	225	139	59	97	36	163	33
9	160	57	255	79	76	32	164	57	183	37
60	83	28	272	82	20	8	153	50	131	27
1	40	13	159	47	35	14	66	20	69	14
2	40	12	92	25	11	4	58	18	12	2
3	16	4	87	23	10	4	36	11	12	2
4	60	15	155	39	16	6	68	20	7	1
5	107	26	193	47	47	18	128	38	25	5
6	59	13	243	57	54	20	200	58	40	8
7	152	32	268	60	89	32	73	21	59	12

	Cardiff		Swansea		Newport		Aberdare		Merthyr Tydfil	
	Plans approved	Plans per 10,000	Plans appr.	Plans per 10,000	Plans appr.	Plans per 10,000	Plans appr.	Plans per 10,000	Plans appr.	Plans per 10,000
1868	152	31	215	46	91	32	67	19	45	9
9	130	25	184	38	76	26	37	11	60	12
70	n.a.	n.a.	199	40	69	23	37	10	19	4
1	277 (277)	48 (48)	214	41	38	13	41	11	58	11
2	251 (251)	42 (42)	213	40	72	24	43	12	144	28
3	270 (273)	43 (44)	337	62	56	18	164	46	162	32
4	531 (539)	82 (83)	380	68	87	28	187	53	90	18
5	635 (648)	94 (96)	820	143	163	51	156	44	26	5
6	509 (552)	73 (79)	365	62	172	53	134	38	176	35
7	596 (611)	82 (84)	330	55	191	58	10	3	17	3
8	553 (564)	74 (75)	189	31	151	45	5	1	40	8
9	585 (618)	75 (80)	113	18	67	20	5	1	10	2
80	762 (771)	95 (96)	129	20	118	34	5	1	137	28
1	860 (904)	104 (109)	179	27	84	24	2	1	56	12
2	(686)	(79)	192	28	87	23	2	1	41	8
3	(980)	(107)	123	17	203	52	1	0	147	29
4	(1445)	(150)	190	26	243	60	3	1	51	10
5	(1345)	(133)	218	29	189	45	29	8	180	34
6	(1201)	(113)	273	35	349	79	12	3	231	43
7	(1226)	(111)	390	48	139	30	39	11	87	16
8	(1062)	(92)	382	46	275	58	6	2	34	6
9	(603)	(50)	414	48	110	22	10	3	107	19
90	(745)	(60)	422	48	183	34	15	4	163	29
1	(730)	(57)	288	32	114	21	36	9	158	27
2	(990)	(75)	420	46	433	77	77	20	193	33
3	(1456)	(107)	479	53	594	104	79	20	247	41
4	(1206)	(86)	459	50	544	93	200	50	297	48
5	(1507)	(105)	473	50	515	86	158	39	162	26
6	(1196)	(81)	319	35	760	125	180	44	222	35
7	(1247)	(83)	134	14	522	84	125	30	255	39
8	(1258)	(82)	62	7	390	61	91	22	446	68
9	(624)	(40)	63	7	300	46	140	33	824	123
1900	(267)	(17)	47	5	307	47	149	35	419	62
1	(230)	(14)	89	9	567	84	109	25	1023	148
2	(185)	(11)	244	26	410	59	161	37	720	102
3	(398)	(24)	182	18	365	52	253	56	283	40
4	(228)	(13)	145	14	426	59	64	14	251	34
5	(389)	(23)	393	38	298	40	149	32	181	25
6	(291)	(17)	305	29	496	66	329	70	185	25
7	(222)	(13)	226	21	481	62	259	54	501	66
8	(307)	(17)	514	47	427	54	233	48	305	39
9	(377)	(21)	447	40	319	40	120	24	632	80
10	(307)	(17)	449	40	261	32	88	18	424	53
1	(208)	(11)	440	38	244	29	94	18	530	65
2	(325)	(18)	311	27	171	20	98	19	209	26
3	(325)	(17)	302	25	199	23	137	26	158	19

The figures in brackets for Cardiff relate to 'Houses and Shops'.

TABLE II

South Wales Building

	4 Towns		6 Towns		15 Towns		20 Towns		28 Towns	
	Plans approv.	Plans per 10,000	Plans approv.	Plans per 10,000	Plans approv.	Plans per 10,000	Plans approv.	Plans per 10,000	Plans approv.	Plans per 10,000
1856	755	61·1								
7	817	64·3								
8	1103	84·5								
9	678	50·6								
60	576	41·9								
1	329	23·3								
2	173	12·0								
3	145	9·9								
4	246	16·5								
5	393	25·8								
6	537	34·6								
7	489	30·9	581	32·6						
8	418	26·0	515	28·3						
9	357	21·8	428	23·1						
70	324	19·4	416	22·1						
1	351	20·7	414	21·6						
2	472	27·6	503	25·9						
3	719	41·7	883	45·0						
4	744	42·8	874	44·0						
5	1165	66·5	1433	71·4						
6	847	48·5	1070	52·7						
7	548	30·8	644	31·4						
8	385	21·5	444	21·4						
9	195	10·8	274	13·1						
80	389	21·4	534	25·3						
1	321	17·5	398	18·6	914	24·6				
2	322	17·0	402	18·2	938	24·4				
3	474	24·3	611	26·9	1421	35·9				
4	487	24·3	702	30·0	1494	36·7				
5	616	29·9	826	34·3	1254	30·3				
6	865	40·8	1017	41·1	1517	35·7				
7	655	30·1	862	33·9	1320	30·2	1800	35·1		
8	697	31·3	861	33·0	1347	30·1	1627	30·9		
9	641	28·0	869	32·4	1424	31·0	1965	36·4		
90	783	33·1	958	34·6	2217	46·8	2849	52·6		
1	596	24·7	1010	35·7	2435	50·2	2819	50·8		
2	1123	45·9	1298	45·2	2553	51·8	2984	52·8		
3	1399	56·4	1859	63·5	3036	60·0	3658	62·6	4249	63·3
4	1500	59·7	2012	67·6	3738	72·4	4203	70·5	5009	72·9
5	1308	51·4	1614	53·4	2829	54·2	3263	53·8	4406	62·8
6	1481	57·4	2068	67·3	3226	60·7	3868	62·5	5554	77·4
7	1036	39·7	1367	43·8	2477	45·8	2833	44·9	5119	69·8
8	989	37·4	1363	43·0	2202	40·0	2526	39·3	3650	48·7
9	1327	49·5	1513	47·0	2396	42·7	2595	39·7	3821	49·9

	4 Towns		6 Towns		15 Towns		20 Towns		28 Towns	
	Plans approved	Plans per 10,000	Plans appr.	Plans per 10,000	Plans appr.	Plans per 10,000	Plans appr.	Plans per 10,000	Plans appr.	Plans per 10,000
1900	922	34·0	1060	32·5	1978	34·7	2329	35·0	2830	36·2
1	1788	65·1	1990	60·1	3326	57·3	3811	56·3	4517	56·7
2	1535	54·8	2005	59·2	3739	62·7	4382	62·9	5779	70·2
3	1083	37·9	1414	40·9	3231	52·9	4175	58·3	5745	67·6
4	886	30·4	1529	43·3	2824	44·8	3606	48·8	5158	58·6
5	1021	34·4	1660	46·0	2958	45·8	3943	52·0	5377	59·3
6	1315	43·5	1849	50·1	3107	46·9	3820	49·0	5123	54·8
7	1467	39·1	1682	44·9	3707	55·1	4743	59·8	6014	62·9
8	1479	38·7	1769	46·2	4283	61·5	5561	67·8	6573	66·4
9	1518	39·0	1744	44·8	4767	67·0	6143	73·1	7590	74·6
10	1222	30·8	1408	35·5	3704	50·8	5198	60·4	6611	63·3
1	1308	32·3	1578	39·0	3286	44·1	4003	45·5	5674	52·9
2	789	19·0	1129	27·5	2300	30·3	3193	35·5	4473	40·8
3	796	19·0	1016	24·3	2215	28·5	2773	30·2	4560	40·6

NOTES

1. The area is defined more fully in Appendix I.
2. Published in the *Scottish Journal of Political Economy*, II, (1955), 104–132.
3. The argument and analysis in this article has since been developed in J. Parry Lewis, *Building cycles and Britain's growth* (Macmillan, 1965).

APPENDIX I

The following notes show the areas included in each series. With the exception of Aberavon M.B. and Oystermouth U.D.C. (which no longer exist), the present name of the Authority is used.

The date given after the name of the Authority is the year in which that local series begins.

Four Town Series (1856–1913): Swansea C.B. (1851), Newport C.B. (1855), Aberdare U.D.C. (1855), Merthyr Tydfil C.B. (1856).

Six Town Series (1867–1913): The above plus: Llanelly M.B. (1865), Mountain Ash U.D.C. (1867).

Fifteen Town Series (1881–1913): The above plus: Blaenavon U.D.C. (1873), Ebbw Vale U.D.C. (1875), Penarth U.D.C. (1877), Rhondda M.B. (1880), Tredegar U.D.C. (1880), Neath M.B. (1880), Abertillery U.D.C. (1881), Neath R.D.C. (1881), Rhymney U.D.C. (1881).

Twenty Town Series (1887–1913): The above plus: Maesteg U.D.C. (1882), Glyncorrwg U.D.C. (1883), Nantyglo and Blaina U.D.C. (1886), Llwchwr U.D.C. (1886), Pontypridd U.D.C. (1887).

Twenty-Eight Town Series (1893–1913): The above plus: Ogmore and Garw U.D.C. (1888), Bedwellty (1889), Llantrisant and Llantwit Fardre R.D.C. (1890), Caerphilly U.D.C. (1890), Barry M.B. (1891), Oystermouth U.D.C. (1892), Aberavon M.B. (1892), Gelligaer U.D.C. (1893).

The following data are also available but are not used in this paper:

Llanelly R.D.C. (1894), Crickhowell R.D.C. (1894), Bridgend U.D.C. (1895), Risca U.D.C. (1895), Penybont R.D.C. (1895), Cowbridge R.D.C. (1896), Pontardawe R.D.C. (1899), Mynyddislwyn U.D.C. (1902), Burry Port U.D.C. (1902), Abercarn U.D.C. (1894–1906 and 1911–13).

No figures are available for the Bridgend U.D.C., Blaenavon U.D.C. and Penybont R.D.C. areas in 1913.

Aberavon Borough and Margam U.D.C. were amalgamated in 1922 to form the Municipal Borough of Port Talbot. Oystermouth U.D.C. became part of the County Borough of Swansea in 1919.

Before 1894 most of the local authorities were administered by Local Boards of Health. The Ancient Boroughs of Swansea, Newport, Neath, Llanelly and Aberavon had Borough Corporations.

The housing Services for Llantrisant and Llantwit Fardre R.D.C. Caerphilly U.D.C. and Glyncorrwg U.D.C., commenced before the areas became separate Local Boards. These districts formed parts of very large Boards where administration was carried out on a regional basis. The regions *later* became independent authorities. Before 1908 the Gelligaer U.D.C. was known as the Gelligaer and Rhigos R.D.C. Llwchwr U.D.C. was formerly known as the Swansea Rural Sanitary Authority and later as the Llangyfelach R.D.C.

SOURCES OF INFORMATION

1. *Council and/or Committee Minutes*

Abercarn, Aberavon, Bedwellty, Blaenavon, Crickhowell, Nantyglo and Blaina, Rhymney, Risca, Tredegar, Swansea (1851–75), Aberdare (1855–1908, 1911 and 1912), Mountain Ash (1867–1902), Abertillery (1881–1911).

2. *M.O.H. Reports*

   A. *Glamorganshire County Council*
   Bridgend, Penybont, Cowbridge R.D.C.

   B. *Local Authority M.O.H. Reports*
   Barry, Swansea (1876–1914), Aberdare (1909, 1910, 1913 and 1914), Mountain Ash (1903–14).

Index